God and the New Biology

God and the New Biology

ARTHUR PEACOCKE

1817

Harper & Row, Publishers, San Francisco
Cambridge, Hagerstown, New York, Philadelphia, Washington
London, Mexico City, São Paulo, Singapore, Sydney

Library of Congress Cataloging-in-Publication Data

Peacocke, A.R. (Arthur Robert)
    God and the new biology

    Bibliography: p.
    Includes index.
        1. Biology—Religious aspects—Christianity.
    2. Evolution—Religious aspects—Christianity.
    I. Title.
    BL255.P43   1987   215'.74   86-45746
    ISBN 0-06-250672-2

87 88 89 90 91 HC 10 9 8 7 6 5 4 3 2 1

Contents

ACKNOWLEDGMENTS

The author and publishers are grateful to the following for permission to quote extracts:

Harvard University Press and The Belknap Press: E.O. Wilson, *Sociobiology* Cambridge, 1975.

University of Washington Press: Francis H.C. Crick, *Of Molecules and Men*, Seattle, 1966.

Allen Lane and Random House: François Jacob, *The Logic of Living Systems*, Allen Lane, London, 1974; *The Logic of Life*, Random House, 1976.

University of Michigan Press: M. Sahlins, *The Use and Abuse of Biology*, Ann Arbor, Mich., 1976.

Clarendon Press: J.H. Crook, *The Evolution of Human Consciousness*, Oxford, 1980.

Darton, Longman and Todd and Crossroad: Karl Rahner, *Theological Investigations III*, London and New York, 1966.

Churchill Livingstone: I.T. Ramsey and R. Potter (Eds), *Personality and Science: An Interdisciplinary Discussion*, Edinburgh and London, 1971.

To Rosemary

Preface

This book represents an attempt to bring together into a coherent whole reflections that I have made during the last decade or so on those developments in biology that have warranted its designation as 'new' and that have in various ways stimulated my own understanding of humanity, nature and God and of their mutual interrelations. This understanding is one which, while being embedded in and informed by the Christian tradition, aspires to be open to new knowledge and perspectives on the grounds that any specifically 'religious' truth about the relationship of humanity, nature and God cannot but be enriched by a genuine widening of our human horizons. It is also based on a 'critically realist' view of both the scientific and theological enterprises. This view I have elaborated elsewhere* but, briefly, it consists in the assertion that the terms of both scientific and theological discourse really refer – they refer to realities – but that the language in which such reference is made is metaphorical, revisable and the result of a continuous development in continuous, linguistic communities – in the context of my own experience, those of the Christian Church and of the historical scientific community.

With such presuppositions it is not surprising that I have myself experienced a continuous inner dialogue between the voices, as it were, of my scientific apprehensions, as expanded by the new biology, and that of my religious perceptions, widened and deepened by the study of theology. The outward results of this dialogue have appeared in the form of a number of articles, or chapters in books, evinced by various conferences and editors and addressed to readers both scientific and theological. I have here melded these various essays into a more ordered and comprehensive presentation in one volume. It is addressed primarily to those who are puzzled and disorientated by the effect of the rapid growth of the biological sciences on their apprehension of themselves,

*A. R. Peacocke, *Intimations of Reality*, University of Notre Dame Press, Notre Dame, Indiana, 1984.

of nature and of God – whether or not they regard themselves as scientists and/or as religious believers.

The exercise involves a certain amount of explaining to each of these groups of readers what is widely known and understood by the other. So I must ask the experts of both kinds to bear with this in the hope, and indeed conviction, that it is the juxtaposition and, if possible, integration of the two perceptions that is particularly fruitful, and indeed necessary, for humanity in this last quarter of the twentieth century. The level of presentation is meant to be such that both the biology and theology should be reasonably intelligible to all those who wish to share this journey of exploration with me. It is only fair to say that part of the argument concerning reduction of scientific concepts in the last part of Chapter 1 may be found to be somewhat heavy going for those not acquainted with that particular philosophical discussion and can well be passed over more quickly for Chapter 2 on the specific and more directly relevant issue of the reduction of biology to physics and chemistry. The text does not discuss at any length the issue of 'creationism' now, amazingly, re-emergent in the USA, for several recent books have attacked that position both frontally and effectively. Recent evidence for biological evolution is adduced and the whole tenor of the book is that this biological percept, far from being opposed to a theistic doctrine of creation, does in fact enhance and enrich it.

For the record, my publications from which this present work has evolved are: 'Reductionism in biology – a review of some of the epistemological issues and their relevance to biology and the problem of consciousness', *Zygon* 11 (1976) 307–324 [Chapters 1, 2]; 'The New Biology and *Nature, Man and God*' in *The Experiment of Life* (ed. F. Kenneth Hare), Univ. of Toronto Press, Toronto, 1983, pp. 27–88 [Chapters 1, 3, 4, 6, 7, 8]; 'The nature and purpose of man in science and Christian theology', *Zygon* 8 (1973) 373–94 [Chapter 6]; 'God's Action in the World', *Epworth Review* 6 (1979) 70–80 and 7 (1980) 72–82, 75–79 [Chapter 6]; 'Biological Evolution and Christian Theology – yesterday and today' in *Darwinism and Divinity* (ed. J. Durant), Blackwells, Oxford, 1985 [Chapters 3, 5, 6]; 'A Christian Materialism?' in *How Do We Know?* (Ed. M. Shafto), Harper & Row, 1985 [Chapter 6]; 'Matter in the theological and scientific perspectives' in *Thinking about the Eucharist*, Report of Doctrine Commission of the Church of England, SCM Press, 1972, pp. 14–37 [Chapters 3, 9]; and throughout, the book involves more detailed and updated considerations of themes in my *Creation and the World of Science* (Clarendon Press, Oxford, 1979; University of Notre Dame Press, 1985).

Finally I would like to pay tribute to the help I have received from Mrs Jean Pike of Cambridge for patiently typing a sometimes wayward manuscript.

Arthur Peacocke
Ian Ramsey Centre
St Cross College
Oxford

Introduction

The panorama of the sciences in the first half of the twentieth century was undoubtedly dominated by the conceptual revolutions of quantum and relativity theory. The reverberations of these paradigmatic shifts in the human intellectual scene continue to echo as their implications in particle physics and cosmology are worked out with new observations crowding in during the second half of this century as a result of the development of new techniques for observing the universe, past and present. Over this, as it were, ground bass of the 'new physics' that underlies the swelling complexity of sound from the sciences, there have entered, since the late 1940s and early 1950s, new themes and motifs that in consort are entirely altering the texture and timbre of what we hear from the sciences. I refer to those developments which may properly be called the 'new' biology.

As Ludwig Boltzman once perceptively wrote, the nineteenth century would be remembered as the century of Darwin and, just when we thought the twentieth was going to be that of Einstein, the biological sciences have burgeoned into a luxuriant growth altering the landscape of human perceptions, particularly on the nature of human life itself. As we shall see (Chapter 3), these new developments resulted from fruitful interaction of the 'modern synthesis' of biology (neo-Darwinism) of the 1930s and 1940s with physics and chemistry – or, more precisely, of biologists with physicists and chemists, particularly the former. The determination in 1953, by a combination of physicists and biologists (J. D. Watson, F. Crick and M. H. F. Wilkins), of the three-dimensional chemical structure of the material (DNA) that carries hereditary biological information led to an explosion of new research that rapidly became known as 'molecular biology'.

This began the transformation of biology into its 'new' form. The process has continued ever since. It is characterised by an increasing apprehension of the labyrinthine complexity of the molecular processes and structures that are involved in the dynamics of a living organism, increasingly powerful techniques for probing these structures at the subcellular and molecular level, and an increasingly quantitative approach. This new spirit in biological investigation has imbued researches over a much wider area than that of the molecular basis of heredity or of a variety of physiological functions. For it has extended to the behavioural patterns of populations (sociobiology/behavioural ecology) and to the study of information-conveying processes and storage, in the human brain in particular (the neuro-sciences).

These developments cast a new light on the organic world in general and on human beings in particular. The perspective has changed so rapidly and extensively that no philosophical or theological reflections on the classical trio of 'nature, man and God' can be unaffected by them. Hence the inquiries with which this book is concerned. However, as soon as one embarks on any such inquiries, one very soon comes up against the questions of both the status of different kinds of knowledge and of their relation to each other. These questions refer not only to the obviously wide cultural gap between the philosophical and theological enterprises, on the one hand, and the natural sciences, on the other, but also to the relations between different natural sciences.

One of the founders of molecular biology, Francis Crick, claimed, as we shall see, that the ultimate aim of the modern movement in biology is to explain *all* biology in terms of physics and chemistry. In making this claim, he was asserting a philosophical position as much as a scientific one, namely, that biological concepts and theories and laws can (and should) be 'reduced' to those of physics and chemistry – that living organisms are 'nothing but' atoms and molecules. It makes an enormous difference to how one assesses the knowledge stemming from the sciences, in this instance from the new biology, whether or not one believes that the relations between different sciences, and the relations between the sciences and other modes of knowing, can be described as 'reduction', in the sense apparently referred to by Crick. That is why the journey on which this book embarks has to begin (Chapter 1) with an examination first of the general issue of reductionism ('nothing-but-ery', as it has been dubbed) and to distinguish different kinds of reductionism. We then proceed to the question, relevant to our main theme, whether or not biology can in fact be reduced to physics and chemistry (Chapter 2).

It is concluded that reductionistic methodology is essential to biological research, but has to be compounded with more holistic approaches. More significantly, for our purposes, it is also concluded that it *is* possible for higher level concepts and theories (applicable, for example, in biology) to be non-reducible to lower level concepts and theories, that is, they can be autonomous. At the same time one has to recognise the applicability of lower level concepts and theories (for example, those of physics and chemistry) to the component units of more complex entities and their validity when referred to that lower level. That is, with reference to biology, it is possible to be anti-reductionist without being a vitalist. Higher level concepts and theories often refer to genuine aspects of reality at their own level of operation and we have to eschew any assumptions that only the so-called fundamental particles of modern physics are 'really real'. To do so is indeed a kind of 'fundamentalism' of a pseudo-scientific kind that is to be as much avoided in impartial inquiry as its religious namesake.

Having, we hope, clarified this issue, we then proceed in the next two chapters (3 and 4) to outline some of the principal features of the new biology* and of the controversies that surround some parts of it. These considerations are divided along the lines of our earlier distinction (Chapter 1) between those scientific research methodologies that are 'holistic', examining entities in their wholeness from the top 'down', and those that are 'reductionistic', examining the parts that make up wholes (from the bottom 'up').

We therefore first examine (Chapter 3) aspects of the new biology that deal with whole organisms, principally evolutionary theory. Arguments that attempt to describe evolution as 'only a theory', and thereby somewhat less than factual, are dismissed in the light of recent evidence and some current controversies concerning evolution are outlined. It is emphasised that the modern synthesis of neo-Darwinism has not been shaken in its broad foundations, though new questions have been posed and it has been much enriched by new developments and studies. Because they are important for our subsequent more theological reflections, the principal trends and features of evolution are then outlined, together with a brief reminder of the web of interconnectedness of living organisms with their environment that modern ecology increasingly and powerfully demonstrates.

The methodology of modern molecular biology is avowedly

*Excluding the neuro-sciences which raise too many issues, both philosophical and theological, to be treated within the compass of this volume. For recent accounts of this area and of some of its philosophical and theological implications, see *How We Know*, Proceedings of the XXth Nobel Conference, Gustavus Adolphus College, ed. M. Shafto (Harper & Row, San Francisco, 1985). Contributors include: G. Edelman, H. A. Simon, R. Schrank, B. Milner, D. Dennett, and the present author.

reductionist, and none the worse for that – indeed it owes its success to its ability to discern the molecular structures and processes that characterise living organisms. Nevertheless, our account (in the first part of Chapter 4) emphasises the historical origins of molecular biology in a marriage of the 'informational school' of investigators, who were concerned with the problems of the transfer of genetic information, and the 'structural school', who were concerned with the three-dimensional structures of biological molecules throughout the evolved hierarchy of living organisms. The very success of molecular biology in describing, amongst other things, the molecular basis of heredity provokes a discussion of reductionism, anti-reductionism and vitalism in relation to these developments. This leads to the conclusion that the 'central dogma' of molecular biology, of the transmission of genetic *information* through molecular *structures*, exhibits precisely that relationship of the non-reducibility of a higher-level concept to a lower-level one which we were concerned to emphasise earlier as legitimate in the interpretation of many biological concepts.

This discussion leads naturally to a consideration of the wide-ranging and much discussed claims of Jacques Monod that molecular biology has so reinforced the role of chance at the molecular level in the evolutionary process that any deductions of significance or meaning in human life are thereby ruled out of court. This deduction, it is argued, does not follow even on Monod's own premises and certainly not when the inbuilt creativity of the increasingly appreciated subtle interplay of chance and law is allowed for, as it must be when developments in theoretical biology, since Monod, are taken into account (the work of Prigogine and the Brussels school on the self-organising propensities of dissipative structures in open systems* and that of Eigen and his Göttingen colleagues on the development of populations of large self-copying molecules).

A second major development in biology that utilises an implicit reductionist methodology is that of sociobiology, which seeks to interpret the behaviour of living organisms (insects, birds, animals, man) in terms of cost-benefit calculations of genetic advantage, arguing, in contrast to much previous biology, that the gene is the unit of selection. This development in biology (described in the second part of Chapter 4) took its name from E. O. Wilson's book *Sociobiology – the New Synthesis*

---

*Elaborated more fully in the Appendix to this book in connection with thermodynamic accounts of living systems and of evolution.

published in 1975, though it rests on significant work by others in the immediately preceding decade and indeed has earlier roots in the 'modern synthesis' of the two or three decades before that. Because of somewhat imperialist claims made by at least some of its protagonists, that sociobiology is now poised ready to reduce sociology, anthropology and the sciences of human behaviour to biology, this whole development has generated much controversy both within and without the community of scientists. Now, more than a decade since Wilson's book appeared, it is possible more clearly to sift the grain from the chaff, and to acknowledge the fruitfulness in research of the basic approach of sociobiology while recognising that it has not yet fulfilled the expectation of those who entertained more extreme hopes that it will take over, by reduction, the social sciences and humanities – for example, the interpretation of cultural evolution.

The second part of the book (Chapters 5 following) attempts to assess the implication of these new biological perspectives for any coherent exposition of our understanding of man and nature, and so of God, since our explicit concepts of God must be sensitive to the best knowledge of the world available to us. This is not to deny that both the perennial unmediated experience of God and that which is mediated through sacred writings, ritual, sacrament and personal experience will continue to be the fountainhead of religious experience. Nevertheless, the intellectual articulation by theology of what, or rather who, is thus experienced remains an essential, if modest, task for any theist today on two counts. First, such conceptual developments are not in practice divorced from the content of the experience of God for there is a mutual interplay, indeed symbiosis, in the individual and in the exchanges of the believing community between the explicit, conscious and conceptual, on the one hand, and the implicit, subconscious and symbolic apprehensions of God, on the other. Second, theists are not intellectually responsible if they attempt to insulate their concepts of God from new apprehensions of nature and of man, stemming in this context from the sciences: if they retreat into an intellectual ghetto it is not surprising if their contemporaries treat their beliefs as irrelevant.

We begin this second part of our journey by examining certain aspects of the understandings of man, God and evolution in their historical perspective (Chapter 5). In particular, we examine the reconciling and conciliatory responses to Darwin's ideas of certain traditions of theology in the nineteenth and earlier part of the twentieth centuries. This is instructive since such responses provided fruitful soil for the growth of a coherent and constructive approach by Christian theology to evolution. Certainly, important questions had been raised for Christian theology by Darwinism, even though the historical development of the controversies is only now being accurately charted and ancient, though strongly entrenched, mythologies concerning it being exploded. After a brief survey of the response of German and French thinkers to evolutionary ideas, a more extended account is given of the somewhat tardy and, at first, cautious response of Roman Catholic thinkers – only now in the later part of the twentieth century constituting any positive integration of Roman Catholic theology with evolutionary ideas.

An earlier and more positive response to Darwin and to the whole concept of evolution came from those theologians in the Church of England who were already emphasising the immanence of God in the processes of an evolving natural world, processes which culminated, in their view, in the incarnation of God in a human person in that world, an event which continues to be perpetually expressed in sacramental worship. Some exponents of this approach are identified and their successors traced well into the twentieth century, in writers such as William Temple and Charles Raven. The development of a distinctive natural theology in the USA based on the 'process thought' of A. N. Whitehead and the 'scientific theology' of Ralph W. Burhoe are also significant twentieth-century attempts to integrate theism with evolutionary perspectives.

However, the growth of the new biology allows no complacent resting even in the insights of these more constructive theological pioneers and a re-consideration of man, God and evolution today becomes imperative, for the Christian life is above all an exploration into God and must always be open to new knowledge of the created world. This continued exploration is pursued in Chapter 6, the aim being coherence and consonance between the scientific and theological perspectives – rather than their total integration, and certainly not the assimilation of one by the other.

As regards 'human being', it is pointed out that the Biblical understanding of man (seminal for the Judeo-Christian tradition) is as a psychosomatic unity with various organs and functions through any of which the person in his or her totality expresses him- or herself – however much Christian theology has subsequently overlaid this Biblical perspective with Hellenistic ones that view human beings as the union of two or three distinct entities, one of which is immortal. It is argued that this basic sense in the Christian tradition of the wholeness of the person is consistent both with much current philosophy of the body/mind problem and with the marked interlocking of the physical, mental and spiritual aspects of human experience that the natural and human sciences increasingly reveal.

Nevertheless, the distinctive sense of being a person, the awareness of being an 'I', the sense of transcendence persons have in relation to their own bodies and of their experience of freedom, are genuinely emergent in evolution, and any discourse concerning the distinctively human and personal, it is again urged (see also Chapter 1), is not to be prematurely reduced to lower-level descriptions. It is at this unique level of the human that distinctive features of the human condition can be identified that go far beyond anything to be found even in the highest primates. Together they constitute the tragedy and comedy of human existence. It is to such needs which differ in quality from those delineated by biology that the religious quest of humanity has responded. Human aspirations and degradations far exceed those of even the 'highest' primates and the Christian understanding of humankind is totally realistic about their respective heights and depths. It is in such a context that ancient myths of the 'fallen' state of humanity have to be re-considered, it is argued, when they can then be understood as extraordinarily realistic in their appraisal of the human condition.

Our understanding of the capability of evolving 'matter' has been transformed from the particulate and billiard-ball conception of the mechanistic models of preceding centuries, to a realisation that, through a process of continuously developing hierarchical complexity, it can, in the human brain, acquire consciousness, self-consciousness, self-transcendence and freedom. All of which, it is argued (Chapter 6), necessitate a revision of what we think matter is 'in itself' for, briefly, it can become *us*. This leads to considerations which are later developed in Chapter 9, where the insights into the significance of matter that are afforded by the Christian sacraments, that is, a sacramental view of the cosmos, provide a fruitful way in which the scientific and theological perspective can be brought into one focus.

After these reflections on evolving matter, Chapter 6 continues with a reassessment of how we think of the relation of God to the world. For the Christian theist – and, indeed, the Jewish and Islamic – God is that which, or rather the One Who (since personal terms are the least misleading, even if inadequate), gives being to the world. The doctrine of creation is a response to questions such as 'Why is there anything at all?' and does not, in spite of popular misconceptions, refer to what happened at a point *in* time, since time, along with space, matter and energy, are all aspects of that which is given being by God. In this sense, God in his ultimate being is other than the world, that is, more technically, he is 'transcendent'. But the world revealed by cosmology and even more so by biology is one in which new forms emerge through the inbuilt natural creativity of its units and processes. So God has to be conceived of as continuously creating in and through the stuff of the world and the inherent properties with which he endowed it. So a re-emphasis on God's 'immanence' in the world is called for by this perception of the world as in process of evolving new emergent forms, with new properties, abilities and powers – not least those of *homo sapiens*. Some models and metaphors that can best express this understanding of God's creative relation to all-that-is in time and space are then elaborated.

One of the recent features of the new biology is, as we mentioned above, the recognition that it is the interplay of chance and law that is creative of emergent complexes of matter in living forms. So God's immanent activity as Creator has to be related to this new perception: this entails a recognition of what we see as the operation of chance in a law-like framework, as a mode of God as Creator. A musical, and other, models are developed to attempt to render this intelligible and the chapter (6) concludes with some reflections on living, as human beings, with chance as an ineradicable and ubiquitous feature of the world we live in.

An increasingly prominent feature of the new biology is the complex web of interrelations that are being discovered between living organisms and their environment, which includes other living organisms, such as man, as well as inorganic nature. So it is that the science of ecology has made human beings more aware of the subtle, intricate, and often catastrophic, character of man's intervention in his environment. This has generated the search for a new basis for values that will operate in regard to man's relation to his environment, that is, for new 'environmental values', and in Chapter 7 it is argued that to see nature *as* created by a transcendent God, immanent within it, provides a cogent basis for such an environmental ethic by generating the requisite values and attitudes.

Sociobiology, being reductionist in method, has tended to be interpreted by many of its leading practitioners in an anti-theistic sense. Yet its evolutionary emphasis poses no problems for belief in God as creator that have not already been absorbed by the developments described earlier (Chapters 5 and 6). Insofar as its exponents use it to give a totally reductionist, and overly deterministic, account of human thought and behaviour, it suffers from the flaws that underlie any such general attempt (Chapters 1 and 2). But, it is argued in Chapter 8, such intellectual imperialism is not essential to impartial inquiries into the genetic component in human behaviour and theists have no particular quarrel with such inquiries or their results when adequately established, provided they are not thought to constitute a *total* picture of the human person. To put it crudely, if God is immanently acting as creator in the stuff of the world, the genetic component in and influences on human behaviour are to be regarded simply as one of the means by which he has, together with other ways, given human beings their specific kind of being, including that of their moral awareness. The reality of this last is not at all undermined if it is eventually established that it is a long extrapolation from, say, the purely genetically determined 'altruism' discovered lower down the evolutionary tree. To suppose so would be to be guilty of the 'genetic fallacy' of explaining the ultimate form of a human development in terms of the concepts needed to explicate its origins – just as science is not magic, so ethics need not be genetics.

After some further reflections on matter in religion and science (Chapter 9), already referred to, our journey ends (Chapter 10) with a retrospective survey of our attempts to find ways of speaking of nature, man and God and their interrelations that are consonant with the new biology which, as with all new perspectives on truth, is found to have widened and deepened the character of that exploration into God which will always be the ultimate concern of groping humanity.

1 *The sciences and reductionism*

Practising scientists are not given to analysing, any more than other human beings, the philosophical presuppositions of their activities, for it has been remarked, with some justification, that the average scientist knows as much about what he does as the average centipede knows how it walks.[1] And there is some truth in this. My own scientific work has been in the borderline between physical chemistry, on the one hand, and biology and biochemistry, on the other – the structure of biological macromolecules (e.g., DNA) and genetic function. I have noticed how easy it is for physical biochemists and molecular biologists, who employ reductionist methodologies (breaking down wholes into parts to analyse them by their own special methods), to transpose this heuristic necessity into a more general philosophical attitude. The procedure of analysis which is required by their own discipline then becomes almost unconsciously a philosophical belief about biological organisms *being* 'nothing but' the bits into which they have analysed them, 'nothing but' a physico-chemical system.

In this sense many practising scientists are unreflective and implicit 'reductionists' – they undergo a very natural psychological transition from the methodological necessities of the way they work to an unanalysed philosophical position. Francis Crick, as a leading molecular biologist, has however been quite explicit in affirming that 'the ultimate aim of the modern movement in biology is in fact to explain *all* biology in terms of physics and chemistry'.[2] It is his argument that our present general knowledge of physics and chemistry is sufficient to act as an exceedingly solid foundation for biology, though he agrees much of the detailed chemistry is incomplete and needs further study.

Another very reductionist statement in relation to another borderline, that between sociology and biology, occurs in the now almost notorious preface by E. O. Wilson to his book *Sociobiology*:

Sociobiology is defined as the systematic study of the biological basis of all social behaviour. For the present it focuses on animal societies, their population structure, castes and communications, together with all the physiology underlying the social adaptations. But the discipline is also concerned with the social behaviour of early man, and the adaptive features of organisation in the more primitive contemporary human societies. Sociology *sensu stricto*, the study of human society at all levels of complexity, still stands apart from sociobiology because of its largely structuralist and nongenetic approach. It attempts to explain human behaviour primarily by empirical description of the outermost phenotypes and by unaided intuition, without reference to evolutionary explanations in the true genetic sense. It (sociology) is most successful in the way descriptive taxonomy and ecology have been most successful, when it provides a detailed description of particular phenomena and demonstrates first-order correlations with features of the environment. Taxonomy and ecology, however, have been reshaped entirely during the past forty years by integration into neo-Darwinist evolutionary theory – the 'Modern Synthesis', as it is often called – in which each phenomenon is weighed for its adaptive significance and then related to the basic principles of population genetics. It may not be too much to say [many people thought it *was* too much to say!] that sociology and the other social sciences, as well as the humanities, are the last branches of biology waiting to be included in the Modern Synthesis. One of the functions of sociobiology, then, is to reformulate the foundations of the social sciences in a way that draws these subjects into the Modern Synthesis.[3]

Then at the end, with a certain amount of humility for which we can be grateful, he wrote, 'Whether the social sciences can be truly biologicized in this fashion remains to be seen'.[3]

Many of our contemporaries see these aims, both of Crick and of Wilson, quoted in their two different contexts, as in fact being achieved all the time. This is indeed the general philosophical outlook of many practising scientists and merits serious examination both on that account and because appraisal of this outlook – 'reductionism', as it is usually called – is crucial to my assessment of the philosophical and theological significance of biology today. Before we analyse further what 'reductionism' amounts to and the different forms it can take, it is worth considering the relevance of this whole question to some of these wider issues.

The relevance of reductionism

Whether explicitly or only implicitly embraced, a reductionist interpretation of the relations among the different sciences can limit and determine any understanding of the nature of man in general and of his consciousness in particular. For if it is true that chemistry is nothing but physics, the biochemistry of cells nothing but chemistry, the biology of organisms nothing but the biochemistry of cells, and ecology and sociology nothing but biology, then the branch from this main line – the statement that consciousness is nothing but neurophysiological events which are nothing but biochemistry, etc., and so on down the chain to physics again – becomes the more plausible and, indeed, attractive to the point of being compelling. This possibly accounts for the popularity of reductionist views among scientists, in spite of the obvious vulnerability[4] of the kind of reductionist circle which the view generates in its crudest forms: physiological processes are merely forms of applied biochemistry, which is merely applied chemistry, which is merely applied physics, which is merely the application of mathematical truth, which is merely the result of rules of thought, which are merely the product of social, cultural and linguistic influences, which are merely the expression of psychological mechanisms, which are merely physiological processes . . . .

All-embracing chains of reduction, such as history-psychology-biology-physics-and-chemistry, have a seductive simplicity which obscures the weaknesses of many of the links. Thus, to take the first of these 'links', even if we had a causal predictive account of the psychology of all particular individuals, the intersection between psychological events and events in the physical world would still often have the character of accidents since the predictability of both psychological and physical event is relative to its own previous variables.[5] The intersection of causal events is an 'accident' relative to one's understanding of the individual psychology and of the nexus of physical events. This unpredictable character of 'accidents' which involve human beings and their encounters with the physical (and biological) worlds is amplified in human history (e.g., *this* head of state killed at *this* point of time, before *that* meeting, had an irreversible, profound influence on human history). Thus, the proposed all-embracing reductive chain lacks even the first link, that between history and psychology.[6] Clearly, in such series of reductive links, more is being affirmed than simply prescriptions for research strategies, and this 'more' is indeed often not what scientists would wish to sponsor. Careful distinctions between different kinds of reductionism seem to be required, if only to ascertain what kind of talk about reducing biological events to physicochemical ones is licensed by the general nature of the relationships among the sciences.

The question is, moreover, not without pressing concern in such a human situation as the relation of a clinician to his patient.[7] Conventional medical education is 'reductionistic' in the sense of attempting to reduce the account of pathological events to physicochemical terms. Medical doctors are trained to believe that there is an 'explanation' in such terms, which is only deficient or not available because of our lack of knowledge and of adequate research. From such attitudes it is very easy to step into the kind of more general, philosophical reductionism with which we are here concerned. In practice, there can be visualized a spectrum of disease – at the one end, purely physical illnesses which could be described in terms of, for example, virulent organisms meeting susceptible hosts with predictable responses and adequately describable in physiological and physicochemical terms; at the other end, neurological and psychiatric illnesses in which our understanding of the chemical and electrophysiological events underlying (however obscurely) mental processes is very elementary or nonexistent. What the clinician knows is that, even if he had a full, physicochemical account of the processes involved in these latter illnesses, it would only be a part (and that a small one in many cases) of coping with the complex interrelation of factors which contribute to the illness and which mar the total integration of a human being.

The clinician becomes acutely aware of this when he has to apply his scientific training, with its reductionistic implications, to individuals with whom he has professional and personal relationships. This personal nature of the doctor-patient relationship may lead to a lack of scientific objectivity, but often the effect of the doctor's personality has an influence on the patient's recovery of health that goes beyond the effects simply of the application of detailed scientific knowledge. The patient responds to the personality of the doctor, explicit or not, in a way in which the contents of a test tube do not respond to that of a chemist.

Certainly, the doctor finds himself at two or more levels in the hierarchy of explanatory schemes and has to act as if human individuals have more value than their constituent elements. This attitude, on the face of it, is not readily derivable from a reductionist philosophy. The medical doctor often faces difficult choices, asking at one and the same time, 'What shall I do for him (the patient)?' and 'How shall I manipulate this (human) physicochemical mechanism?' The manipulative approach of the second question has been successful enough to engender a world view according to which 'how?' seems to be the only question to ask; but the quesion of what a doctor *should* be doing is not readily answered in a manipulative-mechanistic framework, which cannot therefore be a full and adequate account of the case.

But even this complex personal dilemma of the clinician can be placed within a broader context. For the very institution within which doctor and patient interact can shape the whole situation. It has been found that some institutions – for example, mental hospitals – themselves often disturb behaviour.[8] Thus the effects of social organisation and systems on human self-understanding and action have to be allowed for; and this, too, implies a hierarchy which the clinician has to recognise.

Types of reductionism

It is clear that the question of reductionism, the query as to the extent to which reduction is possible, can be raised in relation to many different interfaces in the natural hierarchy of complexity of which the natural world is increasingly shown to consist. The sequence of complexity (atom . . . molecule . . . ecosystem) represents a series of levels of organization of matter in which each successive member of the series is a whole constituted of parts that precede it in the series. The issue is 'whether the theories and experimental laws formulated in one field of science can be shown to be special cases of theories and laws formulated in some other branch of science. If such is the case, the former branch of science is said to have been reduced to the latter.'[9] Academics such as myself from time to time can be irritated by those of our colleagues who, coming from another discipline, claim that our discipline X is 'nothing but' an example and application of their discipline Y. Thus X may be sociology and Y individual psychology; or X may be psychology and Y neurophysiology; or X may be neurophysiology and Y may be biochemistry; or X may be biology and Y physics and chemistry; and so the game goes on. The game is called reductionism. It is what is being urged upon us when we are told that 'study X is nothing but study Y', hence the colloquial name of 'nothing-but-ery'.

Analysis of what is being affirmed in such assertions turns out to be more complex than first appears, as witness the vast literature on the subject,[10] and some careful distinctions clearly need to be made to avoid rendering confusion worse confounded. Clarification will be attempted in what follows before dealing more fully with the question of whether biology really is 'nothing but' physics and chemistry.

Methodological reductionism

This is simply, as mentioned above, the necessity the practising scientist finds of studying problems that are presented to him at a given level of complexity, particularly that of the living world, by breaking down into pieces the entities studied. The breaking down of unintelligible, complex wholes into their component units, the determination of the structures of those pieces and what functions they can perform, and then the fitting of them together as best one can, hypothetically at least, in order to see how they function together in a complex whole, are such common ploys in experimental science that most practising scientists would consider it scarcely worth remarking upon.

This programme, this methodological approach, has been supremely successful in the sciences, and notably in biology, and above all in molecular biology and the neurosciences. It is a prescription for research that has been vindicated through a wide range of the sciences and is scarcely a matter of controversy. In particular, even the most holistic of biologists would not deny the value of the unravelling of the molecular basis of heredity in DNA (deoxyribonucleic acid) or the protein-structural basis of immunological response. Indeed, this strategy is an inevitable consequence of the natural world consisting of a hierarchy of organised systems at multiple levels, one system (e.g. biological macromolecules and living organisms) constituting the interacting units from which more complex systems are assembled at the next level (i.e., in single living cells and in ecosystems of populations of organisms in their environment, respectively).

Such relationships, which emerge empirically, necessitate an analytical strategy of a methodologically reductionist kind. So each 'science' becomes a relatively autonomous interlocking network of theories, descriptions, concepts, experimental techniques, fields of observations, and (one should honestly add) also of individual scientists and their network of personal relationships. There is nothing wrong in this, and it is widely accepted as the way in which a science progresses, even though the relationship of the hierarchy of *systems* which are studied and the hierarchy of *theories* may not be well understood and has been grist to the mill of arguments about reductionism. In this methodological form reductionism is a prerequisite of research.

Most practising scientists, whatever their philosophy or religious beliefs, in practice are methodologically reductionist in their approach, but this does *not* preclude a more holistic (or 'compositionist') methodology. Even the strongest exponents of a reductionist philosophy do not deny that. Crick, for example, a few pages on from that quotation from *Of Molecules and Man*, writes as follows:

> Tactics dictate whether one studies an organism as a whole or breaks it up into bits and studies the bits. In molecular biology the spectacular recent advances have mainly come because the combination of these two approaches has been used, in this case applied to such relatively simple organisms as a bacterial cell. Studying the cell as a living unit enables us to see in a broad way what it does. The system is usually too complicated to enable one to deduce from such experiments the exact details of the mechanisms inside the cell. Breaking open the cell and studying the bits enables one to find the exact behaviour but the breaking process may produce artefacts. To avoid these one must go back to the study of the intact cell. Eventually one may hope to have the whole of biology explained in terms of the level below it and so on, right down to the atomic level.[11]

Another exponent of the reductionist view, K. F. Schaffner, affirms similarly:

I do think there's still an enormous amount of work to be done at the macroscopic, non-molecular level. It is only because of the genuinely *biological* techniques that were developed in the areas of genetics and cytology that molecular biology has made such startling breakthroughs . . . . The antireductionist biologist, accordingly, seems to be restricted to asserting a type of 'make believe' autonomy. He may plan, execute, and interpret his experiments without worrying about reduction to a molecular level, but this is no reason for maintaining that a biological entity is anything *more than* something ultimately characterisable and explicable by molecular biology . . . . This make-believe autonomy [of the whole biological structure] may well be heuristically valuable, though perhaps relative to a particular stage of development of the sciences. There seems to be no positive evidence, either logical or empirical, for any real autonomy.[12]

Popper, who does not usually link himself with the reductionist view, argues[13] that scientific reductions are in fact rarely successful; even the most obvious one, of chemistry to physics, he claims, is not completely successful, because chemistry could not be what it is if the galaxies had not had a certain history leading to the formation of the heavy elements. But he then goes on to say that it is vital to go on attempting reductions, because we learn an immense amount in making such attempts. Thus methodological reductions are vindicated even if they are never entirely successful because we learn so much by trying to do them.

Controversy on methodological reductionism begins only when exclusive claims are made that the analytical reductionist prescription for research is the only fruitful and legitimate mode of investigation, in biology in particular. Then biologists such as Dobzhansky, who was not intellectually comfortable with a reductionist methodology and explanations, have to urge the claims of a contrasting methodology, which can be broadly called 'holistic' (he actually called it 'compositionist'). The holistic approach recognises that in biology there are several hierarchically superimposed levels of integration of structures and functions. For example, the use of adaptations, of both structures and processes, to the whole organism for survival and reproduction in an environment has to be the focus of attention at a level of combination of many factors. A trait of the whole organism can only be described and known as 'adaptive' in relation to this whole. (It is, in fact, a trait which enhances the probability of survival and reproduction in this milieu.)

Dobzhansky argued that the biologist does not really have to choose between a reductionist and holistic (compositionist) approach: both are equally necessary; they are complementary to each other; each is incomplete without the other; and, indeed, at the present state of knowledge, each is incomplete by itself.[14] Such a view recognises that the various levels of integration of structure and function (e.g., along the series – ecosystems, populations, individuals, cells and organelles, macromolecules) necessitate methods, both intellectual and experimental, which are specific to those levels, namely (in the same order as in the parenthesis above), community ecology, zoo and plant geography; population ecology, population genetics; morphology, physiology, cell physiology; biochemistry, biophysics. Understanding of both the pattern and the component units of any one level is required.

This eirenic approach rejects the extreme, methodological-reductionist view that complete knowledge of components will automatically reveal the patterns which they compose. The very complexity of organismic patterns of structure and function should deter one from adopting this extreme position, and few will be found to do so. But some reductionists, while recognising the complementarity of reductionist and holistic methodologies, nevertheless do so only as a kind of concession to the present incompleteness of our knowledge and still believe, however vaguely, that the expectation is that all the sciences, in particular biology, will be reduced to physics and chemistry. In what sense this view has been propounded and what its validity is can emerge only if we examine other, more philosophical forms of reductionism. These raise much broader questions of the kind, 'Is the relation between theories at different levels purely linguistic, for example, a relation between biological statements and physicochemical statements?' and 'What do we count as explanations, and do they operate in the same way at different levels of complexity?' Clearly, the issue of reductionism in this more philosophical mode implicates many major problems in the philosophy of science. In what follows, I shall try to isolate the issue of reductionism as far as possible but with the warning that, in the long run, it is a Pandora's box in the philosophy of science.

Ontological reductionism

Put crudely, ontological reductionism consists in the view that complex wholes (in particular, and in our focus of interest, biological organisms) are 'nothing but' their component parts. It is a statement about what certain entities *are*: hence the designation of this form of reductionism as 'ontological,' that is, concerned with being. Everything, however, then turns on how the 'nothing but' in this (too) brief statement of ontological reductionism is elaborated and unpacked. In the literature on this subject, the term 'ontological reductionism' has been used in two ways, which must now be discussed with the relation of biology to physics and chemistry especially in view.

The first implies that the laws of physics and chemistry apply to all biological processes at the atomic and molecular levels and excludes all 'vitalist' views which suggest that some entity or substance is added to atoms and molecules to constitute them as living organisms. There would be wide agreement upon this form of ontological reductionism which simply asserts that complex wholes are indeed made up of units that obey their own particular laws which are not abrogated by their assembly into these larger wholes – that, e.g., physicochemical entities and processes underlie all living phenomena. Such 'ontological reductionism' 'implies that the laws of physics and chemistry fully apply to all biological processes at the level of atoms and molecules'.[15] The physicochemical features of life are then focused upon as in its description by the physical chemist C. N. Hinshelwood:

> One might in very general terms regard a mass of living matter
> as a macromolecular, polyfunctional free radical system, of low
> entropy in virtue of its order, with low activation energy for
> various reactions in virtue of its centres, and possessing a degree
> of permanence in virtue of a relatively rigid structure.[16]

This view is distinguished particularly by what it excludes – namely, that certain entities other than physicochemical ones operate and are present in biological organisms and so constitute them as 'living' organisations of matter. This latter view (denoted as 'vitalism') is almost totally rejected by biological scientists even when they take up positions opposed to other forms of reductionism. However, there is still the possibility that one can be both antireductionist and antivitalist, as will be shown.

It is important to note that what is excluded by this view is the existence of any ontological entities (be they ethereal soul stuff, élan vital, life force, or entelechy), the addition of which to the organisation of atoms and molecules then constitutes them as living. This is tantamount to asserting that no extra 'substance' is added to atoms and molecules when they adopt the complex organisation which is characterised as 'living'. If that is what is being rejected, then this form of ontological reductionism must, and indeed does, command almost universal assent among both scientists and philosophers. For the biological sciences have scored their most spectacular successes by acting on such nonvitalist assumptions. For these reasons, this form of ontological reductionism is acceptable even to those who are antireductionist, in the sense that they deny some of the philosophical forms of reductionism yet to be described. However, it is important to be clear that the foregoing, true though it is, does not entail a second, and stronger, form of ontological reductionism which asserts that biological organisms are 'nothing but' atoms and molecules in the sense that a physicochemical account of their atomic and molecular processes is all there is to be said about them.

This is a natural enough conclusion for any scientist trained in physics and chemistry to adopt through any investigations he makes of biological organisms. As it happens, I started my research career by studying how physical chemistry could be applied to the biologically highly significant molecules of DNA. We took very biological entities, herring roes, and we ground them up, filtered and extracted them. We eventually obtained sticky solutions from which, by freeze-drying, one could obtain in a bottle DNA as a fibrous material, rather like blotting paper. Then we tried to study the physical chemistry of its solutions. As time went on, we came to understand that in these bottles we had the very molecules which carried the genetic information. In other words, we had a bit of the hereditary material in the test-tube, behaving not unlike a synthetic macromolecule, in some respects; so we used the methods of macromolecular physical chemistry to examine them. Chemistry was being applied to this key molecule of life. It would have been a very natural transition to have thought that physics and chemistry were really going to explain all.

However, because complex wholes are made up of constituent units which obey their own laws at their own level (in this instance, biological organisms are made up of molecules which obey physicochemical laws), this need not mean that merely instancing the component units (molecules, etc.) of a complex whole (living organism) and their mutual relations at that level entails there being nothing else to be said. It is indeed true that the answer to 'What else is there?' – e.g., other than atoms or molecules in a living organism – is 'no-*thing* at all', but this need not mean that describing the molecular constituents and their properties is all there is to be said (i.e., that there is *nothing more* to be said).[17]

Such a strong form of ontological reductionism, which has been dubbed colloquially as 'nothing but-tery' by D. M. MacKay,[18] is opposed by those who wish to assert, as I do, that, even while recognising that the constituent units of a complex whole (such as atoms and molecules in a living organism) obey their relevant laws at their own level, there is indeed much more to be said. It may be true that even the Archbishop of Canterbury is 59 percent water, but so also are President Reagan and the latest Nobel laureate. There is something more to be said, even if one does not want to say that there is some special extra entity present in living organisms.

At the beginning of this chapter, I quoted Crick's remark, 'The ultimate aim of the modern movement in biology is in fact to explain *all* biology in terms of physics and chemistry', as a typically strongly reductionist statement. Indeed, it would amount to an avowal of strong ontological reductionism if, as it seems superficially, the 'physics and chemistry' in terms of which he claims biology is to be explained are the laws of physics and chemistry of atoms and molecules and their processes only as we know them at present and only as they are applied to atomic and molecular processes as such. So interpreted, this remark has often been regarded as a classic statement of such strong ontological reductionism and has been opposed by many authors.[19] However, if by 'physics and chemistry' Crick meant – and the research activities of molecular biologists would be consistent with this – a much expanded form of these sciences, then what he is asserting becomes more obscure. Is the expansion of physics and chemistry going to absorb into its conceptual schemes more purely biological concepts such as adaptation, immune response, and so on? If so, the designation of that according to which biology is to be explained as 'physics and chemistry' becomes a purely semantic operation and a misleading one at that. However, even this statement by Crick, which has often been taken as typical of strong ontological reductionism, is explicitly about explanation and not ontology as such, although it is a natural conclusion and often also a hidden implication that biological organisms *are* 'nothing but atoms and molecules' if they are fully explained in terms of the sciences of atoms and molecules. So this nest of ambiguities leads us inevitably into epistemological considerations concerning reductionism.

In brief, and with reference to biology, the form of ontological reductionism, which asserts that the laws of physics and chemistry fully apply to all biological processes at the level of atoms and molecules, seems scarcely to be in dispute; but strong ontological reductionism, which, in asserting that biological organisms are 'nothing but' atoms and molecules, seems to be implying that a physicochemical account of their atomic and molecular processes is all there is to be said, is widely regarded as inadequate, and is much disputed. It is often expressed ambiguously, for it is also concerned with explanation. This leads naturally to a consideration of the 'something more' that has to be said over and beyond purely physicochemical accounts of living organisms.

Epistemological reductionism

The philosophical debate on reductionism has centred principally on 'whether the theories and experimental laws formulated in one field of science can be shown to be special cases of theories and laws formulated in some other branch of science', and, 'if such is the case, the former branch of science is said to have been reduced to the latter'.[9] This is an epistemological – even linguistic – kind of reduction and, not surprisingly, it touches on important problems in the philosophy of science.

Philosophical discussions of reductionism are often, for example, associated with the theme of the relation between wholes and parts. The laws that explain the behaviour of the whole, it is often suggested, cannot be derived from the laws that explain the behaviour of the parts, acting separately. This is what defines an organic whole or unity to which epistemological reduction is inapplicable. The meaning and usage of the terms 'whole', 'parts', 'sum', and 'organic unity' were carefully analysed by Nagel.[20] The fundamental issue of relevance here is whether the analysis of 'organic unities', of organic wholes, necessarily involves the adoption of irreducible laws for these systems and whether their organisation is of such a kind as to preclude a simple summation of their parts to yield the whole.

Such an 'additive' analysis appears to be one which accounts for the properties of a system in terms of assumptions about its constituents, taken in isolation from the system; and 'a "non-additive" analysis seems to be one which formulates the characteristics of a system in terms of relations between certain of its parts as functioning elements in the system'.[21] Nagel concludes that, although there is no doubt that there are functional wholes whose constituent parts are internally related, in the sense that these constituents stand to each other in relations of mutual causal interdependence, 'some functional wholes certainly can be analysed in that manner [from the additive point of view] while in the case of others (for example, living organisms) no fully satisfactory analysis of that type has yet been achieved. Accordingly the mere fact that a system is a structure of dynamically interrelated parts does not suffice, by itself, to prove that the laws of such a system cannot be reduced to some theory developed initially for certain assumed constituents of the system.'[22] This conclusion, modest though it is, shows that the issue of the relation of wholes to parts, whether 'additive' or 'nonadditive', is not one which can be settled in a wholesale and *a priori* fashion. Each system needs to be examined on its own merits in this regard, even each biological system and level of inquiry.

Now the expansion of our knowledge of the natural world which has occurred particularly in this century has shown it more and more to consist of a hierarchy of systems, and this is particularly true of the various levels of organisation to be observed in living organisms. The sequence of increasing complexity to be found in the living world (atom, molecule, macromolecule, submolecular organelle, cell, multicelluar functioning organ, whole living organism, population of organisms, ecosystem) represents a series of levels of organisation of matter in which each successive member of the series is a 'whole' constituted of 'parts' preceding it in the series (for convenience, let each member of this series be called 'higher' than the one preceding it in the list above). The higher members are 'wholes', in Nagel's sense of being 'pattern[s] or configuration[s] formed by elements standing to each other in certain relations' and, more to the point, being 'organised systems of dynamically interrelated parts'.[23] The issue, with respect to the biological level, is whether biological organisms and systems are indeed 'organic unities', which require nonadditive analysis in Nagel's sense.[24] To resolve this issue, it is necessary to distinguish carefully the hierarchy of systems from the hierarchy of the theories of the sciences concerned with the systems.

The *hierarchy of natural systems* has been described frequently and needs no further elaboration, especially as it is not in dispute among scientists.[25] The concept of a set of hierarchically organised systems has also been thoroughly investigated from a more abstract viewpoint, and the conditions for a set of part-whole relations to constitute a 'perfect hierarchy' were formulated by Beckner.[26] After affirming that, with some inadequacy of fit (e.g., not all the tissues of an organism are composed of cells), biological organisms may be regarded as cases of such hierarchies, Beckner continues,

> The hierarchy model has historically provided a large part of the framework of discussion in the philosophy of biology. It is involved in a wide range of connected ideas: levels of organisation, sequences of boundaries . . ., autonomy at one level with respect to lower ones, a temporal order in the arrival of the higher levels on the cosmic scene, the emergence of higher-level entities, etc. The existence of hierarchical systems is certainly connected with the hierarchical arrangement of theories. But I do think we lack a detailed philosophical account of the connections, in part because the relations between higher and lower-level theories are not too well understood.[27]

Our view of what constitutes a *hierarchy of theories*, he argues, is influenced not only by notions of scope and generality but also by the empirical fact that there are very many hierarchically organised systems, and these provide us with a way of arranging sciences (and their associated theories) on a kind of ladder (see Figures 1, 2). A science at a particular level is then one largely concerned with systems at a particular corresponding level in the hierarchy of natural systems, and is composed of theories and experimental laws pertaining to that level.[28]

The reducibility of a theory at a higher level to a theory at a lower level has been a central concern of philosophers of science.[29] If a theory (or experimental law) within the science applicable to a higher level can be shown, in some sense (see below), to be a special case of a theory (and law) formulated within the science applicable to a lower level, then the higher level theory (or law) is said to have been reduced to the lower level theory. Possible samples of such pairs, of higher and lower level theories, might be, respectively: (much of chemistry) – (physics); (geometrical optics) – (physical optics); (gas laws) – (laws of molecular motion); (classical thermodynamics) – (statistics of molecular motion); (Mendelian genetics) – (DNA structure, coding, and transcription). More precisely, Nagel formulates reduction as the *explicability* of all the laws of the higher in the lower level theory, and the logical conditions for

Figure 1

h = 'higher'
l = 'lower'

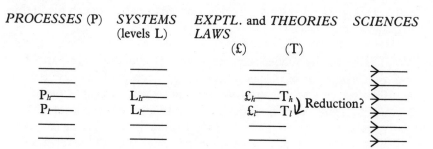

| PROCESSES (P) | SYSTEMS (levels L) | EXPTL. and LAWS ($£$) | THEORIES (T) | SCIENCES |

P_h——— L_h——— $£_h$——T_h $\Big\}$ Reduction?

P_l——— L_l——— $£_l$——T_l

Figure 2

SYSTEMS	SCIENCES	
	Non-Human – – – – – –Human	
1. Ensembles of eco-systems		Social anthropology
2. Eco-systems	Community ecology zoo- and plant geography	Sociology
3. Populations	Population ecology population genetics ethology	Sociology
4. Individual organisms	Cell biology, physiology, ethology	Psychology
5. Cells and organelles	Cytology, cell physiology	
6. Biological macromolecules and small molecules	Biochemistry and biophysics	
7. Molecules and atoms	Chemistry	
8. Atomic structure and sub-nuclear 'particles'	Physics	

this which he has formulated have commanded wide assent,[30] although Hempel, at least, has regarded them as an over-simplification and overly linguistic.[31]

The foregoing represents only a small, although central, sample of the discussions by philosophers of science about the question of reduction of theories in science. This not inconsiderable activity[32] has contributed valuably to our understanding of science and also has implications for interpreting its history as well as for assessing the actual success of attempts at reduction.[33]

Similar issues have arisen when practising scientists have reflected on the *hierarchy of the sciences*.[34] Thus Medawar notes that as one goes along the series physics-chemistry-biology-ecology/sociology, each represents a subclass within the possible interaction of the units of the preceding level, and 'the sciences become richer and richer in their empirical content and new concepts emerge at each level which simply do not appear in the preceding science'.[35] Corresponding to each level in the hierarchy of systems, the appropriate science employs concepts which are peculiar to it and indeed have little meaning for levels lower down (or even higher up in some cases). As new forms of matter, non-living and living, emerge in the universe, new categories of description of their form and properties are necessary and these categories will be other than those of the physics and chemistry appropriate to the subnuclear, atomic and molecular levels. Moreover, every statement true in a science earlier (or lower) in the series of the sciences is true in the later (or higher), but these statements are usually not the focus of interest for the practitioners of a higher-level science because they do not constitute their distinctive problem. For such reasons, sociologists have insisted on the distinctiveness of sociological concepts from biological, and biologists the distinctiveness of their concepts in relation to physics and chemistry.

Apparently, what many practising scientists are concerned to emphasize is this distinctiveness of the concepts of their own science, of which they are only too well aware when they try to communicate with scientists of other disciplines. This distinctiveness has been more precisely delineated by Beckner as *theory autonomy*, the autonomy of higher-level theories with respect to lower-level theories in the sense that the higher are not epistemologically reducible (according to Nagel's criteria) to the lower.[36] This analysis stresses theory autonomy as a relation between parts of scientific languages and is carefully distinguished by Beckner from *process autonomy*, which 'has nothing to do with the languages we choose to describe [processes] but rather with some sort of causal independence'.[37] He defines a higher-level process as being autonomous with respect to processes in a 'lower' level if, and only if, the laws of the higher-level processes are not fully determined by the laws of processes (of a different kind) at the lower level.[38] The autonomy of processes is about what 'we may as well call real relations (causal, identity, spatial, temporal, part-whole, etc.) between the events and other phenomena that our languages describe',[39] whereas the reduction of theories can certainly be called *epistemological*, for it is about 'the logical relations that hold between theories, descriptions, conceptual schemes and other instances of language'.[39]

Much of the confusion in the discussion of reductionism has resulted from a failure to distinguish adequately between, on the one hand, the hierarchy of *sciences*, with their associated theories, concepts, descriptions, etc., and the logical relationships among them (i.e., the question of autonomy of theories) and, on the other hand, the hierarchy of actual *systems* and the real relations (causal, spatial, temporal, part-whole, identity) among the events, processes, etc., occurring at each level in this hierarchy (i.e., the question of the autonomy of processes). Causal connections have to be more carefully defined and analysed for hierarchical systems than they do for pairs of systems which have no parts in common.[26]

Since the non-reducibility of a higher-level theory to a lower-level theory may be due to differences in their conceptual structure and not to lack of determination of processes in the higher level by processes in the lower level, the autonomy of higher-level *processes* is not necessarily linked with the non-reducibility of higher-level *theories*. So there are four hypothetically conceivable combinations of the two types of relation of higher- to lower-level *processes* (autonomy or non-autonomy) with the two types of relation of higher- to lower-level *theories*. Three of these are indicated by the lines in Figure 3 (the fourth has, not surprisingly, never been proposed as applicable to any higher-level/lower-level relation). Of these three relations, one is that of plain reduction, namely, when higher-level theories are reducible and higher-level processes are not autonomous: such a strong form of epistemological reduction becomes indistinguishable from the second kind of ontological reduction described in the previous section. Of the other two relationships represented by lines in Figure 3, one (the lower horizontal) represents a form of non-reduction whereby not only are the higher-level theories non-reducible to lower-level ones but the higher-level processes are autonomous with respect to lower-level processes. Beckner[39] has little difficulty in showing that those who hold this 'strong' form of non-reduction (or 'strong organicism') are driven to postulating a non-material cause operating in the higher-level system. In other words the 'strong organicist' is driven to vitalism.

Figure 3

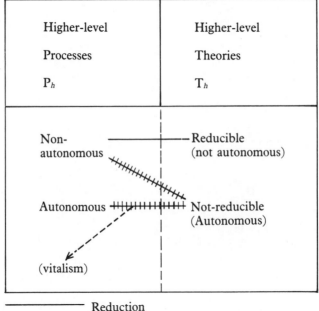

However, the diagonal combination in Figure 3 represents a form of non-reduction that has to be seriously considered in our present context; it is the case when the higher-level processes are not autonomous (i.e., the regularities of the higher-level processes are fully consistent with the laws of the lower-level processes) but the higher-level theories themselves are not reducible. It is clearly possible to be an anti-reductionist, in this weaker form, without being a vitalist in regard to biology. The categories of description and the concepts appropriate to the higher level are, in this case, not reducible (à la Nagel) to those applicable at the lower level, although the processes at this lower level fully operate in it, and do not have to be augmented (under their lower-level descriptions) at the higher level.

2 Is biology nothing but physics and chemistry?

Reduction of biology to physics and chemistry

In the light of the analyses of reductionism in the previous chapter where does biology stand in relation to physics and chemistry? We have seen that an attitude of methodological reductionism toward biology is permissible, indeed often necessary for research, but needs always to be balanced by compositionist methodologies. We have seen that forms of ontological reduction of biology, whereby the atomic and molecular components of biological systems obey the laws of physics and chemistry, are not disputed. The argument among biologists concerned with this question then centres chiefly on epistemological reductionism and what I have called 'strong' ontological reductionism. Beckner's distinction between theory and process autonomy is here of special value.

The biological scientist is certainly keenly conscious not only that biological organisation is a hierarchy of parts making wholes at different levels but also that dynamic processes are themselves interlocked dynamically in space and time in more complex networks. Thus processes at the molecular level, such as enzymatic reactions, are part of a network of interlocked reactions of this kind in a metabolic web, itself distributed spatially over a structurally hierarchical framework of organelles, which are themselves inter-connected by structures and by chemical messengers in a larger whole (the cell), which is itself incorporated into organs – and so on. Hence, regarding the hierarchy of systems as simply a static assembly of building blocks constituting different kinds of parts at different levels, so that within each 'part', so conceived, particular processes go on and are then just added together to make the next level, does not correspond to the dynamic complexity which the biologist observes in living organisms.

Is biology nothing but physics and chemistry?

The biologist is bound, therefore, to stress the special concepts he has to employ to describe and understand such complexities. He finds that, at each new level of biological organization, new kinds of interlocking relationships emerge, and these require new concepts to order them and render them coherent – as well as distinctive experimental techniques and designs of experiment. Such a biologist would therefore strongly support the autonomy of biological concepts; that is, he is *epistemologically* antireductionist, at least in the sense of the diagonal of Figure 3. It is this autonomy of biological theory in relation to physics and chemistry which numerous biologists have been concerned to emphasise. There are, indeed, distinctive ideas in biology which simply cannot be envisaged or translated into the conceptual terms of physics and chemistry.[1] This perception has been particularly well and forcibly expressed by François Jacob, one of the architects of molecular biology in its crucial developments in the 1960s:

> From particles to man, there is a whole series of integration, of levels, of discontinuities. But there is no breach either in the composition of the objects or in the reactions that take place in them; no change in 'essence'. So much so, that investigation of molecules and cellular organelles has now become the concern of physicists. . . . This does not at all mean that biology has become an annex of physics, that it represents as it were, a junior branch concerned with complex systems. At each level of organization, novelties appear in both properties and logic. To reproduce is not within the power of any single molecule by itself. This faculty appears only with the simplest integron deserving to be called a living organism, that is, the cell. But thereafter the rules of the game change. At the higher-level integron, the cell population, natural selection imposes new constraints and offers new possibilities. In this way, and without ceasing to obey the principles that govern inanimate systems, living systems become subject to phenomena that have no meaning at the lower level. *Biology can neither be reduced to physics, nor do without it.* Every object that biology studies is a system of systems. Being part of a higher-order system itself, it sometimes obeys rules that cannot be deduced simply by analysing it. This means that each level of organization must be considered with reference to the adjacent levels. . . . At every level of integration, some new characteristics come to

light. . . . Very often, concepts and techniques that apply at one level do not function either above or below it. The various levels of biological organization are united by the logic proper to reproduction. They are distinguished by the means of communication, the regulatory circuits and the internal logic proper to each system.[2]

Such autonomy of biological *processes*, we have been urging, is a philosophically defensible view, but some authors have moved over from stressing the autonomy of biological *theory* to basing their arguments on the fact that biological organisms evidence new, complex relationships between their constituent parts, and it is these relationships *per se* which, being logically distinct, are then assigned an autonomy of a kind which moves their position closer (although often obscurely so) to the lower horizontal line of Figure 3, that is, towards 'strong organicism'. We have seen that the kind of antireductionist position which argues for theory autonomy is not at all logically committed to process autonomy. Yet some authors, in arguing for the former, slide gently into the latter through an emphasis on the new relationships which biological organisms manifest. They are then vulnerable to the attack of philosophers, for whom it is almost trivial and obvious that, as Smart puts it, 'new qualities emerge when samples are put together to form a complex',[3] as when the pieces which constitute a radio set are connected in the proper sequence and then receive signals. Yet this point, regarded by such philosophers as a very modest one, is often the one which, for example, biologists want minimally to affirm when told that their subject is nothing but 'physics and chemistry'.

One form of antireductionist argument which makes this kind of stress on relationships has been developed by Polanyi, who says that there are 'boundary conditions' which characterise machines in relation to their components, and he then transfers the same argument to the relation of biology to physics and chemistry.[4] His initial point is that for machines (say, a steam engine) the principles ('boundary conditions') which determine the spatial relationships of the constituent units are those of mechanical engineering and are distinct from the properties of the separate units, described in physicochemical terms. Further kinds of description are required to explicate the relations between parts peculiar even to that level of organisation of matter which is a machine.[5] This initial stage of Polanyi's argument is vulnerable to the criticism that the concepts of mechanical engineering are reducible to physics and chemistry, at least in principle; for given the parts with their physicochemical properties *and the relationships between these parts*, the operation of the machine can be deduced. It would then seem plausible to argue that mechanical engineering is indeed reducible to physics and chemistry. However, the italicized phrase is crucial to his argument, for the differentiating characteristic of the concepts of mechanical engineering is that they are concerned with these relationships between parts and are, to that extent, distinct from those of physics and chemistry. Whether or not this is sufficient to establish theory autonomy and so lead to the epistemological antireductionism of the kind represented by the diagonal in Figure 3 is the question at issue.

Polanyi would regard himself as an antireductionist, yet we find Schaffner making almost the same point, although he clearly sees himself as a reductionist.[6] He defines the 'biological principle of reduction' as that, 'given an organism composed out of chemical constituents, the present behaviour of that organism is a function [causal or theoretical?] of the constituents as they are characterisable in isolation *plus* the topological causal inter-structure of the chemical constituents. (The environment must, of course, in certain conditions, be specified.)'[7] Yet the crux of the question is his '*plus*' – not to mention the 'environment', which must be taken to include that larger part of biology concerned with the interaction of living creatures with one another and with the physical world, in fact in ecosystems. For it is the very nature, character, and existence of what Schaffner calls the 'topological causal interstructure' to denote the spatial arrangements and causal signal influences. This is what requires biology to be a distinctive science needing concepts of a quite different kind from those of (say) chemistry, which has to understand molecular behaviour in relation to atomic arrangements.

However, this form of the stress on the relationships of the parts has not always impressed philosophers. There is a real problem here, it seems, about the logical character of biological theory and to what extent biological theories can be regarded as autonomous (i.e., not reducible in Nagel's sense), simply and only on the grounds that they have to concern themselves with the special kinds of biological interrelationships between units. This is not a question that can readily be settled for all biological theory *in toto* but is a matter for investigation in each case.

Polanyi's argument has more force and is certainly less superficially vulnerable to the foregoing criticism when he applies it not to a machine but to a biological system – for example, a living cell with its complex configuration in space and time, with its flow of constantly changing substances both within and across the cell membrane, and with its possession of an individual 'life cycle'. He has based a similar argument on certain molecular structures with biological specificity.[8] The chemical structure of DNA, the covalent (—) and hydrogen bonds (represented by a dot) which link them, thereby enabling specific bases to be paired (A·T, G·C), are describable in terms of the categories of physics and chemistry and are studied on this basis by physical biochemists and biophysicists. Within the double helical structure, there are sequences of base pairs. For example,

$$A — G — C — A — G — T — \ldots$$
$$T — C — G — T — C — A — \ldots$$

All such sequences of these four base-pair 'units' are equally permissible physicochemically (within certain minor limits which do not affect the argument) and can fit equally well into the structure. Yet, in the nuclei of any particular cell of a given organism, within its DNA double helices there are particular specific sequences which perform a unique set of coding functions (for the construction, say, of a particular enzyme). *This* particular base sequence in *this* DNA has a 'meaning' (i.e., a defined readout via the code) only when the DNA has been assembled in *that* organism and can have its biochemical function as a genetic 'blueprint' for the production of, for example, a specific protein only when it functions in the milieu of the whole organism. Chemical processes are, indeed, the means whereby bases are incorporated into chains of DNA (so that there is no case here of process autonomy), but the sequence in which the bases are assembled in the DNA is a function and property of the whole organism. Since no 'laws' or regularities of physics or chemistry describing the nature and stability of the chemical bonds in the DNA as such can specify the actual *sequence* of base pairs in any particular case, this analysis supports the kind of epistemological anti-reductionism which affirms theory autonomy. The concept of 'information transfer' which is needed to understand what is going on *biologically* when DNA functions in an actual cell cannot be articulated in terms of the concepts of physics and chemistry, even though the latter explain how the molecular machinery (DNA, RNA and enzymes) operates to convey information. For the concept of 'information' is meaningless except with reference to the functioning of the whole cell, itself conceived in relation to its genetic and evolutionary history. In no textbook of chemistry or physics, *as such*, would (indeed, do) the concepts of 'information theory' have to be expounded to understand molecular chemistry or atomic physics. It is a concept applicable to the molecular system of DNA-RNA-protein only when these complex structures are linked in networks of interrelations constituting the whole cell.

Thus there does seem to be a *prima facie* case for arguing that some biological concepts, and so theories, are autonomous, are not reducible in the strict sense; certainly, biological concepts and theories are distinctive of the biological level in the natural hierarchy of systems, as many have argued.[1] Because of this distinctiveness, it is not likely that all biological theory is going to prove to be reducible to physics and chemistry.

New bottles for new wine?

What the conceptual schemes will be which can deal with the 'topological causal interstructures' (Schaffner[7]) of the many different kinds discovered, and yet to be discovered, in biological organisms is still an open question, as is their autonomy or otherwise with respect to lower-level theories. These new conceptual schemes will have to integrate into a single framework the multi-level mode of operation of a biological organism, of which *ex hypothesi* the molecular level described by physics and chemistry would be only one, and will also have to include, in some way as yet unknown, the purposeful exploratory activity of at least the higher organisms. There is no special reason why the molecular level should be selected out arbitrarily as that at which alone explanation is necessary to understand all the other levels.

The application of thermodynamic and kinetic principles, for example, to the study of the existence and evolution of something as complex as living organisms, has exemplified repeatedly the need to stretch the characteristic concepts of thermodynamics and kinetics to situations never envisaged in classical physics and chemistry.[9] At many points entirely new concepts have to be devised, e.g., that of dissipative structures and 'order through fluctuations' of the Brussels school[10] and of 'selection' and the 'quality factor', as applied to an assembly of macromolecules by Eigen and his colleagues.[11] Sometimes these involve the juxtaposition of ideas drawn from quite different sources, as when electrical-network theory and thermodynamics were combined by Katchalsky and his colleagues to create network thermodynamics with biological applications in mind.[12] There seems to be here a case for recognizing that new non-reducible concepts are being required to allow these classical physico-chemical disciplines to cope with biological complexity. Or, to put it another way, the physics and chemistry in terms of which living systems are being interpreted is a 'physics' and 'chemistry' so profoundly modified by the incorporation of characteristically biological concepts that it is as much a question of whether physics and chemistry have been taken into biology as whether biology has been 'reduced' to physics and chemistry. In the end, this may come only to a semantic quibble, but the developments described here certainly do not warrant a naive reductionism. For the physicochemical investigator of living systems is again and again baffled by the lack of conceptual resources in received physics and chemistry to deal with such complexity and with the demanding intellectual need for new ones.[13] Benno Hess, who has made important contributions to understanding the complexities of a particular biological system, that of glycolysis, has expressed the situation cogently thus:

> The analysis of many of [the] properties of 'large' living systems is experimentally and theoretically limited by currently available techniques. While the lower limits of reductionism in the description of biological order seem clearly defined in the concept of dissipative structures, an understanding of the function of the large complexity of biological systems is lacking. Although it is clearly recognized that biological systems are irreversibly organized (they do not explode or decay under ordinary conditions but seem to grow and evolve toward a singularity or limit cycle if energy and matter is available), the rules of their network composition, their underlying network hierarchy, and their order in time and space remain to be understood.[14]

What is 'for real'?

Because of widely pervasive reductionist pre-suppositions, there has been a tendency to regard the level of atoms and molecules as alone being 'real'. However, there are good grounds for not affirming any special priority to this level of description. Indeed it has been argued by Wimsatt[15] that there should be a *prima facie* recognition of the need for a variety of independent derivation, identification, or measurement procedures[16] for examining the existence and character of any phenomenon, object, or result with the aim of looking for what is invariant over (or identical in) the outcome of these procedures. What is invariant, at whatever level the procedures are directed, Wimsatt calls 'robust', implying that what is yielded by the procedures appropriate to each level of investigation can be said to be real. In other words 'reality' is, on this view, what the various levels of description and examination of living systems actually refer to. It is not confined to the physicochemical alone. One must accept a certain 'robustness' (Wimsatt) of the entities postulated or, rather, discovered at different levels and resist any attempts to regard them as less real in comparison with some favoured lower level of 'reality' (which, if it is that of atomic and subatomic particles, turns out anyway to have its own kind of elusiveness, as any particle physicist will confirm). There is no sense in which subatomic particles are to be graded as 'more real' than, say, a bacterial cell or a human person or, even, social facts. Each level has to be regarded as a cut through the totality of reality, if you like, in the sense that we have to take account of its mode of operation at that level.

Emergence and other interfaces

The foregoing has been principally concerned with that 'X/Y' interface[17] which lies between biology, on the one hand, and physics-and-chemistry, on the other, for this is one of the central concerns of the new biology. Insofar as biological concepts and theories are not reducible, in the sense already discussed, to the concepts and theories of physics-and-chemistry, the distinctive biological phenomena to which these concepts and theories refer can be said to be 'emergent', where this term is synonymous with the 'theory autonomy' of the preceding discussion. The term 'emergence' is, of course, particularly appropriate when the time sequence of evolution is being attended to, for then it serves to point especially to the fact that biological evolution (and indeed cosmic evolution, too) is characterised by an increasing complexity of organization of the new forms of living matter that appear at the various stages of evolution, this succession of forms itself constituting a hierarchy of complexity.

But what is true about the interface between biology and physics-and-chemistry is also true of interfaces higher up in the scale of complexity of the hierarchy of natural systems. There is again no automatic and inevitable possibility of reducing the concepts and theories of the science of a higher level to the concepts and theories of a science at a lower level. Just as when we move from the physiological to the neurophysiological, or from the latter to the psychological, or from this latter to the sociological, new phenomena characteristic of the higher level may well be 'emergent', in the sense defined above, that is, the concepts and theories applicable to them may not be epistemologically reducible to lower-level theories. If they are not so reducible, are genuinely 'emergent', then, by the argument above, it will be appropriate gradually to attribute reality to that to which they refer. It will be as much in order to predicate the adjective 'real' of the distinctive terms and entities that the higher-level concepts and theories employ as of those employed in the lower-level concepts and theories. It will be a matter of investigation in any particular case whether or not the higher-level concepts and theories are not so reducible: some, but not all, will prove to be so in the course of the critical sifting processes of the scientific community.

Thus terms such as 'consciousness', 'person', 'social facts' are not prematurely to be dismissed from the vocabulary used to describe the human condition since in all three of these instances a strong case can be made for the distinctiveness and non-reducibility of the concepts they denote. For example, as we shall argue later, consciousness is not to be dismissed as 'nothing but physics-and-chemistry, or neurophysiological interconnections', but may properly be regarded as a genuinely emergent, real feature at that level in the hierarchy of complexity which is the human brain in the human body (and perhaps lower down and earlier on in evolution). So the biologist who adopts, entirely consistently with his science, a theory-autonomous antireductionism concerning biological concepts should also be open to viewing consciousness as an emergent, in the way already defined.

Furthermore, such concepts equally become candidates for being regarded as referring to emergent realities. Hence the special terms and language used to refer to these higher levels of integration can command our respect in that we do not prematurely, without further evidence, reduce their conceptual content to those appropriate to lower levels. In particular, the languages human beings have developed to articulate their states of consciousness and their interactions with each other, the languages of the arts and of personal and social relations (the 'humanities' in general), have an *ab initio* claim to be taken as seriously at their own level of reference as the languages of the sciences have at theirs.[18]

We can, I would urge, go further. I refer to that most complex and all-embracing of the levels in the hierarchies of 'systems', namely the complex of nature-man-and-God. For when human beings are exercising themselves in their God-directed and worshipping activities they are operating at a level in the hierarchy of complexity which is more intricate and cross-related than any of those that arise in the natural and social sciences which are in the province of the humanities. For in his 'religious', i.e., God-related, activities man utilises every facet of his total being: his solitary, inner self-consciousness; his interaction with other people at the most personal level; his interaction with nature and the universe; and his relation to what he regards as ultimate. For religion is about the ultimate meaning that a person finds in his or her relation to all-that-is. 'Religion is a relation to the ultimate'[19] and that ultimate is usually denoted, in English, by the word 'God'.

It seems to me that no higher level or dimension of integration in the hierarchy of natural systems could be envisaged than that between the human person (whose brain-in-body constitutes the most complex organization of matter in the known universe), the whole natural non-human order, and God the ultimate ground of all being and source of all-that-is. Theology is concerned with the conceptual and theoretical articulation of the processes and characteristics of this subtle unity-in-diversity and diversity-in-unity which we call 'religion'. It therefore refers to the most integrated level or dimension we know in the hierarchy of relations. So it should not be surprising if the concepts and theories which are developed to explicate the nature of this activity are uniquely specific to and characteristic of it. As with other higher levels and dimensions, the concepts and theories theologians develop to describe this unique integration should not be prematurely reduced, without adequate proof, to the concepts and theories of other disciplines appropriate to man, society and nature. For, only detailed inquiry could establish which theological concepts and theories, if any, are reducible to (say) those of sociology and psychology.

This putative autonomy assigned here to theology does not, *should* not, preclude the careful study of the component 'units', as it were, of religion, namely, men, society and nature. Knowledge of these can then interact fruitfully with the results of the theological enterprise. We have to set 'religious' affirmations and ways of depicting and understanding the world *alongside* those changing perspectives of human beings in the world which the sciences engender through studying the various levels that occur in the natural hierarchy of systems – in this volume it is the biological level we have particularly in focus. Theology, the explicit intellectual articulation of religion, should be neither immune from the changing outlook of the biological sciences, nor should it be captive to them. The ensuing chapters seek to investigate this subtle and mobile relation.

3 *The new biology – 'holistic'*

In this and the following chapter I shall attempt to pick out some of the leading features of the biology of the second half of the twentieth century – a biology so enlivened by new concepts and techniques that it has (giving a hostage to fortune?) come to be known as the 'new biology'. This designation covers a wider range than what came to be called, in the 1930s and 1940s, 'neo-Darwinism', or the 'synthetic theory' of evolution, or just the 'modern synthesis'. This modern synthesis was an amplification of Darwin's theory (of 'natural' selection through interaction with the environment: see F. Jacob's definition below) by the chromosome theory of heredity, by population genetics, by a revised biological concept of a species and by other new ideas – a synthesis that was at the time mainly the work of Theodosius Dobzhansky, Edmund Ford, Julian Huxley, Ernst Mayr, H. J. Muller, Bernhard Rensch, G. Gaylord Simpson and G. Ledyard Stebbins. The new biology incorporates all these features but also that vigorous new child of biology, biochemistry and physics which was called 'molecular biology', as well as sociobiology, the neuro-sciences and, in general, a vastly more sophisticated, quantitative approach to living organisms, coupled with a greatly enhanced appreciation of the labyrinthine levels of control and of complexity that are gradually being unveiled in even the most apparently simple living organism.

It is already apparent even from this brief description of the 'new biology' that only a few of its features can be picked out for comment because of their significance for wider philosophical and theological reflection. It is convenient, for our present purposes, to subdivide our consideration of the new biology into two areas, using the distinction of Dobzhansky[1]: those ideas and perspectives which result principally from a 'holistic' (or 'compositionist') methodology, in which whole organisms are broadly examined in their total environments; and those perspectives which result principally from a 'reductionist' methodology which encourages the attempt to reduce the concepts and theories of a higher level science (in this case, biology or sociology and the study of behaviour) to those of a lower level science (that is, to physics-and-chemistry in the case of biology, or to biology itself in the case of sociology and the study of behaviour). This distinction within the methodological approaches of the two styles of biological investigation provides a convenient binary classification of the 'new biology', without, in itself, prejudging any general philosophical or theological conclusions about the implications of the biology itself. This chapter will be concerned with the more 'holistic' aspects of the new biology, and the following with the 'reductionist' ones.

Evolution – 'fact' or 'theory'?

To be clear what it is we are referring to when we use the word 'evolution' in relation to living organisms, I can do no better than preface my discussion with a definition from one of the best recent expositions of biological ideas, that of the French Nobel prize-winner François Jacob:

> There are many generalizations in biology, but precious few theories. Among these, the theory of evolution is by far the most important, because it draws together from the most varied sources a mass of observations which would otherwise have remained isolated; it unites all the disciplines concerned with living beings; it establishes order among the extraordinary variety of organisms and closely binds them to the rest of the earth; in short, it provides a causal explanation of the living world and its heterogeneity. The theory of evolution may be summed up essentially in two propositions. First, that all organisms, past, present or future, descend from one or several rare living systems which arose spontaneously. Second, that species are derived from one another by natural selection of the best procreators.[2]

Darwin's proposal of 'natural selection' as the natural process by which evolution, that is, the transformation of species (or 'speciation'), occurred had the impact it did in the history of biology because – although the idea of the evolutionary interconnectedness of living organisms had been widely courted, on the basis of the geological record and morphological

33

similarities, since the time of Lamarck (1744–1829) and of Darwin's own grandfather, Erasmus Darwin (1731–1802) – the idea had seemed implausible without a reasonable *natural* mechanism for its occurrence. That is what Darwin provided.

The proposition that living, and extinct, species of all living organisms are connected by evolutionary relationships became surprisingly and rapidly accepted by biologists as being the only broad concept that made any sense of the burgeoning data of biological observation, even though the acceptability of natural selection as its means had many ups and downs (not least in Darwin's own mind!) until by the end of the nineteenth century the laws of heredity were established by Mendel and, belatedly, became widely promulgated. The advent of the science of genetics, as a quantitative, statistical analysis of hereditary transmission, based on the Mendelian concept of discrete hereditary factors ('genes') controlling such transmission, combined with cytological and genetic investigation of the role of the chromosomes in the cell nucleus in hereditary transmission, led to the 'modern synthesis', already referred to, of Darwinian natural selection with Mendelian genetics as the basic explanation of evolutionary change.

As we shall see, there are today different views about the rate and mechanism of evolution and some of these question *inter alia* the validity of Darwin's own belief that evolution occurred by the gradual, slow accumulation of change (a view that made his theory statistically vulnerable until the Mendelian laws of heredity had been established). Darwin regarded as 'natural' the selection effected by the environment operating on the spectrum of individual differences present in any biological population of a given species, in a way analogous to the human selection of 'sports' among pigeons, dogs or cattle to utilize them for breeding. These changes he regarded as random with respect to the needs of the organism in relation to its environment (its physical, nutritional and biological ambience), but he saw the environment as selecting them 'naturally', by allowing some organisms with particular characteristics to reproduce more readily than others and thus establish themselves as predominant in subsequent populations. We now know that there are discrete hereditary controlling factors, the genes, that these undergo sudden, once-for-all, mutations (caused by various physicochemical agencies) which are random with respect to the 'survivability' of the organism (that is, its ability to live long enough to reproduce). As we shall see, 'randomness', of *this* kind, is now better established than in Darwin's own day, and even than in the 1940s when the 'modern synthesis' was proposed, through knowledge of the underlying molecular mechanisms that has come through *molecular* biology.

We shall have cause to discuss later the interpretation of this mechanism of evolution and its general implications. But, for the moment let me stress that the proposition of evolution – that all forms of life, current and extinct, are interconnected through evolutionary relationships – is not in dispute among biologists. As a group of British Museum (Natural History) biologists said in a letter to *Nature* (defending, be it noted, their use of the phrase 'If the theory of evolution is true . . .' for which a *Nature* editorial had taken them to task): 'What we do have is overwhelming circumstantial evidence in favour of it [the theory of evolution] and as yet no better alternative'.[3]

Much play has been made by 'creationists' of the proposal that the evolutionary account of biological relationships is 'only a theory'. There are a number of confusions locked up in such a view. Any scientific account of the past must be based on inferences from present-day observations. On such reckoning the whole of historical geology and much of modern cosmology would be 'only a theory'. However, inferences of this kind can lead to near-certainty and then it becomes proper to speak of our having inferred what actually happened, 'facts' if you like. By the nature of the case, the postulate of past biological evolution cannot be falsified in the sense of Karl Popper, by performing repeatable experiments whose outcomes are inconsistent with the postulate – nor can most theories of geology and of cosmology. These two sciences share with evolutionary biology a *historical* character, that is, they are concerned with reconstructing what *has* happened to living organisms, the Earth, the solar system, the galaxies, and so on. Such theories cannot be subjected to either verifying or falsifying procedures of an experimental kind, though they can nevertheless be judged by their consistency with present observations and with reasonable extrapolation of current conditions to the past, by their ability to make the most comprehensive sense of the widest range of observations, and by their own internal consistency. Popper's criterion of 'falsifiability' is here quite inadequate and widely recognised to be such.

The idea of biological evolution refers principally to the past and, in its general form, simply affirms the existence of genetic relations between the different organisms we now see on the Earth or know from fossils to have been there in the past. The relationship inferred is, to use Darwin's phrase, that of 'descent' with modification, *by whatever mechanism*. That the mechanism is that of natural selection is another matter and must be substantiated by other means. Whatever controversies there may or may not be about mechanisms of evolution and of its speed, biologists are agreed about the *fact* of evolution itself, that is, that all forms of life, current and extinct, are interconnected through evolutionary relationships.

It is true that when Darwin propounded his theory the evidence for evolution was circumstantial rather than direct. Until the advent of modern biochemistry and molecular biology, the observations with which the postulate of evolution had to be consistent were drawn mainly from comparative anatomy and the morphology of living and extinct organisms (the last mentioned mainly confined to those with hard, skeletal remains), considered in relation to their locality and inferred climate and other environmental conditions.

But twentieth-century biochemistry has now demonstrated fundamental similarities at the molecular level between all living organisms from bacteria to man: for example, in many of their shared *mechanisms* for storing and using energy and for conveying substances across membranes; and in the *structures* of their working proteins, structural macromolecules (both proteins and polysaccharides and their genetic material). As François Jacob has put it: 'Over and above the diversity of forms and the variety of performances, all organisms use the same materials for carrying out similar reactions, as if the living world as a whole always used the same ingredients and the same recipes, originality being introduced only in the cooking and the seasoning'.[4]

Moreover, the phase of this science that called itself 'molecular biology' demonstrated not only that the prime carriers of hereditary information in all living organisms are the nucleic acids (DNA and RNA) but also that the code that translated the information from base sequences in DNA, via messenger RNA, to amino acid sequences in proteins (and thence to their structure and function) was the *same* in *all* living organisms.[5] Now all searches for an explanation of why a particular triplet sequence of bases in the nucleic acids codes for the placing of a particular amino acid in a growing protein chain have failed to provide a completely unambiguous chemical basis for the same code to be operating in all present living organisms. The simplest and widely accepted reason is that all living organisms have derived from an original, particular living conglomeration of matter that became self-reproducing (perhaps in the kind of way suggested by Eigen and his colleagues – see below) and just happened to have at that time (though not necessarily without *some* chemical basis) the coding relation now imprinted into all subsequent living organisms. Since this code is arbitrary in just the same way as a human language, its universality is explicable only as the result of evolution: the code employed is the one which happened to be present in those primitive organisms that first out-reproduced other rivals. Its current universality is the result of what has come to be called a 'frozen accident'.

No other scientific explanation appears to be available. Furthermore, molecular biology has also provided another independent and powerful confirmation of evolutionary relationships through its ability to compare the amino acid sequences in proteins with the same function[6] (for example, the beta-globin chains in proteins related to oxygen-carrying human haemoglobin and the enzyme cytochrome C) in widely different organisms. If these organisms are connected in some kind of evolutionary tree and if, as is known to be the case, the amino acid sequences of a given protein class accumulate variations with time (because of the action of various physicochemical agencies) in the regions less critical to their function, then the more the same protein (defined by its function) differs in sequence in two species, the more widely are the species likely to be separated on any evolutionary tree. In this way, and through a much more careful statistical analysis than I have been able to indicate here, 'trees' of relationships between living organisms have been constructed entirely on the basis of such *molecular* evidence. The striking fact is that evolutionary phylogenetic trees so constructed from such macromolecular sequences usually resemble, with regard to branching order, those based on purely morphological (often palaeontological) evidence concerning the phenotype, the chief evidence on evolutionary relationships which had been available to biologists since Darwin.

It must be stressed that these macromolecular sequence studies provide entirely independent evidence for divergent evolution (by duplication and sequence divergence) from common origins – indeed from *a* common origin in many cases, such as the extensively studied globin polypeptides found in a wide range of species. So this now provides cogent support for an evolutionary relation between many forms of life. Oddly, in one case, it is the remarkable *constancy* of the amino acid sequences of the histone proteins in eukaryotic cells (the proteins that surround, and possibly control, the DNA in the chromosomes of all such cells) that is intelligible on the basis of evolution. For their having the same function in a highly protected milieu in all eukaryotic organisms is entirely understandable within the context of an evolutionary process that protects and eliminates variations, thereby preserving this special function in its restricted location.

Confidence in this approach is now such that the amino acid sequences so determined for a given class of protein in different organisms can be used as a molecular 'evolutionary clock'. For comparison of sequences from species whose time of evolutionary divergence are known from palaeontological evidence allows an estimate of the rate at which changes have been accumulating in the sequences (and so in the genes).[7] Hence in addition to allowing reconstruction of phylogenetic trees from determined sequences, that is the approximate *order* of branching of lines leading to modern species, it is also possible from the rates of mutation to estimate the *times* of other branching events, if that of one is known. For example, the branching event separating the human lineage from that leading to apes is thereby estimated to be 5 million years[7,8] ago and genealogies of bacteria,[9] otherwise totally inaccessible, can now be constructed from knowledge of amino acid sequences in proteins and also from nucleotide sequences in the genes themselves. This latter technique must now be discussed.

With the development of techniques allowing the determination of nucleotide sequences in DNA, and so in genes controlling the production of specific proteins, it has become possible to compare the structure of particular genes (or pairs of genes) over a wide range of organisms. In this way, accounts of evolutionary relationships within a gene family have become available that are based entirely on direct comparison of nucleotide sequences in the genes themselves (e.g., the human β-like globin gene family[10,11] and the preproinsulin genes[12]). Such nucleotide gene sequence studies necessitate a new refinement in the description of evolutionary relationships with respect both to corresponding amino acid protein sequences and to the phenotype. The relationships between these three levels of evolution – of the phenotype and the macromolecular sequence of both proteins and DNA – are varied and often indirect.[6] Changes may occur at different rates and major changes at the various levels are not always synchronous on the time scale of evolution. These studies are being actively pursued but it is already clear that the only rational basis for rendering coherent this new body of knowledge is the assumption of evolutionary relations between all forms of life.

Again and again, the evolutionary hypothesis (if that is what we still prefer to call it) has survived the test of consistency with observations of a kind unthinkable even four decades ago when the 'modern synthesis' first emerged. This does not preclude controversy about the tempo of, mode of and constraints upon evolution, but it renders entirely reasonable our basing our philosophy and theology on what we can presume to be the 'fact' of biological evolution, including human evolution.

Some contemporary controversies about evolution

The evidence, therefore, for the evolutionary connectedness of all living forms is extremely strong and must provide the basis for any new philosophical assessments of the relations between the classical trio of 'nature, man and God' to which we shall subsequently advert. What of the *mechanism* of natural selection of the more rapidly procreating mutant forms through the mutual interplay of whole organisms and their environments? The neo-Darwinian 'modern synthesis' is extraordinarily powerful and represents an integration of a wide range of well-established and well-understood processes in genetics, molecular biology, population genetics, palaeontology and ecology. There is no other mechanism for evolutionary change in living organisms that can remotely rival it in its comprehensiveness and cogency, especially in view of our now sure knowledge of the prime role of the nucleic acids in the genome as the carriers of hereditary information from generation to generation.

However, this confidence in the centrality of the neo-Darwinian explanation of the evolutionary process in principle is entirely consistent with acknowledging ignorance about how particular transformations came about in the inaccessible past. The existence of natural selection has now been established both in selection in various media of mutants of bacteria whose rapidity of multiplication allows very large numbers of generations, and so large changes, to be monitored; and also in wild populations with larger organisms (e.g., Kettlewell's experiments on melanism of moths[13]) when growth rates are necessarily slower, and only smaller, less striking, changes can alone be observed during the limited time available for observation. Yet it continues to be astonishing that those who are unaccustomed to the probings and questionings of scientific research find it so difficult to understand how, in this instance, the broad neo-Darwinian mechanism can be regarded as established for all living organisms while our ignorance of its application in detail can at the same time be recognised. This recognition of ignorance of the application of neo-Darwinian ideas to every observable, or inferrable, biological transformation in no way detracts from its proven power as an explanatory principle elsewhere. It is, apparently, difficult for many non-scientists to grasp that an idea may be accepted as established as broadly true in science while its detailed application in every conceivable instance can remain problematic.

An instance of this kind of lack of understanding of that blend of confidence and scepticism that constitutes the scientific enterprise is to be found in the chapter concerning the evolution of species in *The Probability of God* by Hugh Montefiore.[14] The whole book is, in fact, a considerable tour-de-force in its account of a wide range of the sciences by one admittedly a layman in those areas and is to be applauded on that score. However, in the chapter in question a catena of puzzles and problems about the evolution of structures, processes and behaviour patterns is described somewhat as a challenge to neo-Darwinians with the implication that the mere existence of these problems in itself undermines the reliability of the neo-Darwinian modern synthesis. This would only be the case if a genuinely non-neo-Darwinian explanation were forthcoming which was scientifically as established as neo-Darwinism itself is. But since in all the instances cited this is not the case, we must follow that author's own advice and recognise probability as the guide to life and not discard a well-established mechanism for an un-established as yet unknown one. In other words, our inability to go back and explain *all* biological transformations of long ago, which are no longer accessible to investigation, cannot be regarded as fatal to a theory which does actually explain so much and is increasingly consistent with wide new ranges of scientific knowledge, as already indicated.

Now – and this is where acquaintance with the organised scepticism that constitutes scientific endeavour is crucial – this confidence in the broad validity of the neo-Darwinian modern synthesis does not at all preclude controversy about many aspects of its mode of application or its development in ways which counter some of the assumptions of those who originally mounted this synthesis, whether Darwin himself or his twentieth-century 'neo-Darwinian' successors. Many authors, including, I fear, the author just mentioned, and notably the press, hear the bell tolling prematurely for neo-Darwinism when they detect the sound of battle among evolutionary biologists. That controversy should exist *within* neo-Darwinian evolutionary biology is not at all surprising in view of the quite amazing complexity of what appear superficially and phenomenologically to be the simplest biological processes or structures and their evolutionary history.

In many areas our ignorance is vast and is widely recognised, but the mere *fact* of our ignorance – for example, about the evolution of complex behaviour patterns, or about embryonic development and growth, i.e., the enigma of morphogenesis (see below) – cannot count as such as an argument against what we do know in other wide areas, namely, the validity and applicability of the neo-Darwinian concepts of the modern synthesis. It is obscuring to raise questions with respect to biological processes and structures of baffling complexity in such a way (as on pages 81ff., ref. 14) as to imply that the mere ability to raise such questions is itself a reason for doubting the real answers to quite different questions which neo-Darwinism can afford in other areas.

This has to be emphasised in view of the widespread misunderstanding among lay onlookers of disagreements between evolutionary biologists. What is not usually clearly understood is that there are many different levels of disagreement.[15] Most of these controversies are within the structure of neo-Darwinian evolutionary theory, heated though they may appear to be to the outsider. Some others, e.g. an attempt to revive Lamarckism, represent an attempt to *add* different mechanisms to that of natural selection in certain specific instances. Others yet again represent a modification of orthodox neo-Darwinism – and the proponents of the new approach may themselves disagree about the extent to which neo-Darwinian selection and principles apply.[16] These debates and controversies merit some description if only to indicate the continuing fruitfulness, as with all good scientific theories, of Darwin's original insights and the range of questions about evolution still open, both within an evolutionary perspective and, more particularly, with a neo-Darwinian interpretation of evolution. It will transpire that even proposed new mechanisms are usually regarded as *additions* to the modern synthesis rather than as alternatives to it. (Discussion of sociobiology, one of the controversial areas, will be postponed to the next chapter since it can be broadly described as 'reductionist' both in its claimed relation to the study of behaviour and sociology and in its taking the gene as the 'unit of selection', the level at which selection is regarded as operating.)

Creationism It is hardly necessary to remind the English-speaking world (and increasingly the German-speaking too) of the renewed eruption in their midst of 'creationism', that is, of the view that species suddenly come into existence and have not evolved by natural processes from other species and that the age of the Earth is orders of magnitude less than the geologists deduce, some few thousands of years, instead of about 4,000 million. Creationists urge that their views are 'scientific', and not simply religious, and on this basis claim a space in biological textbooks and teaching in the schools and colleges of the United States. The motivation of this campaign is clearly ideological, linked as it is with the emergence of the so-called moral majority with its mix of ethical, political and religious conservatisms.

The existence of this phenomenon, which is far from being confined to the United States, for there is an active pressure group of this kind in Great Britain, and now in Germany, serves to exemplify the vast confusion that exists both about modern evolutionary ideas in biology – the evidence for evolution, the status of the theory of evolution as such and of ideas about its means and mechanism – and about the relation of biological evolution to theistic doctrines of creation. This fog of confusion can permeate quite exalted levels. For example, an exhibition on evolution in 1981 at the British Museum (Natural History) was prefaced by an excellent introductory display which raised the question of biological evolution as an *alternative* to the biblical doctrine of creation in the book of Genesis. Nothing more, quite properly, was said on this matter in the displays that followed, but it was intriguing to see a scientific exposition even hinting that it has fallen into the tactical trap of entering the debate on the terms of the creationists – namely, of opposing evolutionary ideas to a theistic doctrine of creation which, as we shall see, can be held entirely consistently with acceptance of biological evolution.

While the claim for 'creation-science' to be given equal time with the theory of evolution in the public school classrooms of some half dozen states in the United States continued in the law courts, with the American Civil Liberties Union as one of the chief antagonists of the creationists (not to mention all leading biologists and theologians[17] and clergy of the principal Christian denominations), the *status* of the theory of evolution also became an issue in the pages of the scientific journal *Nature*.[18] The controversy there was between the British Museum (Natural History) and the writer of an editorial in *Nature* who attacked the staff of the former for including the phrase 'If the theory of evolution is true' in one of their recent exhibition brochures, on the grounds that the theory of evolution could scarcely still be an 'open question among serious biologists'.

Why the writer of the editorial took (so emphatically) this view, which is also the view of the present writer, may be judged from the weight of the evidence already briefly described. Nevertheless, the argument of 'serious biologists' with the creationists continues and has at least had the virtue of eliciting some spirited responses in defence of biological evolution, especially from writers on the western side of the Atlantic, in works which form very useful and up-to-date compendia of the positive evidence for biological evolution and the neo-Darwinian mechanism.[19]

Cladism　The water of these disputes was further muddied by a more technical one about 'cladism' (or 'phylogenetic systematics'), which is a recent method of classification (or rather a revised version of that of W. Hennig of 1966) that was emphasized in the literature accompanying that British Museum exhibition in 1981, a method that is in direct conflict with the older school of 'evolutionary systematics' of Simpson and Mayr, Cain and others.[20] According to cladism, the 'amount of difference between forms is directly proportional to the age of their common ancestor (the further apart, the earlier the ancestor) as if rates of evolution were constant' (so Cain[20]). It is based on the assumption that only shared, derived homologies indicate branching relationships within any group of organisms and that classification of any such group of organisms should be directly related to the branching diagram indicating such affinities. (A 'clade' is the name for a branch of the evolutionary tree.)

This dispute about cladism might seem to have been an example only of esoteric in-fighting among biological taxonomists, but it nevertheless provoked accusations of crypto-Marxism against the supporters of the, admittedly disputed, cladistic classification. So although cladistics is strictly 'not about evolution, but about the pattern of character distribution in organisms, or the recognition and characterization of groups'[21] (that is, cladistics is a method of systematics and is not concerned with process), nevertheless debate concerning it acquired ideological overtones.

Leaving aside these latter, which are peripheral to the content of the scientific argument itself, the dispute between the 'transformed cladists' and the evolutionary systematists is about whether or not evolutionary relationships, already inferred on whatever basis, should be directly involved in the classification of species in the higher taxa – genera, families, orders, classes etc. The former believe that procedures for constructing trees representing relationships ('cladograms') can be deduced without reference to evolution by systematic comparison of shared features between organisms, because such 'features shared by organisms (homologies) manifest a hierarchical pattern in nature'.[22] Needless to say, there is an implicit, and often explicit,[23] criticism intended of Darwinism in the transformed cladist's methodology.

43

However, as Maynard Smith[24] has pointed out, features shared by organisms 'manifest a hierarchical pattern in nature' only because organisms *are* evolved. He continues: 'the transformed cladists . . . are in the illogical position of saying that evolution is irrelevant to taxonomy, while accepting as an axiom a proposition which is true only because evolution happened'.[24] So this controversy hardly seems likely to shake the foundations of Darwinism, let alone neo-Darwinism.

Punctuated equilibrium Ideological accusations were also generated in another evolutionary controversy, this time not in the pages of *Nature*, but one that erupted at a conference on 'Macroevolution' held in Chicago's Field Museum of Natural History in October, 1980. This controversy, or rather group of controversies, was and is still concerned with the tempo of, mode of and constraints upon evolution.[25] First Eldredge and Gould, and then others, postulated that evolution with the branching of a new species from an established one – 'speciation' – occurred relatively rapidly over short periods, not well or easily represented in the fossil record, rather than by the gradual accumulation of the small changes that Darwin regarded as constituting differentiation of species.

These small, slow changes are well represented in the fossil record, but are considered by Eldredge, Gould and others as inadequate in themselves to represent speciation.[26] Evolution is regarded by these biologists as a 'punctuated equilibrium' – long periods (of the order of five to ten million years) of biological equilibrium, virtually 'stasis', which are characterized by minor adaptations to a slowly changing environment, punctuated by relatively short bursts of rapid change (over periods of about fifty thousand years) during which speciation occurs. *How* such rapid evolution ('macroevolution') might occur in, for example, small populations isolated either geographically or reproductively, and what constrains the range of biological blueprints actually existing also gave rise to controversy at this notable conference.

We need not go into the details of these controversies here – for example, the fascinating question of whether 'hopeful monsters' are the clue to a speciation, that is, members of an established species that have undergone a mutation (presumably in a gene controlling a crucial developmental pathway) so as to cause a markedly idiosyncratic morphology or metabolism of the individual, but a change that did not impair its fitness to reproduce. On this postulate, the mutated gene of such a 'hopeful monster' in a reproductively isolated zone would spread through a wider population, even if it had no extra survival value at the time – but came to be utilised and manifested as favourable only under some later changed environmental conditions or habitat (itself, of course, dependent on the creature's *behaviour*, as constantly emphasised by Sir Alistair Hardy[27]).

This 'hopeful monster' postulate, which implies that the characteristics of new species are random relative to the overall direction of macroevolutions, involves a 'decoupling' of macroevolution (the large-scale features of evolution) from the processes occurring within populations that are studied by population geneticists and ecologists.[28] So presented, it would represent not so much a development within neo-Darwinism, as a major new departure from the more gradualist approach of Darwin himself and of many leading neo-Darwinians in the second phase of the modern synthesis in the late 1940s and the 1950s, Gould urges.[29] The idea depends on the notion of selection acting among *species* under constraints that are independent of the environment, for example, those imposed by the process of embryological growth. If accepted – and the hypothesis in the form of this major claim still continues to be highly controversial – this would certainly represent a development of evolutionary theory going beyond that of the neo-Darwinian synthesis which, nevertheless, could still be regarded as applicable to speciation in which natural selection acts in individuals.[30]

The minor claim of the proponents of punctuated equilibrium is that the fossil record frequently exhibits periods of stability ('equilibrium') of little or no evolutionary change; it is consistent with Darwin's own views and does not imply the 'major claim'[28] already described. As Jones has pointed out,[31] however, there is an important difference in the way in which those dealing with fossils and those who experiment on living organisms assess the rate of evolutionary change. Thus intermediary forms of Cenozoic molluscs were shown by P. G. Williamson to undergo 'major phenotypic transformations of at least as great a magnitude as those now characterizing different extant species of the genera concerned' over periods of 5,000 to 50,000 years,[32] which are much shorter than those of evolutionary stability in each lineage. Yet these periods of transition actually correspond to an average of 20,000 generations, which a geneticist would regard as more than sufficient to enable 'gradual' changes to lead to the phenotypic transformations under consideration. As Jones has put it, 'Depending on the time scale to which the investigator is accustomed, one man's punctuated equilibrium is another's evolutionary gradualism'.[31] He concludes that Williamson's 'extraordinarily complete page in the history of evolution [of the molluscs[32]]' does not 'force us to change our views on the genetic mechanisms of the origin of species [i.e., the modern synthesis]'.[31] So the debate continues: clearly the funeral rites over neo-Darwinism are premature in this context too.

As before, it is interesting to note how in this particular controversy purely scientific issues have again been mixed with ideological ones when, for example, one critic of 'punctuated equilibrium' expressed the scientifically irrelevant fear that Marxists who espouse major political changes through rapid and abrupt leaps from one form of social and political organization to another, might 'be able to claim the theoretical basis of their approach was supported by scientific evidence' for punctuated equilibrium, if this were established.[33]

The new Lamarckism and the effect of behaviour The subtleties of how evolution occurs have long been known to biologists who accept the neo-Darwinist 'modern synthesis' – for example, the intricacies of the interplay between genetic constitution and environment via the phenotype involving the possibility that the predisposition to adapt to the environment is itself under genetic control.[34] But even those who have long recognized such subtleties (and Prof. J. Maynard Smith protested that many of the ideas presented as new at the Chicago 'Macroevolution' conference were, in fact, part of the 'modern synthesis' of the last three or so decades) must have been somewhat startled by the proposal of Gorczynski and Steele that an acquired characteristic (tolerance to a specific antigen) can be inherited in mice. The Lamarckian thesis, widely thought to have been finally discredited, was thereby resuscitated. The experimental evidence is disputed,[35] but even if Gorczynski and Steele were vindicated, these ideas 'are not a threat to the central dogma of molecular biology [DNA makes RNA and RNA makes proteins] nor do they really conflict with the existing framework of evolutionary theory . . . . [The theory of Steele] . . . is not intended to be more than an addition to natural selection. If valid, the new mechanisms merely would speed up evolution by allowing a more rapid adjustment of bodily structure to new habits adopted by the organisms.'[36]

Some authors, such as H. Montefiore,[37] influenced by Arthur Koestler,[38] have been disposed to accept Steele's ideas because they seem to be an antidote to the supposed mechanistic and materialist bias of neo-Darwinism.

However, not all neo-Darwinists can be so characterised, for the statistical interplay between genetic mutations and environmental pressures as the sole mechanism of evolutionary change has appeared increasingly inadequate also to some neo-Darwinists. This interplay, even when elaborated by game theory in terms of the concept of 'evolutionarily stable strategies', conceives of evolution as an 'unfolding' of the basic internal genetic programme of the organism, a programme that is already present in its genes. Nevertheless, some biologists have urged that 'unfolding' is an inappropriate metaphor for development. For example, Richard Lewontin[39] stresses that organisms are consequences of *themselves* – that is, of their state at any given moment, with all its dependence on historical accidents – *as well as* of their genotype and environment. Thus the evolution of organisms cannot be understood as a movement towards a fixed point; organisms are not climbing a peak with a fixed summit but, Lewontin suggests, rather impacting a trampoline that changes with the impact. In so speaking, Lewontin is close to an earlier stress of Sir Alister Hardy[40] on the role of innovative behavioural patterns in evolution. This debate still continues and we have not heard the end of it yet. But it is worth drawing attention to, if only to show that even amongst biologists a purely mechanistic account of evolution has its critics among those who favour a more holistic and sophisticated interpretation of neo-Darwinism.

Neutral mutations   The genetic code is redundant: that is, some amino acids are coded, with respect to their placing in a growing polypeptide chain (a nascent protein), by any one of a number of triplets of DNA units (the four nucleotide bases). So a mutation which leads to an alteration of one of these sets of triplets, which thereby generates another triplet also coding for the same specific amino acid, will not alter its placing in the polypeptide chain. Hence (provided a different transfer RNA is not needed) this so-called 'silent' mutation will be real at the level of DNA, but have no effect at the protein, and so phenotypic, level. It will be a 'neutral' mutation having no selective advantage or disadvantage. Whether or not such mutations will survive into succeeding generations depends on chance fluctuations. The chance of perpetuation by chance fluctuations is greater in small populations; such fixation is called 'genetic drift' and a number of apparently selectively neutral features of organisms (for instance, arrangement of bristles in *Drosophila*, the 169 recorded variants of human haemoglobin amino acid sequences, butterfly wing details, human fingerprint patterns) have been attributed to it. This neutral theory of *molecular* evolution[41] distinguishes between the laws of evolution at this level and those at the phenotypic level, at which

Darwinian selection through the environment acts. The existence of several forms of a different protein having the same functions is regarded as the consequences of 'silent' mutations and it is argued that mutation rates can be calculated from rates of amino acid changes. The theory encompasses removal of harmful mutations and selection for the small proportion of advantageous ones.

This somewhat classical theory, in which variation is removed by selection and genetic drift, is rival to the selectionist theory in which a variety of balancing selection mechanisms acting at the level of populations preserve genetic diversity in nature (for a full account of these theories see that of R. C. Lewontin[42]). The two explanations of genetic diversity are not in fact mutually exclusive but the relative contribution of each remains controversial,[43] not least because of the difficulty of mounting experimental tests of finely graded differences in fertility.

Morphogenesis and other mysteries The controversies described so far concern aspects of evolution where rival theories compete as explanations of evidence that is, in principle, obtainable. However, there are other areas where, although empirical observations are not lacking – indeed, are overwhelmingly rich and diverse – it is still exceedingly difficult to formulate theories at all, the biological phenomena in question being baffling in their complexity and still capable of exciting that wonder which only the inexplicable, or at least the unexplained, can induce.[44] The whole area of morphogenesis is an example, whether in its epigenetic (appearance of new structures), or its regulatory (embryonic) or regenerative (restoral of damaged structures) aspects – and the genesis of the organization of nervous systems, especially brains, is the most baffling area of all. The last mentioned is connected, of course, with the daunting problem of behaviour (instinct, behavioural regulation, and new patterns of behaviour inexplicable in terms of preceding causes).

The approach to such problems varies from the determinedly reductionistic, such as F. H. C. Crick's previously quoted 'the ultimate aim of the modern movement in biology is in fact to explain all biology in terms of physics and chemistry'[45] (however much new conceptual frameworks have to be provided to incorporate the physicochemical accounts of highly complex systems), to the avowedly holistic, such as that of Sheldrake[46] who, repudiating even the attempts of an organismic biology to begin to explain the problem of morphogenetics and behaviour just indicated, resorts to a hypothesis of 'formative causation'. In his view, specific morphogenetic fields are responsible for the characteristic form and organization of systems at all levels (not only biological, but also physicochemical) and these morphogenetic fields are derived from those of previous similar systems; that is, past systems influence the form of present systems acting across space and time. This latter, very unconventional theory, is regarded by the author as 'scientific'[47] – even though there is no evidence for any continuous changes over the decades in, say, the rate constants of chemical reactions, as would be required by the theory, nor is he able to offer any conceptual framework of the mode whereby these 'morphogenetic fields' propagate and whether or not they do so at a speed which obeys the Einsteinian canon of not exceeding that of light. If they do not obey it, then various curious time-reversal effects should be (but are not) observed in biology; if they do do so, why are these fields not detectable in the range of the electromagnetic spectrum? Be that as it may, the fact that a biologist has had to resort to such a hypothesis at least emphasizes the radical and fundamental nature of many problems still facing biologists.[48]

As a matter of fact, the enterprise of understanding morphogenesis appears not to be entirely hopeless ever since a whole new way of understanding pattern formation during growth as the interplay of reaction and diffusion processes was opened up over thirty years ago by A. M. Turing in a paper entitled 'The chemical basis of morphogenesis'.[49] This seminal paper, which long lay neglected, predicted that diffusion of substances participating in chemical reactions could, if the parameters of reaction and of diffusion and of the containing space were related in specified ways, bring about, in an originally homogeneous system, the formation of temporal and spatial patterns of concentration of these substances (and so, potentially, of precipitation and so of structure formation).

Investigation of many chemical systems has fully confirmed this prediction and has been widely applied to biochemical systems, such as oscillations in glycolysis; to embryonic pattern formation that affects structures and patterns in adult organisms (e.g., animal coat markings); as well as to the concerted apparently 'social' behaviour of the simple cells of amoebae, the cellular slime moulds, which, when their food supply runs out, aggregate spontaneously and rhythmically to form a slug-shaped mass of cells which in a synchronous fashion then moves to a new centre in the soil, richer in food, where the cells then disperse to operate individually again.[50] These concepts of 'symmetry breaking', the generation of stable, spatial patterns through the interplay of reaction rates and diffusion, have also had application in neurobiology for it turns out that the properties of nets of neurons are very similar to those of diffusion – coupled reaction systems and, in the case of the visual cortex, the patterns of neuronal excitation induced by drugs can be exactly correlated with the concomitant drug-induced visual hallucination patterns.[51]

There is no dearth of new ideas to account for cell differentiation and pattern formation: for example, the notion of 'positional information';[52] joint diffusion of activators and inhibitors that afford an explanation of the formation of bristle patterns and of hydra buds;[53] models of 'cellular automata' which consist of many identical, simple components that together are capable of complex behaviour (the beginnings of a theory to describe the nature and generation of complexity)[54]; and the idea of the 'homoeo' box of genes, a group of genes regulating development and differentiation that are highly resistant to mutation and which appear to be much the same in organisms separated by millions of years of evolution (*Xenopus, Drosophila*, chickens, mice and human beings)[55] – so that the *genetics* of development is turning out to be significant and to involve conservation of fundamental similarities in the processes of pattern formation during evolution.

I hope this account of some recent controversies in evolutionary biology, inadequate though it must be for the expert, at least gives an indication to the non-specialist of their standing in relation to the neo-Darwinian modern synthesis. Discussion of such developments and openness to them is a proper characteristic of any active science, but is frequently misunderstood by the popular and, more reprehensibly, the intellectually sophisticated media to represent, in this case, another attack on the status of the whole theory of evolution and of Darwin's explanation of the basic mechanism by which it occurred. I hope the foregoing account makes it clear that one can still regard the neo-Darwinian modern synthesis as the established core of the explanation of evolution while at the same time being open to new developments that, including it, yet go beyond it conceptually and empirically in order to encompass the many unsolved mysteries of the biological world, most notably that of morphogenesis in its various modes.

Trends in and general features of evolution

We are bound to ask if there are any trends discernible in the processes of cosmic development and, in particular, of biological evolution and whether any of them are particularly relevant to man. This is, of course, a notoriously loaded question which men are only too ready to answer on the basis of their own significance in the universe grounded on their own importance to themselves! Is there any objective, non-anthropocentrically biased, evidence for directions or, at least, trends in evolution?

Biologists are cautious about postulating 'progress' in evolution, for the criteria of progress are often already chosen with man's special exemplification of them in mind, deliberately or otherwise. As G. G. Simpson says, 'Within the framework of the evolutionary history of life there have been not one but many different sorts of progress'.[56] He instances the kinds of progress as: the tendency for living organisms to expand to fill all available spaces in the livable environments; a succession of dominant types in biological evolution; the successive invasion and development by organisms of new environmental and adaptive spheres; increasing specialization with its corollary of improvement and adaptability; increasing complexity; increase in the general energy or maintained level of vital processes; protected reproduction-care of the young; change in the direction in which increase in the range and variety of adjustments of the organism to its environment occurs; individualization.[57]

As the investigations of man's biochemistry, physiology, nervous system and behaviour patterns burgeon, striking similarities and continuities are more and more being observed between what had previously been regarded as very distinctly human characteristics and parallel characteristics of the higher mammals, especially the primates. But it is also becoming increasingly apparent that there is a distinctive transition in passing from the most intelligent primates, or dolphin, to human beings. The most Herculean efforts of devoted investigators rarely seem to be able to train a highly domesticated chimpanzee beyond the level of that of a 1½-year-old child.

Distinctive transitions have, of course, occurred at other stages in evolution and have given rise to the notion of 'emergence' – the recognition that, with the development of new forms of life, there arise new modes of existence, new activities and new kinds of behaviour, and that new modes of investigation and new conceptual language are required for their proper and appropriate understanding. It is clear that evolution has occurred, concomitantly with increasing levels of consciousness and that in man self-consciousness emerged. In this connection, the judgement of the evolutionary biologist G. G. Simpson is pertinent:

> Man has certain basic diagnostic features which set him off
> most sharply from any other animal and which have involved
> other developments not only increasing this sharp distinction
> but also making it an absolute difference in kind and not only
> a relative difference of degree. . . . Even when viewed within
> the framework of the animal kingdom and judged by criteria
> of progress applicable to that kingdom as a whole and not
> peculiar to man, man is thus the highest animal.[58]

Because of our ability to transmit culture, with all that implies in
mankind, evolution has become 'psycho-social', as Julian Huxley used
to put it; that is to say, in the case of man we have a creature that shapes
its own evolution by willingly shaping its own environment. With man
biology has become history.

One broad feature seems to be common to both the cosmic and
biological development, as pointed out by Simpson. It is the tendency
for more and more complex structures to emerge in the world. Attempts
to find a suitable measure of the complexity of structures by means of
information theory have not been as useful as was earlier hoped. More
fruitful may be a suggestion of Denbigh[59] who has pointed out that,
although we have concepts of orderliness, or order, and of disorder, we
do not have any satisfactory measure of *organisation*. He has therefore
proposed, as a measure of complexity, a quantity he names *integrality*,
which is the product of the number of connections in a structure and
the number of different *kinds* of parts. Integrality is not identical with
'information', nor with entropy, it can increase in a closed system (e.g.,
when an egg develops into, say, a chick) and its total value on the earth
has increased since life began.[60]

The need for clarity here is provoked by the proposal that there is a
connection between 'complexity' and consciousness. This has been
strongly urged and gained wide currency through the writings of Teilhard
de Chardin, who calls this his 'law of complexity-consciousness'.[61] This
'law' is certainly an impression, though an imprecise one (what *kind* of
complexity is to be correlated with consciousness?), that is given by the
broad sweep of evolution, but Teilhard's pan-psychic assumptions give
grounds for doubting such a sweeping generalization. Until we can quantify 'complexity' better it is unwise to promote our impressions into a
'law' that can then tempt us into applying it to the, undoubted,
complexity of intra- and inter-communicating human societies.

This increase in organisational complexity that occurs in the course of biological evolution has often seemed a paradox in view of the general increase in 'disorder' in natural irreversible processes that the Second Law of Thermodynamics affirms as a general feature of *all* such processes, for living organisms are in no way exempt from the laws of thermodynamics. The relation of the science of thermodynamics to life is described more fully in the Appendix and the interested reader is referred there. Some recent developments in irreversible thermodynamics that affect our appraisal of the possibility of living matter emerging naturally on the Earth by chemical processes will also be discussed in the next chapter, when the creative interplay of 'chance' and 'law' will be elaborated. For the moment, it suffices to point out, with J. Wicken,[62] that there are some natural processes (including some chemical reactions) in which there is an overall increase in entropy, which nevertheless manifest an increase in molecular complexity or, better, 'organization'. In fact, the Second Law *necessitates* such an increase at the molecular level in associative chemical reactions, in spite of the general trend to increased 'randomness' which it also elaborates and quantifies through appropriate concepts (see Appendix).

In addition to the increase in complexity in both cosmic and biological evolution, that is, the emergence in time of higher levels of organization of matter, already referred to and the creative interplay of chance and law (to be discussed in the next chapter), there are some other broad general features of the whole process which need to be explicitly noted because of their significance for any subsequent philosophical or theological reflection on that process. I refer to the *continuity* of the whole evolutionary process, its *open-ended character* and the fact that new life appears through *death of the old*.

The *continuity of biological evolution* follows on from that of the cosmological processes producing stars such as the Sun and its satellite planet, Earth. The continuities of biological evolution extend now to the molecular domain, where increasingly the principles that govern the emergence of self-reproducing macromolecular systems are now well understood both kinetically (Eigen and colleagues at Göttingen)[63] and thermodynamically (Prigogine and colleagues at Brussels).[64] I have already presented the overwhelming evidence for the interconnectedness through time of all living organisms originating from one or a few primeval simple forms. The 'gaps' in the scientific account of this evolution of the multiplicity of living forms that scientists yesterday thought they detected continue to have the habit of being closed by the work of scientists today – and those of today will, no doubt, share the same fate tomorrow. The 'gaps' for any intervening god to be inserted go on diminishing. For we see a world in process that is continuously capable, through its own inherent properties and natural character, of producing new living forms – matter is now seen to be self-organizing.

That there is a certain looseness in the causal coupling that physics describes is widely recognized and this feature of the world becomes more noticeable in the *open-ended character of biological evolution*. In retrospect each emergence of a new form of the organisation of living matter is, in principle, intelligible to us now as the lawful consequence of a concatenation of random events. This involvement of randomness means that, although in retrospect the development is intelligible (at least in principle) to modern science, yet in prospect the development would have been not strictly predictable. The development of the world as a whole has not unfolded a predetermined sequence of events, like the development of a mammalian embryo from the fertilised ovum. As Dobzhansky put it: 'The chief characteristic, or at any rate one of the characteristics, of progressive evolution, is its open-endedness. Conquest of new environments and acquisition of new ways of life create opportunities for further evolutionary developments.[65]

As one goes up the scale of biological evolution the open-ended character, unpredictability and creativity of the process becomes more and more focused in the activity of the biological individual. For in the biological sequence, the increase of complexity becomes increasingly accompanied by an increase in consciousness culminating in human self-consciousness, the power of language, and rationality. This aspect of the process reaches its apogee in man's creativity and his sense of freedom in taking responsibility for his decisions. Such a perspective on evolution still therefore attributes a special significance to man's emergence in and from the material universe but recognises he has arrived by means of an open-ended, trial-and-error exploration of possibilities – an exploration devoid neither of false trails and dead ends nor, as consciousness emerges, immune from pain, suffering and struggle.

The processes by which new species appear is a process of *new life through death of the old*. It involves a degree of competition and struggle in nature which has often offended man's moral and aesthetic sensibilities. It has taken modern biologists to restore the balance in our view of the organic world by reminding us, as Simpson said: 'To generalise . . . that natural selection is over-all and even in a figurative sense the outcome of struggle is quite unjustified under the modern understanding of the process. . . . Struggle is sometimes involved, but it usually is not. . . .

Advantage in differential reproduction is usually a peaceful process in which the concept of struggle is really irrelevant.'[66] The death of old organisms is a prerequisite for the appearance of new ones.

There is indeed a kind of 'structural logic' about all this, for we cannot conceive, in a lawful, non-magical universe, of any way for new structural complexity appearing except by utilising structures already existing, either by way of modification (as in the evolutionary process) or of incorporation (as in feeding). Thus the law of 'new life through death of the old' is inevitable in a world composed of common 'building blocks', but in biological evolution this does not happen without pain and suffering and both seem unavoidable. For death, pain and the risk of suffering are intimately connected with the possibilities of new life, in general, and of the emergence of conscious, and especially human, life, in particular. Moreover, the very order and impersonality of the physical cosmos which makes pain and suffering inevitable for conscious and self-conscious creatures is, at the same time, also the prerequisite of their exercise of freedom as persons. Again, it seems hard to avoid the paradox that what theologians used to call 'natural evil' is a necessary prerequisite for the emergence of free, self-conscious beings.

Ecology

It is hard to be a reductionist ecologist, according to Dr Norman Moore, an eminent ecologist, and this increasingly important branch of biology – amazingly *un*fashionable even two decades ago – certainly qualifies as one for which a 'holistic' approach is essential. For it is the study[67] of the dependence of all living forms not only on the continued supply of energy from the sun and on the physical and natural environment, but also on each other. All plants and animals, including man, live in intricate systems consisting of many cross-flows and exchanges of energy and matter, of a labyrinthine complexity that has, until recently with the advent of computers, defied analysis. The impact of man on evolved, natural ecosystems has been dramatic, often catastrophic, and frequently disastrous – though not always, as in the (until recently) successful maintenance of the fertility of agricultural land in many parts of Europe over hundreds and, in some areas (for instance, northern Italy), thousands of years of careful husbandry. What we now consciously realize, which past generations had only intuitively sensed, is that through his technological power man is today forced into becoming a manager of the earth whether he likes it or not, for almost everything man does to natural ecosystems for his own presumed benefit has long-term global effects for better or for worse.

It is the *interconnectedness* of the whole biosphere with itself and of the biosphere with all the physical cycles and organisation of planet Earth that have been so urgently manifest to our generation. Moreover, photographs of the Earth from outer space have brought home strikingly to our imaginations the already cerebrally accepted fact of the limitedness of the Earth's surface. It is to this we have to adjust to survive.

4 *The new biology* – '*reductionistic*'[1]

Molecular biology

Its history and present state   'Molecular biology' is the name given to that phase in the development of biology in which largely physicists and chemists turned their attention to the molecular basis of fundamental biological processes. It is scarcely distinguishable from the science of biochemistry except for the attitudes of the pioneers of this phase of biological science, among whom at least one group was, oddly, antipathetic to biochemistry as it had developed during the first four decades of this century. This was what G. S. Stent has called the 'informational school' in a 1968 article reviewing the stage molecular biology had then reached, an article entitled, it must be noted, 'That Was the Molecular Biology, That Was'.[2]

This 'informational school' consisted mainly of physicists who were, Stent affirms, 'motivated by the fantastic and wholly unconventional notion that biology might make significant contributions to physics'.[3] He traces back to Niels Bohr[4] this motivation which was transmitted to his pupil Max Delbrück, who in 1938 started his work on bacteriophages and so initiated what Stent calls 'the romantic phase' of molecular biology. In this phase the informational school, which was largely German in origin and later based in the United States, thought that the *real* problem requiring explanation was the physical basis of genetic information – and this phase was vastly stimulated in 1945 by the immensely influential *What is Life?* written during the war by the famous quantum physicist Erwin Schrödinger, then in Ireland.

The other principal strand in this phase of molecular biology, from about 1938 to 1952, was the 'structural school' which was mainly of British provenance (under the influence of W. T. Astbury, J. D. Bernal and their pupils) and later also American (for example, Linus Pauling). Indeed, W. T. Astbury was the one to coin the label 'molecular biology' for the study 'concerned with the *forms* of biological molecules and with the evolution, exploitation and ramifications of these forms in the ascent to higher and higher levels of organization. Molecular biology is predominantly three-dimensional and structural. . . .'[5] In contrast to the 'informational' molecular biologists, members of this school were preoccupied with structure rather than information and 'reflected a down-to-earth view of the relation of physics to biology – namely, that all biological phenomena, no matter what their complexity, can ultimately be accounted for in terms of conventional physical laws'.[6]

These two schools of molecular biology converged personally in the meeting in 1951 in Cambridge, England, of the American biologist J. D. Watson, seeking the basis of genetic information and its transmission by the hereditary mechanism, and the English physicist F. H. C. Crick, studying biological structures by X-ray diffraction. The story of how they came to postulate the double-helical *structure* of that material, DNA, which turned out amazingly to be the conveyor of genetic *information* by virtue of its structure, has been told at least three times – once autobiographically (and not a little scurrilously) by J. D. Watson, in a more historical perspective by R. Olby, and in great detail, based on interviews with many of the participants, by H. F. Judson.[7] So there is no need for me to recall this fascinating history – of which I had a grandstand view as an investigator, at the time, of the solution properties of DNA.

The publication of the structure of DNA by Watson and Crick in 1953 (in association with the X-ray diffraction studies, by M. H. F. Wilkins and others in London, on which it was based) led to a veritable explosion in 'molecular biology' and initiated a second 'dogmatic phase' (as Stent designates it). This phase of molecular biology, which lasted approximately until 1963, was dominated by the 'central dogma' of molecular genetics, of Watson and Crick, that DNA replicates its unique sequence of units (nucleotides) autocatalytically by copying one of its two intertwined chains and also acts as a template for single RNA chains, which then control the synthesis and amino acid sequences of proteins. The properties of proteins depend on these sequences, so

$$DNA \rightarrow DNA \rightarrow RNA \rightarrow protein$$

would be the sequence of transfer of information. The 'dogmatic phase' saw this proposal vindicated, enriched by F. Jacob and J. Monod's ideas on messenger RNA and the operons. So the molecular machinery that transmits the information came to be elucidated.[8]

If this phase represented one of Kuhn's paradigmatic shifts in the history of biology, the period since 1963, the 'academic phase' (Stent), sees molecular biology re-integrated with biochemistry and becoming 'normal science', with a high increase in the number of its practitioners and range of study – and with medical and technological consequences of which we are hearing more and more. Those with a pioneering spirit that prefer to confront mysteries in the natural world rather than to solve problems it poses, are turning to the study of the genetics, development, and mode of operation of the higher nervous system and to morphogenesis. These are regarded by some as the last frontiers of biology, but past experience has shown only too often that such frontiers, like the false summits well known to the slogging mountaineer, almost always give way to yet others as the vista changes.

In all of this development no new laws of physics or chemistry had had to be propounded to unravel the molecular processes of genetic information storage and transfer and to this extent the 'romantic' aspirations of the informational school had not been fulfilled – although, in fact, it was they as much as any who largely elucidated, during the 'dogmatic phase', how phage DNA replicates itself and controls the synthesis of the specific proteins of such viruses. Most molecular biologists would now agree with Sidney Brenner when he wrote, in the 1974 issue of *Nature* surveying molecular biology, that

> Much has been written about the philosophical consequences of molecular biology. I think it is now quite clear what the enterprise is about. We are looking at a rather special part of the physical universe which contains special mechanisms none of which conflict at all with the laws of physics. That there would be new laws of Nature to be found in biological systems was a misjudged view and that hope or fear has just vanished.[9]

No 'conflict at all with the laws of physics' – agreed; but does this judgement mean that all accounts of biological systems are to be subsumed into physics? Does the triumph of molecular biology really imply the long-term demise of all 'holistic' approaches and the final victory for a reductionist interpretation of biology in the terms of F. H. C. Crick already quoted?

Reductionism, anti-reductionism and vitalism Certainly Crick thought so and prefaced his 1966 *Of Molecules and Man* with a quotation which, judging by the subsequent contents, as indeed by Crick's well-known attitudes, leaves us in no doubt that it is meant to be taken ironically. The quotation is from Salvador Dali: 'And now the announce-ment of Watson and Crick about DNA. This is for me the real proof of the existence of God.' The irony arises because Crick identifies belief in God with vitalism – the view that living organisms have some special added entity or force over and beyond non-living matter – for, as Crick saw it, molecular biology had triumphantly demonstrated the *molecular* basis of the most distinctive feature of living organisms, their ability to reproduce, and thereby rendered all such proposals of vitalism null and void. This equation of vitalism with theism is, I think, simply false, though understandable because Christian apologists have unfortunately had, and still do have, a tendency to attempt to insert 'God' into the gaps of biological explanation.

Oddly, Stent thinks Dali is right but, in my view, for the wrong reason.[10] For Stent simply identifies 'God' with the rationality of the universe and its amenability to rational explanation – 'God' is the single principle that regulates everything and makes science possible. Belief in 'God' so formulated is the axiom from which it follows that an expla-nation of the world is accessible to human reason. Stent thinks the structure of DNA, and molecular biology as a whole, is further proof for such a 'God', even when, as for Crick himself, this 'God' is identified with 'Nature', without remainder. But Stent himself wishes to empha-sise, not the triumph of molecular biology over vitalism (which, inciden-tally, he agrees with me is *not* implied by theism), but rather 'the apparent inaccessibility of the human psyche to scientific study' and looks to Eastern philosophical-ethical systems (Confucianism and Taoism) as providing for man's harmony, both inner and outer, with his environ-ment and the possibility of abandoning the Platonic 'God' of rationality.

Stent is unrepresentative among molecular biologists in taking this line and most, when they comment on philosophical or theological matters, follow Crick in finding reinforcement of their reductionist views from modern molecular biology. K. F. Schaffner seems to argue the reductionist case with respect to the non-autonomy of the *processes* going on at the higher level in relation to molecular processes, but goes on to recognise that a 'compositionist' (holistic) methodology is often the most pragmatically feasible, even allowing the formulation of 'specifically biological theories'.[11] He appears to me not to distinguish clearly enough between the reducibility (= non-autonomy) of *processes* in higher levels to lower levels, with which I would agree, from the autonomy (= irreduc-ibility) of *theories* concerned with the lower levels (for instance, physics and chemistry). As we saw in Chapter 1, the discussion of these matters is often confused because of a failure to make this distinction of Morton Beckner,[12] and one finds Schaffner, who describes himself as an in-principle reductionist, using the same arguments for his position as Michael Polanyi, who regarded himself as being on the opposite side of that fence.[11]

But the climate has changed since the successes of the 'dogmatic phase' of the 1960s and one finds increasing recognition of the need for entirely new concepts to describe the complexities of living matter, concepts not even 'in principle', conceptually reducible to those of the physics and chemistry we have hitherto known. This is what I, following Beckner, would regard as genuine 'theory autonomy', that is, non-reducibility of higher level concepts; such views have been propounded in relation to both dissipative systems and the application of network thermodynamics to biological systems.[13]

In my view, the real irony is that the autonomy of at least some of the concepts applicable to the higher levels of complexity of biological systems is, in fact, implicit in the inbuilt dichotomy that we saw charac-terised the pioneering days of molecular biology – namely the different aims and directions of the informational and structural schools. The convergence and union, already mentioned, of these two movements in the information-carrying structure of DNA shows precisely what the non-reductionist is trying to argue. For, as we saw in Chapter 2, in no way can the concept of 'information', the *concept* of conveying a message, be articulated in terms of the *concepts* of physics and chemistry, even though the latter can now be shown to explain how the molecular machinery (DNA, RNA, the appropriate enzymes etc.) operates to convey information. Thus (and *this* is the irony) the marriage of 'infor-mation' and 'structure' which characterises molecular biology is a classic illustration of the kinds of distinction we had to make in Chapter 2 concerning the autonomy of some higher level *concepts, theories* and so on (for instance 'information') and the non-autonomy, that is, reduc-ibility, of *processes* (there is 'nothing else' going on in the replication of DNA, for example, except re-arrangement of atoms and molecules obeying the laws of physics and chemistry). The anti-reductionist position requires no mystical affirmation of vitalism, or any like 'non-natural' hypotheses, but it does require the recognition in many cases of the autonomy, and so of the validity, of the concepts and language we apply to the higher levels of complexity of the natural world, in this case the biological. As we said earlier, there are simply not just grades of 'reality' of which atoms are the 'most real', biological entities less so, and persons the least.[14]

Chance, law and the origin of life   Until the recent past, chance and law (necessity or determinism) have often been regarded as alternatives for interpreting the natural world. But the interplay between these principles is more subtle and complex than the simple dichotomies of the past would allow. In any particular state of a system, we have to weigh carefully the evidence about the respective roles of these two principles in interpreting its present and past behaviour. The late Jacques Monod, in *Chance and Necessity*, contrasted the 'chance' processes that bring about mutations in the genetic material of an organism and the 'necessity' of their consequences in the law-abiding, well-ordered, replicative mechanisms which constitute that organism's continuity as a living form.[15] He pointed out that mutations in the genetic material, the DNA, are the results of physicochemical events and that their locations in the molecular apparatus carrying the genetic information are entirely random with respect to the biological consequences to and needs of the organisms. The two causal chains are entirely independent and so Monod was correct, to this extent, in saying that evolution depends on chance. This is the basis on which he stressed the role of chance: 'Pure chance, absolutely free but blind, at the very root of the stupendous edifice of evolution'.[16] There is, according to Monod, no general purpose in the universe and in the existence of life, and so none in the universe as a whole. It need not, it might not, have existed nor might man.

However, there is no reason why this randomness of molecular event in relation to biological consequences has to be raised to the level of a metaphysical principle interpreting the universe. For in the behaviour of matter on a larger scale many regularities, that have been raised to the level of being describable as 'laws', arise from the combined effect of random microscopic events, which constitute the macroscopic. The involvement of chance at this level of mutation does not, of itself, preclude these events manifesting a law-like behaviour at the higher levels of organisms, populations and biosystems – which may also be presumed to exist on the many planets throughout the universe that might support life.

Instead of being daunted by the role of chance in genetic mutations as the manifestation of irrationality in the universe, it would be more consistent with the observations to assert that the full gamut of the potentialities of living matter could only be explored through the agency of the rapid and frequent randomisation which is possible at the molecular level of DNA. This role of chance is what one would expect if the universe were so constituted that all the potential forms of organisations of matter (both living and non-living) which it contains might be explored. In principle, this is the only way in which all potentialities might eventually, given enough time and space, be actualised. Since Monod wrote his book, there have been developments in theoretical biology in the last decade that cast new light on the interrelation of chance and law (or necessity) in the origin and development of life.

Ilya Prigogine and his colleagues at Brussels, who were already well known for their work on the thermodynamics of irreversible processes, have in recent years increasingly turned their attention to the analysis of living systems.[17] They asked how it was that such highly ordered systems as living organisms could ever have come into existence in a world in which irreversible processes always tend to lead to an increase in entropy, in disorder. They have been able to show that there exists a class of open systems, 'dissipative structures', which can maintain themselves in an ordered, steady state far from equilibrium. Under certain conditions they can undergo fluctuations that are no longer damped, as they are near to equilibrium, but are amplified so that the system changes its whole structure to a *new* ordered state in which it can again become steady and imbibe energy and matter from the outside (that is what is meant by being 'open') and maintain its new structured form. It turns out that the conditions for such instability and transition are not so restrictive that no systems can ever possibly obey them. Indeed, systems such as those of the first living forms of matter, which must have involved complex networks of chemical reactions, are likely to undergo such changes.

Because of the discovery of these dissipative systems, and of the possibility of 'order-through-fluctuations', it is now possible to regard as highly probable the emergence of ordered, self-reproducing molecular structures – that is, of living systems. To this extent, the emergence of life was inevitable but the form it was to take remained entirely open and unpredictable. Prigogine and Nicolis go further: 'We are led to a first parallelism between dissipative structure formation and certain features occurring in the early stages of biogenesis and the subsequent evolution to higher forms. The analogy would even become closer if the model we discuss has further critical points of unstable transitions. One would then obtain a hierarchy of dissipative structures, each one enriched further by the information content of the previous ones through the "memory" of the initial fluctuations which created them successively.'[18]

But how can a molecular population have 'information content', and how can it store a 'memory'? It is to problems of this kind that Eigen and his colleagues at Göttingen have directed their attention.[19] They have examined the changes in time of a population of biological macromolecules each capable of carrying the information required to make a copy of itself (as can DNA). Their treatment is based on the theory of games and of time-dependent random processes, but they have been able to illustrate the principles involved by inventing actual games that the novice can play (with, for example, octahedral dice!).[20] They have been able to delineate fairly precisely what kind of combination of chance and law will allow such a population of information-carrying macromolecules both to develop into one 'dominant species', and yet to have enough flexibility for further evolution. Moreover, they have been able to propose what kind of self-organising cycles of macromolecules would most likely be viable and self-reproducing. Eigen concludes thus: ' . . . the evolution of life, if it is based on a derivable physical principle, must be considered an *inevitable* process despite its indeterminate course . . . it is not only inevitable "in principle" but also sufficiently probable within a realistic span of time. It requires appropriate environmental conditions (which are not fulfilled everywhere) and their maintenance. These conditions have existed on Earth.'[21] According to this analysis, although the emergence of living systems may be 'inevitable', it is nevertheless 'indeterminate'. For it is impossible to trace back the precise historical route or to predict the exact course of future development, beyond certain time limits, because of the involvement of time-dependent random processes.

The work of Prigogine and Eigen and their collaborators now shows how subtle can be the interplay of chance and law (or necessity), of randomness and determinism, in the processes that lead to the emergence of living structures. These studies demonstrate that the mutual interplay of chance and law is in fact creative within time, for it is the combination of the two which allows new forms to emerge and evolve – indeed, natural selection appears to be opportunistic. This interplay of chance and law appears now to be of a kind that makes it 'inevitable' both that living structures should emerge and that they should evolve – given the physical and chemical properties of the atomic and sub-atomic units in the universe we actually have. The end result of this process is in fact the kind of complex, conscious life of the higher mammals, including the primates and man. It appears that the universe has potentialities which are becoming actualised in time by the joint operation of chance and law, of random, time-dependent processes in a framework of law-like determined properties – and that these potentialities include the possibility of biological, and so of human, life.

Sociobiology

Earlier I discussed evolutionary theory as 'methodologically holistic', since it is a view of the biological scene that certainly looks 'from the top down', that is, it deals primarily with whole organisms in their total environments. One of the all-pervasive problems in the history of evolutionary theory is the identification of the unit that is being selected as subject to evolutionary laws. Nearly all of the possible levels of analysis have, at some time or another, been chosen by some biologist as *the* unit of selection – genes, parts of chromosomes, whole chromosomes, genotypes, organisms, Mendelian populations, biological species, and so on.[22]

In the last decade this area of biology has witnessed sharp controversy emanating from the confrontation of the theory, until then widely accepted by biologists, of 'group selection' with the theory of 'individual, or gene, selection'. As we shall see, the latter theory has largely been expounded by its supporters in a reductionist manner not only in relation to animal behaviour but also in relation to human behaviour, ethics, sociology and anthropology – and even wider aspects of culture. Hence its classification here as exemplifying a reductionist methodology. Broadly, sociobiology (sometimes now denoted as 'behavioural ecology') may be defined, with Wilson,[23] as the systematic study of the biological basis of all social behaviour and, in relation to human beings, aims at exploring the relationships between biological constraints and cultural evolution. But it has a more particular origin in biology itself, as we shall see in the following.

The controversy was initially associated with different interpretations of biologically 'altruistic' behaviour which, for these purposes, may be defined as behaviour by an individual organism of a kind that increases the chances of survival of another like individual, with increased risk to its own survival. 'Survival' is taken here in its Darwinian sense, namely, 'survival in order to reproduce' and it is now well established that quite small increments in the chance of survival, in this sense, lead surprisingly rapidly to the dominance in biological populations of individuals possessing the genetic factors responsible for these increments. In the 'group selection' theory, altruism was explained on the supposition that a group (for instance, a species, or a population within a species) whose individual members were altruistic was less likely to become extinct than one whose members were non-altruistic, that is, 'selfish'.[24]

But there was a paradox here – for altruistic behaviour reduces the chance of an organism surviving (to reproduce) and so, eventually, organisms that behave thus should disappear from the group, or species. In recent years, a very active group of biologists have resuscitated Darwin's own emphasis on 'individual selection' and now represent altruistic behaviour as *genetic* selfishness. In this theory, what we call altruistic behaviour on the part of an individual, apparently on behalf of other organisms in the group, is simply behaviour which enhances the chance of survival (and so of the reappearance in the next generation) of the genes in those other organisms that they also share with the 'altruistic' individual.[25] So those on behalf of whom the altruistic sacrifice is made must be genetically kin to the altruistic individual. The 'altruism' of, for example, a bird emitting a warning cry to the rest of its kin-group of the approach of a predator, thereby attracting the attack to itself, is simply, on this view, a mechanism for enhancing the chances of survival of genes that are like its own but are carried by those other, related, individuals.

As is often recalled in this context, J. B. S. Haldane once affirmed he would lay down his life for two brothers or eight cousins![26] No special 'motivation', or any special awareness of the group, needs to be attributed to the organism – the selection processes and their statistical features ensure this result (the increased chance of reproduction of the genes that the 'altruistic' individual shares with the rest of the group) – and to introduce teleological or group language is simply a *post ipso facto* gloss on what is actually going on. These ideas have been powerfully argued in E. O. Wilson's monumental work *Sociobiology*[23] and, more popularly, expounded in Richard Dawkins's *The Selfish Gene*.[27]

The argument for individual, or gene, selection as the appropriate interpretative category of behaviour rests on the assumption that one can properly speak of a gene for a particular kind of behaviour, even if we have no knowledge of the actual causal chains linking genes and behaviour.[28] Thus a 'gene for altruistic behaviour' would be one that transmits information that affects the development of the organism's nervous system so as to make it more likely to behave altruistically – and so might have its effect at a number of levels.[29] In fact, studies of genetic variations for ecologically important behavioural traits are only in their infancy and it remains to be seen what changes may be required in the theoretical structure of behavioural ecology.[30] For the time being the postulate remains plausible in principle for non-human organisms, though likely to be complex in application. Its application to humans is much more controversial, smacking as it does of biological determinism of human behaviour.

The basic ideas of sociobiology that are used in the analysis of animal societies have been summarised by J. Maynard-Smith[31] as: first, societies consist of relatives – cooperation and altruistic interactions are more likely to occur between relatives; secondly, both partners in a cooperative interaction may benefit, so that neither would gain by defection; and, thirdly, the concept of evolutionary stability can be used to analyse those cases in which the best thing for an individual to do depends on what others are doing – the most 'evolutionarily stable strategy' (ESS). The theory of games has been applied to work out the ESS which is that behavioural policy which, if adopted by most members of a population, cannot be bettered by any other strategy from the viewpoint of gene *and* population survival.[32] These ideas were very quickly applied to interpreting a wide range of behaviour, in addition to altruistic, for example: aggression, the 'battle of the sexes', parental policies, feeding habits, the relation between old and young, etc.

There is no doubt that an enormous stimulus was given by this constellation of ideas to experimental investigations of biological societies and the behavioural patterns of their members. It became experimentally established[30] that kinship plays a central role in most instances of altruistic helping and that individuals, in a wide variety of taxa, are able to recognise close kin as siblings (human society is discussed separately below). The phenomenon of reciprocal altruism ('tit for tat'), whereby an organism behaving altruistically selectively dispenses benefits to those who reciprocate, was also established to be operative in primates. Conflicts of interest, with consequent disharmony in 'cooperative' groups, and so a subtle balance between costs and benefits, have also been observed and analysed in detail – for example when female birds cooperate to lay eggs in the same nest, and then surreptiously remove the eggs of their 'colleagues' from it.

Different systems of mating and reproduction strategies are now better understood in the light of the conflict of interest between males and females, the former having a genetic vested 'interest' in fertilising as many females as possible and the latter in setting a balance between having a succession of males to fertilise them and at the same time needing to stay with the young to rear them to independence. The concept of the optimisation of use of resources for a biological community has been found to be interpretatively fruitful, amongst other things, in providing quantitative predictions about how much time an individual will spend searching for food or mates.

There is therefore no doubt of the fruitfulness of the sociobiological component of the 'new biology' in generating new ideas and meaningful investigations – such fruitfulness being an important criterion of a worthwhile scientific hypothesis.

In recent years, some sociobiologists, after rebutting the attempts of recent decades to reduce biology to the molecular sciences, have taken upon themselves the role of the Unjust Steward and have appeared to be attempting to reduce sociology, anthropology, and the sciences of human behaviour to biology. Perhaps this assertiveness should not be taken as an attempt at outright reduction of these sciences in biology, for Wilson has, subsequent to the publication of *Sociobiology*, argued for the value to any discipline of its 'antidiscipline' (referring to the special, creative, adversary relation that exists initially between the studies of adjacent levels of organization) – with biology as the antidiscipline to the social sciences.[33] Moreover, in the same article he explicitly repudiates any reductionist ambitions of biology with respect to the social sciences, which he recognizes as 'potentially far richer in content' than biology. For Wilson is quite aware that the properties of societies are emergent and hence deserving of 'a special language and treatment'[34] but he, nevertheless, wishes to give a prime and determinative role to the biological basis of human social behaviour and patterns.[35] Such apparent intellectual imperialism has provoked strong reactions from the native denizens of anthropology and sociology – not to mention political opposition from the left which sees sociobiologists as reincarnated nineteenth-century social Darwinists.

One of the earliest weightiest attacks on sociobiology from within one of the 'threatened' sciences was that of Marshall Sahlins, an anthropologist. To Wilson's question[35] of 'whether the social sciences can be truly biologicized in this fashion [of sociobiology]', Sahlins responds: 'The answer I suggest here is that they cannot, because biology, while it is an absolutely necessary condition for culture, is equally and absolutely insufficient: it is completely unable to specify the cultural properties of human behaviour or their variations from one human group to another.'[36] For, he argues: ' . . . the central intellectual problem does come down to the autonomy of culture and of the study of culture. *Sociobiology* [E.

Wilson's book] challenges the integrity of culture as a thing-in-itself, as a distinctive and symbolic human creation. In place of a social constitution of meanings it offers a biological determination of human interactions with a source primarily in the general evolutionary propensity of individual genotypes to maximize their reproductive success.'[37] Scientific sociobiologists who attempt to place social behaviour on sound evolutionary principles (notably the self-maximization of the individual genotype) do so, Sahlins asserted, by assuming that human social behaviour can be explained as the expression of those needs and drives of the human organism which have been imprinted by biological evolution:

> [In sociobiology] The chain of biological causation is accordingly lengthened; from genes through phenotypical dispositions to characteristic social interactions. But the idea of a necessary correspondence between the last two, between human emotions or needs and human social relations, remains indispensable to the scientific analysis . . . The interactions of organisms will inscribe these organic tendencies [aggressiveness, altruism, male 'bonding', sexuality, etc.] in their social relations. Accordingly there is a one-to-one parallel between the character of human biological propensities and the properties of human social systems . . . For him [E. O. Wilson], any Durkheimian notion of the independent existence and persistence of the social fact is a lapse into mysticism. Social organization is rather, and nothing more then, the behavioral outcome of the interaction of organisms having biologically fixed inclinations. There is nothing in society that was not first in the organisms.[38]

He claimed that this position did not correspond to the results of anthropological study then available (1976) and as evidence of this he cited *inter alia* the absence of any relation between war and individual human aggressiveness. The latter may be mobilized to pursue a war but its existence does not in itself explain the existence of war, in general, and the causes of any particular war. For

> the problem is that there is no necessary relation between the phenomenal form of a human social institution and the individual motivations that may be realized or satisfied therein. The idea of a fixed correspondence between innate human

dispositions and human social forms constitutes a weak link, a rupture in fact, in the chain of sociobiological reasoning.[39]

. . . Aggression does not regulate social conflict, but social conflict does regulate aggression.[40]

Many sociobiologists (Wilson, Trivers, *et al.*) had argued that kin selection – an essentially cost-benefit analysis of an individual's behaviour towards genetic relatives, the 'selfish gene' model – is the deep structure of *human* social patterns and behaviour. Sahlins, by ranging over the actual arrangements in a number of carefully studied human cultures, claimed to demonstrate that 'sociobiological reasoning from evolutionary phylogeny to social morphology is interrupted by culture'[41] so that any claims for sociobiology to be the key to all the human sciences, and indeed all the humanities, are exaggerated.

Sahlins argued against sociobiology's pre-eminence on the grounds that (1) no system of human kinship relations is organized in accord with the genetic coefficients of relationship as known to sociobiologists; (2) the *culturally constituted* kinship relations, which govern production, property, mutual aid, and marital exchange, have an entirely different calculus from that predicted by genetic kin selection; (3) kinship is a unique characteristic of human societies, distinguishable precisely by its freedom from natural (genetic) relationships; (4) human beings reproduce not as physical or biological beings but as *social* beings, that is, human reproduction is engaged as the means for the persistence of cooperative social orders not vice versa, and so, finally, (5) culture is the indispensable condition of systems of human organization and reproduction. For, he would argue, 'Human society is cultural, unique in virtue of its construction by symbolic means', and 'Culture is biology plus the symbolic faculty'[42]; the importance of the symbolic is to generate meaning, not merely to convey information, as Wilson seems to want to say.

Sahlins' attack focused the debate on important questions: Is the claim of sociobiologists that social patterns are emergents from causally prior biological, and specifically genetic, factors exaggerated? Are human social systems autonomous from biological causation? Moreover, as one reviewer of Sahlins put it, 'Can anyone explain how genes are supposed to "tell" humans how to organize their social life?'[43]

This gauntlet, thrown down by Sahlins in the debate following the publication of Wilson's book, led to a controversy that stimulated new work. It was not likely that, given the vast complexity of human societal patterns, a clear-cut decision was going to emerge, but at least further investigations of certain simpler societies *have* revealed an influence of the degrees of genetic relatedness on formal kinship systems and behaviour in certain small-scale human societies.[44] Awareness of genetic distance seems to be at least one factor in the complex ecological and social patterns that characterise such human groupings.

But what about more complex, stratified human societies, both traditional agrarian and modern industrial? In the former, the social movement of women upward by dowries and the celibacy or infanticide of women in the highest levels of society can be interpreted[45] in terms of the investment males and their families make in their assured offspring in societies where inheritable descent is through males and where there is polygyny amongst the wealthier of them. There is not much work available on modern industrial societies, which is not surprising in view of the methodological problem of measuring 'fitness' in such studies. Such investigations as have been made seem to yield results conforming with sociobiological predictions in the limited range over which they necessarily operate.

As we saw in the quotations above, the gravamen of the charge by the anthropologist Sahlins against sociobiology was its inadequacy to describe and account for the evolution of human culture with, at any time, its unique nexus of culturally constituted 'social facts' (conventions, taboos, laws, kinship relationships, property dispositions, etc.). The most ambitious attempt to bring culture within the orbit of sociobiological interpretation with its emphasis on genetic determination of human behaviour has been that of E. O. Wilson and C. J. Lumsden.[46] If human behaviour changes under cultural pressures, they argued, then genetic changes that cause the new behaviour will follow, so that a genetic constitution *predisposing towards these behaviour patterns* will rapidly be acquired – i.e., culture speeds up genetic change in a 'synergistic' way. (This proposed effect is distinct from the obvious feature of human society that human beings uniquely, rapidly and continuously alter their environment and this in itself generates selective changes in the human genetic constitution.)

As might have been expected, Wilson and Lumsden's book provoked strong reactions[47] and some were highly critical.[48] The most objective, thoroughgoing, and necessary, analysis of Wilson and Lumsden's mathematical model, crucial to their thesis, was made by the mathematical biologist J. Maynard Smith with N. Warren, an anthropologist.[49] Maynard Smith and Warren concluded that Wilson and Lumsden's model only has the particular kind of synergistic effect they proposed for cultural changes speeding up genetic changes if extremely implausible assumptions are made and they do not think the experimental observations sufficiently support the model. So this particular model for the relation between genetics and human cultural changes seems to be flawed but that, clearly, does not rule out the possibility of interactions between genetic and cultural processes in human evolution. There is clearly need for more investigations of this relation but these do not have to presume a biological determinism that implies that a particular gene (or group of genes) alone *causes* an individual human being to perform a particular act or to exhibit a certain regular pattern of behaviour, professions, or even belief. But this need not preclude genetic 'biostrategies' being at work beneath the surface layer of culture.[50]

The controversy concerning the sociobiological interpretation of human behaviour and culture has continued sharp and furious not only between sociobiologists and philosophers,[51] but also amongst biologists themselves[52] – not to mention the political antagonism it has aroused from American groups such as 'Science for the People' who gratuitously attribute political motivations to the scientists involved.[53] Crook's summary of the situation is still one of the fairest:

> The tentative explanation[54] of human conduct that stems from the sociobiological paradigm relates man to behavioural and social evolution in the animal kingdom generally and thus for the first time anchors the study of society in evolutionary biology through a fundamental theory. None the less the enormous variety of cultural processes cannot be interpreted solely by sociobiological explanation. Cultures express the attempts of individuals to find meaning in their lives and to produce collectively systems of meaning that make life comprehensible and legitimize action. The capacity to construct interpretative systems rests in the advanced cognitive capacities of man which have evolved in relation to a need to represent social relations in language. The study of what people say in accounting for their actions . . . gives an understanding of the processes of culture while sociobiological theorizing gives an insight into the ultimate meaning of culture itself . . . . Cultural evolution comprises the historical process which provides the sociobiological environment within which the basic biological strategies of the species find varied expression.[55]

5 *Man, God and evolution: yesterday*

Any assessment of the relation between biological evolution and Christian theology today cannot be made without an adequate historical perspective. Fortunately that perspective has been greatly enriched by historical investigations in recent decades,[1] and these have resulted in a significant reappraisal of the impact of Darwin and of the Darwinians on the thought of their day. It is sufficient here simply to recall that evolutionary ideas, as expounded by Darwin, were widely seen as a threat to religious belief in the mid-nineteenth century, not only by their apparent impugning of the veracity of Scripture, as literally read, but also by their undermining of traditional ideas about the nature and origin of human beings. For many of Darwin's contemporaries believed his ideas called into question human dignity and moral freedom. Instead of dwelling on this familiar confrontation, I shall begin by recalling some of the more conciliatory theological responses to Darwinism in the last century. For the stage has been occupied too often by those who want to stress the negative reactions of many Christians, both theologians and lay people, to Darwinism in the Victorian era. The reconciling responses are worth recapitulating because many of them provided fruitful soil for the growth of what I consider to be a more coherent and constructive approach by Christian theology to evolution. Then we can return in the next chapter to questions such as 'What is it to be a Christian theist in a post-Darwinian world?'

The constructive responses of those Christian theologians who, in the phrase of Gertrude Himmelfarb,[2] wished to be 'reconcilers' rather than 'irreconcilers' were not based on any mood of defeatism or any sense of accommodation of Christian truth to a new and overwhelming force. Rather, they were based on a conviction that has always motivated the best and, in the long run, the most influential theology – namely that, to be intelligible and plausible to any generation, the Christian faith must express itself in ways that are consistent with such understanding of the nature of the world as is contemporarily available. For the constructive theological responses to Darwin's ideas represent a better-established way of doing theology than some of the more extreme denials that then filled the stage (and often still fill our headlines).

However, the theological questions were real enough: How could one believe in Darwin's hypothesis and still hold the account of creation in Genesis to be true? How should God's action as Creator be conceived in relation to an evolutionary formation of new creatures? How could one continue to use the popular argument for the existence of God, namely, that the presence of design and apparent purpose in the mechanisms of living organisms shows them to have been fashioned by a Cosmic Designer of an intelligence and power attributable only to a Creator God? Moreover, if human beings had evolved from the animals to a higher state of intellectual and moral consciousness, how could there be any place for the supposed historic Fall, as thought to be described in the early chapters of the book of Genesis, and much elaborated in Augustinian strands of Christianity, both Catholic and Protestant? If human higher capacities have evolved by natural means from those of animals, how could we go on supposing that they had any special ultimate value or significance? So although Darwin himself was careful never to debate these issues in public, while his own Christian belief gradually and privately ebbed away, it is not surprising that the publication of his ideas provided a new tiltyard for those who wished to enter the lists on behalf either of supposed Christian truth or of free scientific inquiry.

Because Darwin was an Englishman writing in England, and his work was published first in London, it was inevitable that the first impact of his ideas on Christian theology was upon the Church of England. But let us begin by examining the fate of his evolutionary ideas in the German and French contexts, and the response of the Roman Catholic Church.

Germany

German readers tended to see Darwin through the spectacles of Ernst Haeckel, who held a monistic world view based on a strongly mechanistic view of evolution. For him the only viable religion was the 'monistic religion of humanity', of 'truth, goodness and beauty'.[3] It was such a pantheistic religion of immanence which alone could form a bond with *Wissenschaft* and create a unity of God and the world. At the same time, the recruiting of Darwinism into the struggle for socialism, atheism and free thinking by Marx and Engels tied evolution into a package which most theologians inevitably rejected.[3] Thus German theology, insofar as it did not reject all evolutionary thought but did reject both Monism and Marxism, was pushed either towards a neo-vitalism, which had its roots in an earlier *Naturphilosophie*, or towards an existentialist dualism of 'belief' and 'knowledge' in the post-Kantian tradition of Albrecht Ritschl.

Those who chose the former option were deeply influenced by Hans Driesch, who saw in evolution the working of a non-material factor – a vital agent or *Entelechie* which could interlock with the material processes of living organisms as understood by physics and chemistry, and was the source of their character as *living* entities. R. Seeberg (1924), for example, saw in this a way of countering a purely mechanistic interpretation of evolutionary causality and so of 'saving' the creative intervention of God.[3] For him, as for Driesch, matter, life and spirit were transformed by the action of an inner, active, teleological principle transcending the laws of physics and chemistry. Driesch's vitalistic concept of wholeness (*Ganzheit*) was also utilized by other theologians, such as Jacob von Uexküll (1920), who regarded the organism and its environment as parts of a concerted unity, linked together by an 'immaterial factor'.[3] Arthur Titius and Karl Heim also invoked the idea of wholeness in order to unite causal and teleological explanations. In his *Das Weltbild der Zukunft* (1904),[4] Heim attempted to integrate the principle of natural selection with a natural theology. For both Titius and Heim mechanistic causality was not enough to explain evolution; an active purposefulness (a *Ganzheitsfaktor*) was also necessary and the introduction of this concept created a bond between science and religion. This emphasis on the *Ganzheit* principle brought both Titius and Heim close to vitalism, which in Heim's case sat rather uncomfortably with his understanding of God as personal. Titius developed the idea of *Ganzheit* to interpret God as the driving force of the cosmos and he saw creation and evolution as different ways of conceiving the same divine activity.[3]

For a long period after the Second World War, German theology (and with it much American and European, though not English, theology) was dominated by the impressive writings of Karl Barth, for whom the relation between the realms of nature and grace, between the sphere of the corrupt human intellect and that of the pure Word of God, between the created and the Creator, was simply and starkly that of a 'great gulf fixed', with no possible traffic between them that man could initiate. Consequently natural theology was relegated to the wings of the theological stage, and even a theology *of* nature was not much pursued. So inevitably from the mid-1940s to about the mid-1960s there was little active consideration in Barthian circles of the relation between evolutionary ideas and Christian theology.

Today, however, under the pressure of environmental problems, that generate the need for a theology of nature, German theology has begun to take a new interest in the findings of science in general, and of evolutionary biology in particular. Thus we have two of Germany's leading theologians, Wolfhart Pannenberg and Jürgen Moltmann, writing on these themes. Wolfhart Pannenberg[5] has carefully worked out the relation between theology and the natural and human sciences. In his view, when natural science and human understanding are emancipated from the spectre of scientific positivism they can regulate each other in a unified perspective in which theology deals with the all-embracing totality of meaning that is implicit in them both. According to Pannenberg[6] this entails theology asking certain questions of the natural sciences, such as 'Is there any equivalent in modern biology to the Biblical notion of the Divine Spirit as origin of life that transcends the limit of the organism?' Whether or not this is the best way to formulate this question is open to debate, but it is clear that German theology has now really begun to come to grips with the actual content of evolutionary biology. Moltmann's work is more confessional and political in tone, dwelling on the practical tasks of understanding and transformation.[7] But he does take account of an evolutionary understanding of what is happening in the world. He sees the natural and biological worlds as open systems with open futures, and examines what this entails for human activity, including political action.

France

In France, biology was dominated in the early nineteenth century by the giant figure of Georges Cuvier, a formidable opponent of the evolutionary scheme and mechanism proposed by Jean Baptiste de Lamarck. The reaction to Darwin in France was bedevilled by the French word *évolution* referring primarily to 'individual development' while 'evolution' in Darwin's sense was there referred to as *transformation* or *transformisme*. Moreover, 'Ever since Ray . . . the definition of the term "species" [Fr. *éspèce*] had entailed that two different species must be *genealogically* distinct: this being so, the theory of *transformisme* could not be stated as a doctrine about "species" at all – let alone throw light on the origin of species'.[8] This semantic stumbling block, which worried the French more than the empirical English, has only been properly circumvented in the mid-twentieth century 'new taxonomy' wherein 'species' are defined in a much more restricted fashion that takes account of the evolutionary process.[8]

Undoubtedly the chief influence in French philosophy of evolution, either as acquiescence or as opposition, was Henri Bergson, who was born in the same year as the publication of *The Origin of Species* and died during World War II. His *Creative Evolution*[9] represented a reaction against any mechanistic understanding of evolution by postulating a vital impulse (*élan vital*) that operates in living organisms and pervades the evolutionary process but not the universe in general: it is the cause and coordinator of variations that produce new organs and new species. He postulated a dualism of life and spirit *versus* matter and regarded the process of evolution as life and spirit diverging and unfolding from matter. Bergson differed from German neo-vitalism in that he was against 'finalism', the belief that the cosmos in general (including the biological world) was moving towards a predetermined and possibly forseeable end. For Bergson, 'finalism' postulated a mechanistically determined process which he saw as an idea opposed to true freedom, and evolution proceeded unpredictably from the one to the many. It was not a creative unification.

Roman Catholicism

French Christianity is largely Roman Catholic, and the official response of that Church to Darwin can be fairly described as a cautious keeping of Darwinism at arms' length with the preserving of belief in a distinctive act of creation for the human species through two historical individuals (traditionally known as Adam and Eve). Thus the Roman Catholic Church virtually 'bracketed off' the whole question of evolution until the middle of the twentieth century when the French Jesuit Teilhard de Chardin, in his own personal synthesis of Christian faith and evolutionary philosophy, through his posthumously published work, stimulated a renewed debate about it in the Roman Catholic world.

Teilhard was, of course, building on the ideas widely popularised by Bergson. But he rejected Bergson's interpretation of evolution as divergent from the one to the many, and he reinstated the idea of evolution as a creative unification. Teilhard was, and is, one of the most widely-read Roman Catholic thinkers to base his thinking on evolution, which he used as a theological category and as a hermeneutical principle to transpose Christian belief out of a static world-view into one that recognized the world as being in process of becoming ('cosmogenesis'). For him, the Christian God was 'a God of cosmogenesis, a God of evolution'. In spite of the plethora of living organisms, the evolutionary process has a spearhead in the human psyche and moves towards an ultimate unification in what he called the 'Omega Point'. For Teilhard, cosmogenesis has taken place in the evolution of life and spirit and potentially it can become a 'Christogenesis'; an emphasis on Christ as Redeemer was replaced by an emphasis on Christ as Evolver; and the idea of salvation was extended from that of 'redemption' to embrace that of 'genesis'. This interpretation of evolution Teilhard saw as giving meaning to what Christ was and is, and how he is expressed in the evolving world. At the same time, Christ himself 'saves evolution' by being its Mover, Animator, Guide, Coordinator, and Uniter. It is not always clear in Teilhard's writings (e.g. *The Phenomenon of Man*)[10] whether the 'God of evolution' and the 'Christ-evolver' are vitalistic, teleological factors, or whether they represent a conjunction of two ultimate, but fundamentally coincident, consummations in human consciousness and in the evolutionary process.

Although Teilhard's ideas were rejected by the official organs of the Roman Catholic Church, both during his lifetime and when they were eventually published posthumously, he has been extremely influential among lay Roman Catholics (and others), and possibly even in the deliberations of Vatican II. The official response of the Roman Catholic Church to Darwinism up to the late 1960s was summarized thus in 1967 by Z. Alszeghi[11]:

Documents after Pius XII touch only indirectly on the problem of evolution. Although taking account of the possibility of hominization [presumably meaning the formation of human beings or their creation] through evolution, they none the less affirm the necessity of proceeding with moderation and they insist on the fact that the question of the reconciliation of the faith with evolution cannot yet be regarded as definitely resolved. A recent allocution of Paul VI to a group of theologians characterises evolution as no longer an hypothesis but a 'theory', and makes no other reservation for its application to man than the immediate creation of each and every human soul and the decisive importance exerted on the lot of humanity by the disobedience of Adam. . . . The Pope observes that polygenism has not been scientifically demonstrated and cannot be admitted if it involves the denial of the dogma of original sin. (p. 16)

A final factor which was to attenuate the diffidence of the Church towards evolution consisted in the deeper under-standing of the Creator's special action in the formation of man. For, on the one hand, it is inadmissable that the human race should spring forth independently of the Creator; and on the other hand, the interpretation of the divine intervention in a determinative manner – as an action of God which is part of the same plane of secondary causes – does not fit in with an evolutionistic vision of the world. This obstacle has been overcome by conceiving the special action of God as one that works through all the generations of living beings, so that everyone shares in this special but continuous action in the great work of universal evolution. (p. 17)

Alszeghi concludes that it is not at all likely that the ecclesiastical *magisterium* would 'in the concrete' declare that evolution is irreconcilable with the faith. A survey of the state of official Roman Catholic thought on evolution by two Jesuit authors, and later than that of Alszeghi,[12] concludes that

> . . . the church, in her official teaching, has never condemned the theory of evolution, as such. Yet, it would be futile to deny that her officials for a long period had a hostile attitude to the theory. . . . However, since about 1950 there has been a marked change of atmosphere. Catholic authors put forward ideas accepting man's evolutionary origins without any inter-ference on the part of ecclesiastical authority.

Amongst these latter, the most significant contribution to Roman Catholic thought was that of Karl Rahner, who in 1966[13] put forward an interpretation of the incarnation of Christ that is essentially 'Scotist', a school of thought among Catholic theologians that 'has never been objected to by the Church's magisterium'.[14] He relates this interpretation of the incarnation positively to evolutionary ideas and is confident that 'it is therefore impossible to say that the view of the Incarnation proposed by us [i.e., Rahner] could arouse some real misgivings on the part of the magisterium'.[15]

Rahner's Christology forms part of an immensely comprehensive and profound Christian theology, and little justice can be done to it here. Rather than attempting to summarise his position, I choose to present his ideas by some excerpts from his 1966 article that, even out of context, may perhaps serve to indicate the gist of a position that adopts a much more positive and welcoming approach to evolutionary ideas of at least this influential Roman Catholic theologian. We must, he says, 'take into consideration the known history of the cosmos as it has been investigated and described by the modern natural sciences: this history is seen more and more as one homogeneous history of matter, life and man. This one history does not exclude differences of nature but on the contrary includes them in its concept, since history is precisely not the permanence of the same but rather the becoming of something entirely new and not merely of something other.'[16]

Thus Rahner assumes the current evolutionary view of the world and emphasises the connections between matter and spirit that it implies and so between its view of the unity of the world, of natural history and the history of man. Because all is the creation of one and the same God, he deems it self-evident for Christian theology that spirit and matter have 'more things in common' than 'things dividing them'. This is shown *par excellence* in the unity of spirit and matter in man himself, who is not a merely temporary composite but is fundamentally so – for the starting point is the one man in his *one* self-realization. By 'spirit', Rahner means 'the one man in so far as he becomes conscious of himself in an absolute consciousness of being-given-to-himself. This man does by the very fact that he is always referred to the absoluteness of reality as such and so to its one root (called God). . . .'[17]

This inseparable, but irreducible, correlatedness of matter and spirit in man itself has a history, for matter develops out of its inner being in the direction of spirit and such 'becoming' must be conceived as something 'becoming *more*' – the coming into being of more reality. This 'more' Rahner describes *inter alia* as the 'self-transcendence by which an existing and active being actively approaches to the higher perfection still lacking to it'.[18] He writes:

> If man is thus the self-transcendence of living matter, then the history of Nature and spirit forms an inner, graded unity in

which natural history develops towards man, continues in him as *his* history, is conserved and surpassed in him and hence reaches its proper goal with and in the history of the human spirit.[19]

Based on this view of the significance of the evolutionary perspective, Rahner tries

to see man as the being in whom the basic tendency of matter to find itself in the spirit by self-transcendence arrives at the point where it definitely breaks through; thus in this way we may be in a position to regard man's being itself, from this view-point within the basic and total conception of the world. It is precisely this being of man, seen from *this* view-point, which – both by its highest, free and complete self-transcendence into God, made possible quite gratuitously by God, and by God's communication of himself – 'awaits' its own consummation and that of the world in what in Christian terms we call 'grace' and 'glory'.

The first step and definitive beginning, and the absolute guarantee that this ultimate and basically unsurpassable self-transcendence will succeed and indeed has already begun, is to be found in what we call the Hypostatic Union [the union of the human nature and divine nature in the one person of Christ]. At a first approximation, this must not be seen so much as something which must happen once, and once only, at the point where the world begins to enter into its final phase in which it is to realize its final concentration, its final climax and its radical nearness to the absolute mystery called God. Seen from this viewpoint, the Incarnation appears as the necessary and permanent beginning of the divinization of the world as a whole.[20]

This positive treatment of a central theological theme in relation to an evolutionary perspective by a leading orthodox Roman Catholic theologian was welcome, even if somewhat delayed, coming as it did just over a century after Darwin and Wallace announced their theory of evolution by natural selection. It has indeed already begun to constitute a new point of departure for Roman Catholic thinking about evolution (see, as an example, ref. 12).

England

Needless to say, the impact of Darwinism on Christian thought was greatest in the England in which Darwin first propounded his views, though naturally the controversy soon spead throughout Britain and to the United States.

There were, in England in the mid-nineteenth century, particular cultural and religious features of the Darwinian debate that are being increasingly better documented by historians of the period – for example, the dominance of the argument from design within traditional natural theology and the increasingly disturbing analysis, emanating from Germany, of the Scriptures by the criteria and methods of historical scholarship. Rather than enter into this intriguing history, study of which is revealing a greater flexibility and openness on the part of orthodox Christian theologians than is purveyed by the inherited mythology about this period,[21] I wish to pick out one thread in the debate. It is that quieter and, in the end, more profound response of those Christian theists who did not reject Darwin but sought seriously to incorporate the evolutionary perspective into their theological reflection.

I am referring to that part of the theological response within the Church of England that was deeply influenced by the doctrine of the Incarnation. A stress on the doctrine of the Incarnation, and on a sacramental understanding of the world with its concomitant emphasis on the sacraments of the Church, had been revived in the second half of the nineteenth-century by the Tractarians. It represented a renewal in the theology of the Church of England of an earlier emphasis on the immanence of God in the natural world and on the sacraments as being but an expression and reflection of that presence of God in the world. This goes back to the very foundations of the reformed catholicism of the Church of England. Some indication of the flavour of this theology is provided by the following selected quotations. Some thirty years after the publication of the *Origin* we find Aubrey Moore writing:

> . . . the scientific evidence in favour of evolution, *as a theory* is infinitely more Christian than the theory of 'special creation'. For it implies the immanence of God in nature, and the omnipresence of His creative power. Those who oppose the doctrine of evolution in defence of a 'continued intervention' of God, seem to have failed to notice that *a theory of occasional intervention implies as its correlative a theory of ordinary absence.*[22]

The same author also wrote in the then controversial collection *Lux Mundi*:

> The one absolutely impossible conception of God, in the present day, is that which represents him as an occasional visitor. Science had pushed the deist's God further and further away, and at the moment when it seemed as if He would be thrust out all together, Darwinism appeared, and, under the disguise of a foe, did the work of a friend. . . . Either God is everywhere present in nature, or He is nowhere.[23]

In the same volume, in an essay entitled significantly 'The Incarnation in relation to Development', J. R. Illingworth wrote as follows:

> The last few years have witnessed the gradual acceptance by Christians of the great scientific generalisation of our age, which is briefly if somewhat vaguely described as the Theory of Evolution. . . . It is an advance in our theological thinking; a definite increase of insight; a fresher and fuller appreciation of those 'many ways' in which 'God fulfills Himself'.[24]

Illingworth saw Christ as the consummation of the evolutionary process:

> . . . in scientific language, the Incarnation may be said to have introduced a new species into the world – the Divine man transcending past humanity, as humanity transcended the rest of the animal creation, and communicating His vital energy by a spiritual process to subsequent generations of men.[25]

Charles Gore, the editor of that same controversial volume, later in his 1891 Bampton Lectures affirmed that:

> . . . from the Christian point of view, this revelation of God, this unfolding of divine qualities, reaches a climax in Christ. God has expressed in inorganic nature, His immutability, immensity, power, wisdom; in organic nature He has shown also that He is alive; in human nature He has given glimpses of His mind and character. In Christ not one of these earlier revelations is abrogated; nay, they are reaffirmed; but they

> reach a completion in the fuller exposition of the divine
> character, the divine personality, the divine love.[26]

In the early twentieth century one of the most positive attempts to integrate evolutionary biology into Christian theology was made by F. R. Tennant[27] who rejected the traditional pessimism about man, as it had been developed from the Bible by the combination of the book of Genesis with the Pauline epistles. Instead, Tennant appealed from the Scriptures, understood in the light of tradition, to the evidence of the evolutionary process. In the original man, he argued, the moral consciousness awakened only slowly: there was no question of some *catastrophic* change for the worse in his relationship with God, nor was there, at a later stage in man's development, a 'radical bias towards evil' because of the Fall. It was as true to say that God was still making man as to say that God *had* made him. Similarly the origin and meaning of sin were to be sought in the process of becoming. This emphasis on the 'process of becoming' was also a major strand in the philosophy of A. N. Whitehead.[28] The theologians William Temple[29] and L. S. Thornton[30] were contemporaries of Whitehead and were deeply influenced by him; like Tennant, they drew upon the tradition of evolutionary interpretation that went back to *Lux Mundi*.

The last name I want to mention in this specifically Anglican tradition is that of Charles Raven, formerly Regius Professor of Divinity in the University of Cambridge, and one whom his biographer, F. W. Dillistone, dubbed as 'naturalist, historian, theologian'.[31] Raven's whole life was devoted to integrating the evolutionary perspective of biology with his Christian theology, for he embraced evolution wholeheartedly and believed that it could serve as the conceptual framework for religious expression.[32] He strove to enhance the place of the life sciences in man's understanding of the universe, then largely dominated by physics, and pioneered in emphasising the need for ecologically wise policies of conversation. The living world was for him the many splendoured sacrament of the activity and presence of the living God. His last words from the pulpit, which I was privileged to hear, expressed with characteristic eloquence his vision of the unity of Christian insight and aspiration with a perspective on the cosmos that was deeply informed by the natural sciences and above all by that of evolution. Such a vision pervades this 'immanentist' tradition of Christian theology in Britain, and this may help to explain why the ideas of Teilhard de Chardin and of Whiteheadian 'process theology' have been generally less significant for an indigenous tradition that was already integrating science and religion, but not under the sway of one dominating metaphysic.

The United States

In contrast, process theology is that particular development of American natural theology which, utilising the metaphysical system of A. N. Whitehead, incorporates both the idea of the natural world as 'in process of becoming' and an emphasis on organicism. The process theologians have taken more seriously than almost any others in recent decades the problem of explicating God's action in a world for which all is describable in terms of law-like evolutionary processes. In process thought, God in His 'primordial nature' is regarded as providing 'aims' for all actual occasions, the ideals which they are striving to become, and in this aspect God is the envisager and fund of universals – he is eternal, absolute, unchangeable. In his 'consequent nature' he is Responsive Love and is temporal, relative, dependent and constantly changing in response to new unforeseen happenings. Process theology is closely interlocked with pan-psychism, a view of the world which sees mental and physical aspects in all entities and events. Although I find the postulate of pan-psychism to be logically flawed,[33] there is no doubting the seriousness with which process theology takes the evolutionary perspective. Process thought has had considerable influence, particularly as developed by Charles Hartshorne at Chicago, and it has subsequently proliferated elsewhere, especially at the Center for Process Studies at Claremont, California. It is still the dominant form of natural theology in America today.[34]

An even more complete welding of theology and evolutionary ideas occurs in the 'scientific theology' of R. W. Burhoe. He regards the sciences of human nature and the increasingly accepted role of religion in human evolution as capable of providing the major religious traditions with the means of interpreting themselves in harmonious relation both to science itself and to one another. He even goes so far as to claim that it makes 'little difference whether we name it [the power that created the earth and life] natural selection or God, so long as we recognise it as that to which we must bow our heads or adapt'.[35]

This has now brought us up to the recent past in our survey of constructive theological responses to evolution. But science never stands still, so there is a continuous need to re-think our understanding of the relation of nature, man and God as our perception of the natural world changes. To this task we now turn.

6 *Man, God and evolution: today*

As far as we can tell, *Homo sapiens* is the only organism that asks itself questions about the meaning of its existence – questions like the penetrating title of the famous story by Tolstoy 'What do men live by?' This is a question about man's needs. Of course, man has biological needs, and the pursuit of their satisfaction has shaped human history. But even when these basic needs have been met man is not necessarily happy. For he has a restlessness which stems from his failure to satisfy other needs which he seems *not* to share with other animals. For human beings need to come to terms with their awareness of their own death and with their finitude, to learn how to bear suffering, to realise their potentialities, and to determine their own directions. It is to the satisfaction of needs such as these that the religious quest of mankind has always directed itself, and this is true *a fortiori* of what I prefer to call the Christian experiment. These fundamental questions about human existence have to be raised because it is as a response to them that the Christian experience has developed and the theological enterprise has unfolded as reflection upon this experience. However, our particular world is informed and dominated by the evolutionary perspective that I have expounded. So the question arises, 'What is it to be a Christian theist in a post-Darwinian world?'

To ask such a question is also to ask how Christian theology is to be related to scientific knowledge, and there are many answers to that. I have elsewhere been able to delineate at least eight different ways in which modern science and Christian faith can interact in relation to their intellectual content and epistemology.[1] Like most scientists, I am a critical, qualified realist with respect to my scientific knowledge; and since I take this same stance with respect to theological affirmations, my approach is to regard science and theology as interacting approaches to the same reality.[1,2] I want to affirm that *both* the scientific *and* the theological enterprises are explorations into the nature of reality. The former is widely assumed, but less frequently the latter. I heartily endorse the initial and controlling statement in the 1976 report of the Doctrine

Commission of the Church of England entitled *Christian Believing* which opened as follows: 'Christian life is an adventure, a voyage of discovery, a journey, sustained by faith and hope, towards a final and complete communion with Love at the heart of all things.'[3]

In what follows in this chapter, I shall indicate how I think Christian theology, evolutionary and other scientific ideas may be incorporated into a coherent view of human beings, the non-human natural world ('nature') and God. Inevitably this can be only a sketch of a style of theological reflection that takes seriously both the scientific and evolutionary perspective and the insights of the Judeo-Christian experience (for a fuller exposition see ref. 4). It must be emphasised that this attempt at synthesis is based on the epistemology expounded in the first chapter. It essays to fulfil the hope, there held out, of a coherent and consonant perspective of 'nature, man and God'. In particular it also assumes the positions adopted in that chapter concerning the relation between our knowledge of different levels of the natural hierarchy of complexity, the non-reducibility of many of the concepts that refer to the realities that emerge at each level in that hierarchy, and the relation between different 'interfaces' – those between the sciences themselves, between the sciences and the humanities, and between the sciences (and much else) and theology.

So we turn now to examine some Christian perspectives and their relation to the scientific, evolutionary world-view.

Human being

The early Christian, and especially the New Testament, understanding of human nature was rooted in its Hebraic background, albeit often overlaid by later Hellenistic influences. It is important to remember, however, that the Hellenistic distinctions between flesh and spirit, body and soul, and indeed those between form and matter and the one and the many, were never made by the Israelites. In particular, the concept of non-material entity, the soul, imprisoned in a material frame, the body, is entirely contrary to their way of thinking. 'The Hebrew idea of personality is an animated body, and not an incarnated soul', affirmed H. Wheeler Robinson[5] some sixty years ago in a famous epigram. Or, in Eichrodt's terms, 'Man does not *have* a body and a soul, he *is* both of them at once'.[6] This is not to say that, within this view of man as a psychosomatic unity, there was no awareness of the distinctive character of the inner life, as contrasted with physical processes. There is a word for the living body of a human being, *basar*, the 'flesh', that not only has a range of usage distinct from, but can even occur in a certain opposition to, other words such as *ruach*, 'vitality', *nephesh*, 'person', or 'living being' and *leb*, 'heart', which have a closer connection with man's inner, psychic life. Thus the principal feature of Hebrew anthropology is that it sees human nature primarily as a unity with various differentiating organs and functions through any of which a person in his or her totality can express him- or herself and be apprehended. The person does not subdivide, however, into immortal and mortal parts. Indeed, for the Hebrews, personal individuality was delineated not by the boundary of the body but by the responsibility of each person to God, and so by the uniqueness of the divine call to that individual – and certainly not by his 'flesh' (*basar*) as such.[7]

Moreover, this Hebraic background is the key to understanding the New Testament writers, especially St Paul in his use of *sarx* ('flesh'), *soma* ('body'), *kardia* ('heart'), *nous* ('mind'), *pneuma* ('spirit') and *psyche* ('soul'). The consensus of careful scholarship agrees that the New Testament view of human nature is very much like that of the Old insofar as a human being is regarded as a psychosomatic unity, a personality whose outward expression is his body and whose centre is his 'heart', 'mind', and 'spirit'.[8] What clearly emerges is an affinity between this view of human nature in the Biblical tradition and that stemming from the sciences. This affinity has often been obscured by the strong influence of Hellenistic thought on the development of Christian ideas, leading to the notion that the Christian view of the individual is that of a union of two entities, a mortal body and an eternal soul. However, this is not in accordance with the Biblical anthropology, even if much popular exposition of Christianity would lead one to suppose otherwise. Biblical ideas about death and its aftermath are also consistent with this background. The Hebrews, unlike the Greeks, did not think of the real core of personality as naturally immortal and therefore existing beyond death in a more liberated form. The most they could imagine was a shadowy existence which was but a pale reflection of life in its fullness. Only gradually did the sense that the timeless character of man's relationship with God could not be ruptured by death come to the fore. Only then did a doctrine of resurrection begin to appear in Jewish thought. And, given Hebrew anthropology, it involved resurrection of the total person and thus had to include what we call a 'body', some form of expression of the total personality.

Biblical views of human nature, and the Christian teaching which stemmed from them, are thoroughly realistic in their recognition of the paradoxical character of human beings. They recognise the greatness of human potential but the infrequency of its realization. They recognise also human degradation and wretchedness, engendering cynicism and a sense of tragedy. And they contrast the eternal longings of humanity with individual mortality. Man, like all other beings, is regarded by Biblical writers as existing by the will of God who sustains the cosmos in being. He is furthermore regarded, especially by the 'priestly' writer of the book of Genesis, as created in the 'image' and 'likeness' of God in the sense that:

> [On man] personhood is bestowed as the definitive character-
> istic of his nature. He has a share in the personhood of God;
> and as a being capable of self-awareness and self-determination
> he is open to the divine address and capable of responsible
> conduct.[9]

From both the Biblical and scientific viewpoints, a human being is a psychosomatic unity that is a part of nature and is conscious and self-conscious.

Such affirmations of the reality of consciousness and self-consciousness are not dependent on any particular philosophy of the relation of an entity called 'mind' to one called 'body'. All I am concerned to emphasise in the present context is that there are human activities and experiences that demand this kind of language, and that what these languages refer to is uniquely and characteristically human. We should note too that many philosophers who accept the idea of an identity between mental states and brain states differ as to whether this is a contingent or a necessary identity,[10] a debate which involves the possible definition and role of rigid designation.[11] They also differ as to whether mental events fall under any laws that would allow a single, particular mental event to be predicted or explained. D. Davidson, for example has argued for an 'anomalous monism' according to which there are no general laws correlating the mental and the physical ('psycho-physical laws'), although mental events are identical with physical.[12]

We have no time, nor do I have the professional expertise, to follow the tracks of current philosophical inquiry. But it does appear that overtly materialist or physicalist views of the body-mind relation have not been able to capture fully what more mentalist and less physicalist views often aim to ensure, namely, the ability of the human brain in the human body to be a self-conscious free agent with inter-connecting mental events linked in a causal nexus of a kind peculiar to themselves. I see no reason why Christian theology should not accept body-mind identitist positions providing they are qualified at least to the extent that Davidson urges, with respect to the 'anomaly' of mental events and to their non-reducibility to the physical,[13] and provided that the autonomy of man as a free agent is preserved. This is in fact the position taken by many of these 'qualified identitists'. For the sense of the self as an agent is a given fact of our experience of ourselves in relation to our bodies and the world and, surd though it may be, demands incorporation into our views of our bodies and the world – even if we recognize that the mental events which are the experience of being an 'I', an agent, are identical, under another description, with neuro-physiological events in the brain.

Such an understanding of both the distinctiveness of the 'I' and, at the same time, its rooting in the physiological and biochemical has been well expressed by the Christian philosopher, I. T. Ramsey:

> All this [the study of the interacting factors operating in shaping human personality] suggests that the one unifying concept, definitive of personality, is not soul nor mind nor body. There is no kind of underlying cushion to which all our bodily and mental events and characteristics are attached as pins; and any basic personality matrix is not static. Rather is personality to be analysed in terms of a distinctive activity, distinctive in being owned, localized, personalized. *The unity of personality on this view is to be found in an integrating activity*, an activity expressed, embodied and scientifically understood in terms of its genetic, biochemical and endocrine, electronic, neurological and psychological manifestations. What we call human behaviour is an expression of that effective, integrating activity which is peculiarly and distinctively ourselves.[14]

In human beings part of the world has become conscious of itself and consciously and actively responds to its surroundings; in human life a new mode of interaction is introduced in the world. Oddly, however, this product of evolution is strangely ill at ease in its environment. Human persons alone amongst living creatures individually commit suicide. Somehow, natural selection has resulted in a being of infinite restlessness, ill at ease with its environment – and this certainly raises the question of whether human beings have properly conceived of what their true 'environment' is. In the natural world, new life and new forms of life can arise only from death of the old, for the death of the individual is essential to the possibility of new forms evolving in the future. Yet to human beings this is an affront and they grieve over their suffering and their own personal demise.

We have the paradox of man as the summit of the cosmic development so far, for his mental activities transcend all, yet at the same time he is tragically aware of his personal and social shortcomings and subject to the tension between the awareness of the finitude of his individual life and the infinity of his longings. He is aware both of that from which he has evolved and of his tendency always to fall short of the full realization of his own individual and corporative potentialities. Thus the incompleteness of the actualisation of the potentialities inherent in the stuff of the universe is, in man, a result of his own decisions, or lack of them, and is quite different from the situation of unrealized potentiality in the molecule or cell which is eventually expressed in, *inter alia*, living organisms. Man constitutes a break in the evolutionary process which had hitherto depended on the continuous operation of natural 'laws'. For man appears to himself to have a free will allowing him to make choices and is free to fail to respond to the challenge presented to him.

Man's dilemma is real, for how is he to know which way to go, to which challenge he should respond, what his real potentialities might be? What does it involve to be a human being, to be fully a person? What should constitute personalness in its richest manifestation? What should human beings strive to become? Moreover, given that we know the answers to these questions, how are we going to overcome our inherent limitations and deficiencies freely to will to move in the sought-after direction? For any such change of direction cannot be imposed if it is to be effective in human 'inner', mental life. The evolutionary sequence clearly shows that the answers to these questions are vital for man and his future but, at the same time, provides nothing from within the process itself which will tell us what human beings *ought to become*, how they should achieve their ends in a way which recognizes their personalness, that psychosomatic unity which differentiates them from the rest of the cosmos.

The evolutionary account of mankind, as depicted in geology, palaeontology, biology, and anthropology, demonstrates unambiguously that man is a creature who has emerged into a self-consciousness that has enhanced his adaptational flexibility and power over his environment, and so his biological survival ability. The only state of primeval 'innocence' that such a scientific account of the emergence of man might allow is of a kind that can be attributed to all non-human, non-self-conscious mammalian organisms, namely, one innocent of any sense of responsible choice and of the relationship of power to moral choice. In the emergence of man, science sees only a gradual awakening to self-consciousness and so to an awareness of freedom of moral and other choice, and also to power over the environment. The traditional theological doctrine of 'the Fall' as a disobedient act by the original man and woman (Adam and Eve) in which they fell from grace and which so altered their state that they transmitted this state of 'original sin' pseudo-genetically to all succeeding mankind is clearly at odds with the scientific account – which sees in man only an emergence from the consciousness of the higher mammals to self-consciousness, language, and deliberate choice. The meaning of what is now regarded as the Genesis myth of 'the Fall' has been widely and profoundly interpreted existentially in our times by both Biblical and systematic theologians as a myth of man's present *state* of alienation from God, and of disharmony both between men and between man and nature.[15]

Evolving matter

The sciences of the twentieth century have confirmed what many in the nineteenth century believed, but without adequate evidence, and what in the eighteenth century was only intimated, namely, that the whole cosmos is in a state of evolution from one form of matter to another, and that a significant point in this evolutionary process occurred on the surface of the Earth where the conditions were such that matter was able to become living. This transition was of a kind that did not require for its occurrence any factors external to the world itself.

Stress on this continuity between the living and non living worlds, with no evocation of any intruding principle, or *deus ex machina*, has been thought by some authors to entail a materialistic interpretation of life and evolution, and I would not demur at this were it not for the implications that have accrued to the word 'materialistic' since the nineteenth century. For there is a hidden implication that we know already what we mean by the word 'matter'. But the whole sweep of cosmic evolution can be regarded as revealing, as the aeons unfold, that of which matter is capable when it adopts new forms of organisation. We do not know all there is to be known about oxygen, carbon, nitrogen, hydrogen, and phosphorus until they adopt the form of the DNA molecule in its biological milieu. From this viewpoint, the continuity of cosmic development serves to reveal the potentialities of the primordial nebular cloud of hydrogen atoms (or rather, of its more fundamental predecessors in the origin of the universe 10–20 thousand million years ago). So the description of the cosmic development, including the biological, as 'materialistic' is acceptable if, and only if, we mean by the noun 'matter', from which the adjective 'materialistic' derives, something very different from the limited billiard-ball concept of a nineteenth-century materialism based on a mechanistic universe governed by Newtonian mechanics. For, just look at what has become of the 'simple' matter of the 'hot big bang'! Each level of the development of the cosmos can, it appears, legitimately be regarded as a manifestation of the potentialities of matter which have been implicit in it from the beginning in its simplest forms and have only gradually unfolded.

Our understanding of matter has been enormously enhanced as a result of this perspective, for matter turns out to be capable of organising itself into self-reproducing systems that are capable of receiving signals, storing and processing information from their environment, and becoming cognitive. In this development, matter in the form of living organisms comes to manifest behaviour to which we attribute consciousness, and eventually self-consciousness when it takes the form of the human brain in the human body with its enormous cognitive powers. These manifestations are as real at their own level as any chemical reaction or sub-atomic interaction at theirs. Self-consciousness cannot lightly be set on one side, and by the very nature of the activity itself cannot but appear to us as one of the most significant features of the cosmos. Paradoxically the arrival of *homo sapiens* as a product of nature must give us pause in thinking that we know all about what matter is 'in itself', for it shows the potentialities of matter in a new light.

There are good scientific grounds for stressing the continuity of the physical with the biological world, so perhaps the cosmic process may be described as 'materialistic', provided the term is understood in the light of this. However, the qualification of 'materialistic' just made may in the end be so drastic that some other less misleading term becomes necessary. For 'matter' appears to be far more subtle and its potentialities far richer and more diverse than can be inferred from observations made at any single particular level of the development of the cosmos, especially the simplest and least complex.

God and the world

The postulate of God as Creator of all-that-is is not, in its most profound form, a statement about what happened at a particular point in time. To speak of God as Creator is a postulate about a perennial or 'eternal' – that is to say, timeless – relation of God to the world, a relation which involves both differentiation and interaction. God is differentiated from the world in that he is totally other than it (indeed *this* dualism – of God and the world – is the only one that is foundational to Christian thought). He is the 'Ground of Being' of the world; or for theists, that without which we could make sense neither of the world having existence at all nor of its having that kind of intellectually coherent and explorable existence which science continuously unveils. But this affirmation of what is termed 'transcendence' has to be held in tension with the sense of God's immanence in the world.

For the process of evolution is continuous with that of inorganic and cosmic evolution – life has emerged as a form of living matter and develops by its own inherent laws, both physicochemical and biological, to produce new forms with new emergent qualities requiring new modes of study (the various sciences) as well as new concepts and languages to describe and explicate them. The stuff of the world therefore has a continuous, inbuilt creativity – such that, whatever 'creation' is, it is not confined to a restricted period of time but is going on all the time (and indeed modern physics would support seeing time itself as an aspect of the created order). So, if we identify the creativity of the world with that of its Creator, we must emphasize that God is *semper Creator*, all the time creating – God's relation to the world is perennially and eternally that of Creator. But to speak thus is to recognize also that God *is creating* now and continuously in and through the inherent, inbuilt creativity of the natural order, both physical and biological – a creativity that is itself God in the process of creating. So we have to identify God's action with the processes themselves, as they are revealed by the physical and biological sciences, and this identification means we must stress more than ever before God's *immanence* in the world. If the world is in any sense what God has created and that through which he acts and expresses his own inner being, then there is a sense in which God is never absent from his world and he is as much in his world as, say, Beethoven is in his Seventh Symphony during a performance of it.

The processes of evolution, initially the physical and cosmological, and then more strikingly the biological, are characterised by the *emergence* of new forms within and by means of continuous developments subject to their own inherent, regular, law-like behaviour that is studied by the sciences. What emerges is usually more complex and, along certain branches of the evolutionary tree, more and more conscious, culminating in the self-consciousness and the sense of being a person that characterizes humanity. In theological terms, God's immanent creative action in the world generates within the created order a being, the human being, who becomes self-aware, morally responsible, and capable of himself being creative and of responding to God's presence. Thus the natural, biological, and human worlds are not just the stage of God's action – they *are* in themselves a mode of God in action, a mode that has traditionally been associated with the designation Holy Spirit, the Creator Spirit. I think that to give due weight to the evolutionary character of God's creative action requires a much stronger emphasis on God's immanent presence in, with, and under the very processes of the natural world from the 'hot, big, bang' to humanity.

If I had to represent on a blackboard the relation of God and the world, including man, I would not simply draw three spheres labelled respectively 'Nature', 'Man' and 'God' and draw arrows between them to represent their interrelation. Rather I would denote an area representing nature and would place that entirely within another area representing God, which would have to extend to the edges of the blackboard and, indeed, point beyond it (to infinity). When I came to depict man, I would have to place him with his feet placed firmly in nature but with his self-consciousness (perhaps represented by his brain?) protruding beyond the boundary of nature and into the area that attempts to 'depict' God, or at least refer to him.

The basic affirmation[16] here is that all-that-is, both nature and man, is in some sense *in* God, but that God is, profoundly and ultimately, 'more' than nature and man – there is more to God than nature and man. God in his being transcends, goes beyond, both man and nature, yet God is either in everything created from the beginning to the end, at all times and in all places, or he is not there at all. What we see in the world is the mode of God's creativity in the world. The analogy with

Beethoven's Seventh Symphony as an expression of Beethoven's own inner creative being is, I think, a fair one. In the actual processes of the world, and supremely in human self-consciousness, God is involving himself and expressing himself as Creator. However, since man has free will we have also to recognise that God put himself 'at risk', as it were, in creatively evoking in the natural world a being who has free will and who can transcend his perceived world and shape it in his own way.

God and chance

How may this understanding of God creating 'in, with and under'[17] the ongoing processes of the natural world be held in consonance with the recognition that new, and increasingly complex, forms of both inorganic and eventually living matter emerge by a combination of what we recognise (see Chapter 4) as 'chance' and 'law' – and that this combination is inherently creative in itself[18] and involves, for sound thermodynamic and chemical reasons, an increase in complexity[19]? How can the assertion of God as Creator be interpreted in the light of this new and profound understanding of the natural processes by which new organised forms of matter appear, both non-living and living? In evolution there is an interplay between random chance at the micro level and the necessity which arises from the stuff of the world having its particular 'given' properties and law-like behaviour. These potentialities a theist must regard as written into creation by the Creator's intention and purpose and they are gradually actualised by chance exploring their gamut.[20]

I have earlier[21] tried to express this situation by seeing God as Creator as like a composer who, beginning with an arrangement of notes in an apparently simple tune, elaborates and expands it into a fugue by a variety of devices. Thus, I suggested, does a J. S. Bach create a complex and interlocking harmonious fusion of his original material. The listener to such a fugue experiences, with the luxuriant and profuse growth that emanates from the original simple structure, whole new worlds of emotional experience that are the result of the interplay between an expectation based on past experience ('law') and an openness to the new ('chance' in the sense that the listener cannot predict or control it).

Thus might the Creator be imagined to unfold the potentialities of the universe which he himself has given it, selecting and shaping by his redemptive and providential action those that are to come to fruition –

an Improvisor of unsurpassed ingenuity. He appears to do so by a process in which the creative possibilities, inherent (by his own intention) within the fundamental entities of that universe and their inter-relations, become actualised within a temporal development shaped and determined by those selfsame inherent potentialities.

The image of creation as an act of composing and of the created order as a musical composition is surprisingly rich and fecund and, since propounding it in my 1978 Bampton Lectures,[21] I have come across a number of other authors resorting to the image of music, as flexible form moving within time, to express what they wish to say about both the created order and the act of creation – authors as diverse as Popper, Capek and Eigen.[22] One recalls in this connection that the music of creation has also been a constant theme of the religions of India, for example the South Indian representations, in bronze, of the dancing Shiva, the Creator-Destroyer, as Lord of the Dance of creation.[23]

Both images, of the writing of a fugue and of the execution of a dance, serve to express the idea of God enjoying, of playing in, creation. This is not an idea new to Christian thought. The Greek fathers, so Harvey Cox argues, contended that the creation of the world was a form of play. 'God did it they insisted out of freedom, not because he had to, spontaneously and not in obedience to some inexorable law of necessity.'[24]

H. Montefiore has criticised this wholehearted acceptance, by the present author and by Dr J. S. Habgood[25], of the creative interplay of chance and law as a sufficient account of the observed growth of complexity as leading to the 'God of the deists'[26] – that is, to a distant 'absentee-landlord' God who, as it were, sets the universe going and leaves it to get on with it – 'a remote, unmoved, unloving' God. He asserts this because he believes 'chance and necessity may produce creativity, but they cannot produce purpose'[26]. But what these new developments actually show is that the interplay of chance and law bring about that increase in complexity which is both inbuilt according to the laws of thermodynamics and chemical kinetics[19] and is also the basis of that increase of sentience and freedom of the individual organism which is the condition for the appearance of all those qualities in and values of man, the eliciting of which in the created order Montefiore quite properly wishes to attribute to the purpose of the creator God of Christian theism.

D. J. Bartholomew (a professor of statistical and mathematical science) has made the most recent and thoroughgoing study of this role of chance in the natural order in relation to the concept of God.[27] He contends that chance is actually conducive to the kind of world which he would expect a God, such as Christians believe in, to create, and that God uses chance to ensure the variety, resiliance and freedom necessary to achieve his purposes. His basic hypothesis is that God uses chance which 'offers the potential Creator many advantages which it is difficult to envisage being obtained in any other way'.[28] Even more strongly, he believes 'God chose to make a world of chance because it would have the properties necessary for producing beings fit for fellowship with himself'.[29] His whole position merits careful study though, in the present author's opinion,[30] it takes too externalist a view of God's mode of action in the world and does not emphasise sufficiently, or develop any understanding of, God's immanence in the natural creative processes. Like Montefiore, whose views are otherwise contrary to his, Bartholomew fails to recognise[28] that the joint emphasis, which I, for one, have been making, *both* on the role of chance in natural creativity *and* on the immanence of God in these same natural processes leads not to deism but to that integration of immanence and transcendence that I have already described (pages 96–7) – that 'the Being of God includes and penetrates the whole universe, so that every part of it exists in Him, but . . . that his Being is more than, and is not exhausted by the universe' ('pan-en-theism').[16]

Living with chance

This theoretical acceptance of the role of chance in creation and in the created world also has implications for our attitudes to the role of chance in human life. Rustum Roy (Director of the Materials Research Laboratory at Pennsylvania State University) entitled his first 1979 Hibbert Centenary Lecture, in London, 'Living with the Dice-playing God'.[32] He urged us to accept that the world displays patterned chance. It is not a chaos, for there is only a 'loose coupling' through statistical laws and patterns, which still allows talk of 'causes'. In human life we must accept, for the stability of our own mental health and of our faith, that reality has a dimension of chance interwoven with a dimension of causality[33] – and that through such interweaving we came to be here and new forms of existence can arise.

This acceptance of chance as part of the mode of God's creativity is more consistent with the fundamental creativity of reality than the belief – stemming from a Newtonian, mechanistic, determinist view of the universe with a wholly transcendent God as the great Lawgiver – that

God intervenes in the natural nexus for the good or ill of individuals and societies.[34] We must learn to accept these conditions of creation and of creativity in the world – 'the changes and chances of this fleeting world'. Such an attitude can rightly be urged not simply as a psychological necessity but also as the outcome of the recognition that we have just been developing, that the creation of life itself, and the creativity of the living, inevitably involves an interplay of chance and law.

A Christian materialism?

The processes of the universe are continuous and evolutionary[17] and in them arise new organisations of matter-energy. Such new levels of organisation require epistemologically non-reducible concepts to articulate their distinctiveness. Any new meaning that God thereby expresses is thus not discontinuous with the meanings expressed in that out of which it has emerged. *Both* continuity *and* emergence of the new are features inherent in the observed world. So we would anticipate continuity, with new meanings emerging out of the old, subsuming them, perhaps, but not denying them.

Now evolved human beings seek such meaning and intelligibility in the world; that is, from a theist's point of view, they seek to discern the meanings expressed by God in creation. These are meanings which, alone among created organisms, we are capable both of consciously discerning and freely appropriating to give purpose and meaning to our lives. Although we should not regard God as more present at one time or place than at others, nevertheless we should not be surprised to find that in some sequences of events in nature and history God unveils his meaning more clearly than in others. Though God as Creator acts in all events, not all events are equally *perceived* as 'acts of God'. Some events will reveal more to us than others.

The aspect of God's meaning expressed by any one level in the natural hierarchy of complexity is limited to what it has the capacity to convey, but how much we perceive of this depends on our sensitivity or responsiveness to that level. Thus, although God must in his own being *ex hypothesi* be supra-personal, we may well expect that in personal experience, personal encounter and in human history, we shall find meanings of God unveiled in a way that we will not perceive through *im*personal events. For the more personal and *self*-conscious the entity in which God is immanent, the more capable it is of expressing God's supra-personal characteristics, and the more God can be immanent in that entity. The transcendence-in-immanence of man's experience furthermore raises the hope among those who seek God in his created work that uniquely in a human being there might be unveiled, without distortion, the transcendent Creator who is immanent; that is to say, that in *a* human being (or beings) the presence of God the Creator might be revealed with a clarity not hitherto perceived.

It is the distinctive affirmation of *Christian* theists that this has actually happened – to Jews a stumbling block and to the Greeks foolishness – to other-worldly 'religious' a demeaning of the Almighty, Eternal One so to enter material existence; to the Western intellectual a unique lawless surd, indeed, an absurdity in a law-abiding universe. Yet is it so anti-theistic, is it so inconsistent with profounder trends and laws and with the concepts of God I have been elaborating to affirm that at a particular time and place in history, the God who had all along been immanent in the whole temporal creative process should have expressed himself directly, personally and concretely in and through a particular person who, humanly speaking, was completely open to him? The effort to describe the nature of that person through whom God so revealed himself constituted a major transition in the way humankind came to think of nature, of God, and of itself.[36] For it profoundly affected man's perception of God, of human destiny, and of nature.

To take just the last, human understanding of nature was gradually transformed in Christian consciousness because, if God was able to express his nature – that is, 'incarnate' himself – in a human being, then the world of matter organised in the form we call human must inherently have a capability of thus being a vehicle of God's action and of expressing God's being. This in itself constituted a repudiation of the attitudes of all who saw the stuff of the world as evil, alien to its Creator, a prison from which a non-material reason, or 'soul', must seek release. God must henceforth be seen as achieving his ends by involvement with, immanence in, expression through, the very stuff of the world and its events in space and time. Moreover, the assertion that Jesus the Christ was the ultimate revelation of God's being to men in a mode that they could understand and appropriate, amounted to an affirmation that nature in its actuality, materiality and evolution, of which Jesus was indubitably a part, is potentially at least both an expression of God's being and the instrument of his action. Paradoxically, the Christian claim asserts that God fulfils human personalness, and satisfies mankind's highest aspirations, by entering the temporal process as a man, made like all human beings of the component units of the stuff of the world.

There is indeed a *Christian* materialism. As David Jenkins put it in his Bampton lectures:

> The Christian discovery on the basis of the givenness of Jesus Christ was that man and the universe hold together because of the involvement of God to that end. Thus materiality and history provide the stuff for the attainment of ultimate reality and the fulfilment of absolute value.[37]

Or, in the words of William Temple:

> It may safely be said that one ground for the hope of Christianity that it may make good its claim to be the true faith lies in the fact that it is the most avowedly materialist of all the great religions. It affords an expectation that it may be able to control the material, precisely because it does not ignore it or deny it, but roundly asserts alike the reality of matter and its subordination. Its own most central saying is: 'The Word was made flesh', where the last term was, no doubt, chosen because of its specially materialistic associations. By the very nature of its central doctrine Christianity is committed to a belief in the ultimate significance of the historical process, and in the reality of matter and its place in the divine scheme.[38]

There is, moreover, in the long tradition of Christian thought, going back to Jesus' own actions and words, a way of relating the physical and the personal worlds that avoids any stark dichotomy between them, seeing them rather as two facets of the same reality. This way of thinking is generally denoted by the word 'sacramental' and to this we shall have to revert later (in Chapter 9). Before we do so, there are two particular areas of the 'new biology' – one holistic and the other reductionist in style – which should engage our attention because they have implications for our understanding of the relation of nature, man and God, and this understanding itself has implications for the way we might regard the aspects of the living world which these areas of biology are interpereting. I refer to ecology (Chapter 7) and sociobiology (Chapter 8).

7 *Nature as creation*

At the end of Chapter 3 we referred briefly to an area of 'holistic' biology of increasing significance today – that of ecology. We mentioned how the interconnectedness of all living systems on the surface of the Earth with each other and their interaction with their physical environment is one expression of a more general unity and mutual interconnectedness and interdependence of all things and events.

That the universe is such a complicated web of relations between the parts of a unified whole has, according to Capra,[1] been a major emphasis in much Eastern mystical thought. But, as I have pointed out elsewhere,[2] there has also been a genuinely Christian mystical tradition which also exhibits many of the 'interconnected' features that Capra attributes only to the East.[3] However, there are good grounds now for amplifying further and enriching the Judeo-Christian doctrine of creation, in the light of the sciences, so we ought to reconsider man's role in creation and the human response to the created from the newer perspectives I outlined in the last chapter.

I developed there an account of our understanding of God's relation to the world in the light of our knowledge of it provided by the natural sciences. We must now look at its various elements in relation both to man's roles in creation and to the kind of response from man to nature these call for. In accord with the traditional Judeo-Christian doctrine of creation, exposition would be based on the conception of God as transcendent creative agent and this properly evokes such terms as *'vicegerent'*, *'steward'*, *'trustee'* or *'manager'* to represent the human role in nature. However, these terms still introduce a nuance of 'domination' into the biblical concept of 'dominion' and, in modern English, do not adequately convey the 'caring' component inherent in the Biblical understanding.[4] So they leave much to be desired in this respect. The exposition also stressed particularly, and intentionally more than has traditionally been the case, that God the Creator is immanent in a world that he is still creating. God is everywhere and at all times in the processes and events of the natural world which is to be seen as the vehicle and instrument

of God's action and as capable of expressing his intentions and purposes
– as our bodies are agents of ourselves.

This immediately suggests that man should respond to nature with a
respect of the same kind as a man accords to his own body and those of
another person – as an agent of that other 'self'. Man's attitude to nature
should show a respect which is transmuted into reverence at the presence
of God in and through the whole of the created order, which thereby
has, as it were, a derived sacredness or holiness. But this is tantamount
to saying that the world is sacramental,[5] to use the traditional term in
Christian theology which by its etymology and its long associations also
conveys the sense of 'holy'.

This complex of proper responses of man to nature also suggests that
man's role may be conceived as that of *priest of creation*, as a result of
whose activity the sacrament of creation is reverenced; and who, because
he alone is conscious of God, himself and nature, can mediate between
insentient nature and God – for a priest is characterised by activity
directed towards God on behalf of others. Man alone can contemplate
and offer the action of the created world to God. But a priest is also
active towards others on God's behalf and in this sense, too, man is the
priest of creation. He alone, having reflected on God's purposes, can be
active in and with the created world consciously seeking to further and
fulfil God's purposes.

> Man is the world's High Priest: he doth present
> The sacrifice for all: while they below
> Unto the service mutter an assent,
> Such as springs use that fall, and winds that blow.
>
> (G. Herbert)[6]

To instil and to practise such reverence is for man indeed to be the
priest of creation and Lord Ashby attributes such attitudes to pragmatic
biologists who, he says, having reflected on complexity, 'regard it as an
act of vandalism to upset an ecosystem without good cause for doing
so'.[7] Considerations such as these, he claims, 'are enough to provide the
rudiments of an environmental ethic. Its premise is that respect for
nature is more moral than lack of respect for nature. Its logic is to put
Teesdale Sandwort into the same category of value as a piece of Ming
porcelain; the Yosemite Valley in the same category as Chartres
Cathedral; a Suffolk landscape in the same category as a painting of a
landscape by Constable.'[8] This represents well the reactions of many

biologists to natural ecosystems, but one questions whether, in itself, it provides the rudiments of an environmental ethic, for could not one always argue against the preservation of any natural ecosystem which man needed to disrupt that, in doing so, man was simply expressing his biological need to survive? Biology *per se* seems able only to generate a human self-survival policy towards nature, whatever the sympathies of individual biologists. That is why we are exploring in this chapter the implication of seeing nature *as* created.

We came to speak of God as actively unveiling his meaning, of speaking his word, to that part of his creation, man, capable of seeing and hearing him. This allows man to see the natural world as a symbol of God's meaning: this understanding is, indeed, included in the concept of the world as a sacrament and suggests further that man is the interpreter of creation's meaning, value, beauty and destiny. Man alone in the natural world reads, articulates and communicates to others the meanings he reads. He has that prophetic function which always complements the priestly in man's corporate relation to God. Like Hamlet's players, his role is 'to hold, as t'were, the mirror up to nature'.

As we have seen, the created world consists of natural hierarchies of complexity, of immense variety and distinctiveness, whose uniqueness often consists in them being describable only by epistemologically non-reducible concepts. 'It is hard to be a reductionist ecologist.'[9] Thus man, in his relation to nature, must make a sensitive response to its integrated complexity. Some authors, appreciating this, have urged him to regard the natural world as a 'Thou' to his 'I'; they press for an I-Thou relation to our environment. These authors are not wanting to personify nature, to write it as 'Nature', in any romanticising manner. But they do want to emphasise the unique non-reducible wholeness and integration of the ecosystems of the Earth and see parallels in personal relations. In a way, they are asking mankind to adopt the role of *lover of nature*, for the lover, supremely in I-Thou relationships, is sensitive to the full personhood of the beloved.

It is this kind of motivation which seems to have led Barbara Ward and Rene Dubos to conclude their book with the following impassioned plea: 'Alone in space, alone in its life-supporting systems, powered by inconceivable energies, mediating them to us through the most delicate adjustments, wayward, unlikely, unpredictable, but nourishing, enliving and enriching in the largest degree – is this [Earth] not a precious home for all of us earthlings? Is it not worth our love? Does it not deserve all the inventiveness and courage and generosity of which we are capable to preserve it from degradation and destruction and, by doing so, to secure our own survival?'[10]

The scientific perspective on the world resuscitated the theme of continuous creation (*creatio continua*) and consideration of the interplay of chance and necessity (law) led us to stress the open-ended character of this process of emergence of new forms. We recognized that creation is still going on – the fugue is still being developed – the choreography is still being elaborated. But man, too, finds himself with creative energies both within and for himself and in relation to nature through his newly acquired technology. So he is faced with a choice – does he join in with the creative work of God harmoniously integrating his own material creations (which are never *ex nihilo*) into what God is already doing? Or does he introduce a discordant note, an entanglement of and confusion within the dance?

It is as if man has the possibility of acting as a participant in creation, as it were the leader of the orchestra of creation in the performance which is God's ongoing composition. More generally, man now has the opportunity of consciously becoming *co-creator* (and *co-worker*) with God in his work on Earth, and perhaps even a little beyond Earth. Man thus could become that part of God's creation consciously and intelligently cooperating in the ongoing processes of creative change, taking due account both of man's and of nature's proper needs, with duly assigned priorities for each. And, in a small way, is it not precisely this that every good gardener and farmer concerned to maintain the fertility of his land has always practised?

We have seen reasons for expecting that the immanence of God's transcendence in the natural order might reach a unique intensity in that least reducible of all the levels of created entities – the human person. Christians affirm that such an 'incarnation' occurred pre-eminently in history in one who was uniquely open to God, Jesus of Nazareth. But, I would also argue that, unique though this was, it was also expressive of an open possibility for and potentiality of all mankind, and means that the transcendent Creator can be immanent in man at the fully personal level. But since God is Creator, and still creating, then we must conclude that the continuing incarnation of God 'in us' is identical with God's creative work in and through us. In other words, when we as persons are most creative then we are fulfilling those human potentialities that were unveiled in Jesus uniquely and seminally as the ongoing creative work of God in man.

Man has a derived creativity from God and all genuine activities of man which attain excellence, and are in accord with God's intentions to build his reign of love (his 'kingdom'), may be regarded as man exerting his role as *co-creator* with God. This seems to be what William Blake had in mind when he spoke of 'building up Jerusalem'. In the doctrine of creation in the light of incarnation we have the basis for a genuinely Christian humanism, in which all human excellence is seen as man making his distinctive human contribution as co-creator to that ceaseless activity of creation which is God's action in and for the world.

Such an apprehension of the life of man engraced by God now allows us to make a more positive assessment of human civilisation, in general, and technology, in particular. For it is not without significance that the Biblical account of man begins in a garden in the book of Genesis, but is consummated in the new Jerusalem – a city, symbol of culture. For one who believes in, is committed to, God as Creator can affirm that it must have been God's intention that human society should have attained its present economic and technological complexity since he created man, through evolution, with just those abilities which made such complexities inevitable and he, at least, must have known that it would be so. Such a believer could thus see his work in a technological society as a genuine *opus Dei* of its own; in building up human society one is joining in that creative activity of God which brought man and society into existence – and this could give human work a new significance and counteract the pointlessness and vacuousness which so many feel about it.

For Christians the life and death – in conjunction with the teaching – of Jesus provide a profounder revelation than that afforded by the evolutionary process of the truth that God as Creator suffers in and with his creations. If that is the case, then man cannot expect to participate in the creative process, to be, as we said, a *co-creator* and *co-worker* with God, without cost and without love. There can then in the long run be no re-adjustment of the relation of man and nature, adequate to their needs, without cost to man, without sacrifice of the selfish ends of both the individual and of the community. Too much contemporary ecological discussion has been in terms of a sophisticated projection of *man's* desire for survival – not wrong in itself, but inadequate for providing the larger perspective the mounting climacteric demands. The investigations of the ecological sciences could provide us, if they were pursued energetically enough, with the knowledge that would actually make possible any implementation of this theologically informed view of nature *as* creation and of man's role in it as *co*-creator – a propitious marriage of theology and science?

8 *God and the selfish genes*

As we saw when we were considering man, God and evolution today (Chapter 6), developments in biology, ever since Charles Darwin, have continued to uncover more and more aspects of the human personality that can be related to its evolutionary origins. The response of theologians to these developments, as we saw, has varied from the pugnacious to the indifferent, and any reading of the history of the dialogue cannot but counsel caution and warn against premature judgments.

The advent of sociobiology accompanied, as in the case of Darwinism, by overtly reductionist and antireligious sentiments on the part of some of its proponents may likewise tempt the theologian into ill-advised and premature opposition. Not that this has indeed been the stance of many theological contributions. One has to be reminded that 'sociobiology' as a distinctive biological discipline or, rather, programme is still a relative newcomer. It is still only a decade or so since E. O. Wilson's volume launched that title for his claimed 'new synthesis'. In this chapter we shall attempt to assess the core of sociobiological arguments that seem to be important for our understanding of man, God and evolution and to point to what might be appropriate responses to this new multifaceted activity.

Sociobiology is concerned with interpreting human social behaviour, with its rich cultural expression and variety, in the light of animal, bird and insect social behaviour, with their more fixed behaviour patterns (often entirely so in the case of insects) that are described in terms of genetic cost-benefit exchanges. By virtue of thus straddling the world of human culture and that of the behaviour of the nonhuman biological world, it inevitably touches, indeed sometimes forcibly strikes, upon many issues concerning the fundamental nature of man. The debate about sociobiology is not entirely a replay of the old controversy concerning the nature-nurture dichotomy as factors in human behaviour because there has been an enormous increase in knowledge of the complexity of the strategy of gene perpetuation and of the many-levelled character of any adequate interpretation of human behaviour (symbolic, psychological, hormonal, neurological, nutritional – not to mention the spiritual, ethical and intellectual). So many of the issues that the proponents of sociobiology touch upon are those that have again and again been raised by both science and philosophy for religion.

The emphatically evolutionary outlook of sociobiology does not, in itself, have any new implications for religion that have not been raised in relation to the general idea of biological (and indeed, cosmic) evolution, namely, questions concerning continuity, chance, emergence, and interconnectedness, with their resulting renewed stress on the immanence of God in the natural processes of creation. However, it is true that the wide-ranging scope of sociobiology and the energy and zest with which its expositors apply and extend it, undoubtedly makes even more urgent the need for Christian (and indeed all) theology to become much clearer and explicit about its relation to such views, that is, to the world view of scientific 'evolutionary naturalism'. This latter is the dominant viewpoint of the contemporary scientific community and has been described by Karl E. Peters in the following terms:

> . . . evolutionary naturalism may be described as follows: First, the realm of nature is all there is; there is no supernatural in the sense of a realm of knowable reality totally other than that which is open to some possible interpretation of every-day experience by some possible scientific theories. Second, nature is dynamic; it evolves. Change is not merely an appearance or an indication of a second-class reality but is essential to the way things are. Third, at least at the level of life, the evolution of nature is best understood by updated Darwinian mechanisms: a continuing inheritance by the replication of major bodies of information; continual, essentially random, small variations of these information systems; and environmental selection pressures favoring the reproduction of some variations over others and thus modifying in small steps the information heritage.[1]

However incomplete we may regard these propositions (and Peters's first, namely 'no supernatural . . .', is to be questioned,[2] as we saw in Chapter 1), the second and third are supported on scientific grounds and their religious implications require exploration. They will not go way, however uncongenial to traditional theology, and increasingly constitute the most widely, generally accepted account of at least how we arrived here, if not why. For myself, it is in its bare outline the best account we have of the natural world of which we now know we are part – and sociobiology, stripped of its reductionist overtones, is certainly a new and positive contribution to that evolutionary naturalism. As Peters points out, such evolutionary naturalism (except for the first clause in his account that I have already questioned) is not by itself definitive of any particular theistic or atheistic position and is, as a matter of observation, shared by at least liberal theists, religious humanists, and agnostic and atheistic humanists – if not always by some Christian theologians. But for anyone who believes that the natural world is the sphere of action of God the Creator, it makes new demands upon theological conceptualization.

Sociobiologists are not a uniform group with respect to their philosophical positions. However, I think it is fair to say that, by successfully delineating the genetic strategies underlying behaviour patterns and roles in many insect, bird, and animal societies, they have often been confidently and explicitly deterministic, reductionist and functionalistic in their interpretation of human behaviour – or, perhaps it is more accurate to say, they have shown a general tendency to favour interpretations of human behaviour that have been easily seized upon by those who are determinists, reductionists and functionalists. Some sociobiologists[3,4] have gone out of their way to disavow such extreme positions, which at times their writings may have seemed to imply. Actually the net effect of sociobiology has been a renewed stress on reducing accounts of biological behaviour to a deterministic level that views it functionally in terms of its contribution to the survival of genes; behaviour is regarded as a strategy, however indirect, for gene survival.

There can be no doubt of the success of many such interpretations in the nonhuman biological field, but, as we saw in Chapter 4, it is with respect to their application to human behaviour that particular controversy arises, as we have seen in the example of kin selection. The theological response to these ideas is, in their general import, that which must be made to any purely deterministic and reductionistic accounts of human behaviour.[5] But in making any such appropriate responses, theologians would do well to recognize, more explicitly than they have done in the past, the complexity of human nature and the fact that its basic foundational level is biological and genetic, however overlaid by nurture and culture. And they must couple this also with an acknowledgement that it is this kind of genetically based creature that God has actually created as a human being through the evolutionary process. God has made human beings thus with their genetically constrained behaviour

– but, through the freedom God has allowed to evolve in such creatures, he has also opened up new possibilities of self-fulfilment, creativity, and openness to the future that requires a language other than that of genetics to elaborate and express.

The scientifically reductionist account has a limited range and needs to be incorporated into a larger theistic framework that has been constructed in response to questions of the kind, Why is there anything at all? and What kind of universe must it be if insentient matter can evolve naturally into self-conscious, thinking persons? and What is the meaning of personal life in such a cosmos? Scientists *per se* are unlikely to seek such incorporation, but at least they may be prepared to recognize that the scientific method is not of the kind that can be directed to answering such questions. Meanwhile theologians have to take more seriously the mode of God's actual creation of human beings through evolution and also our new understanding of the creature thus formed – even though, in the past, words such as *determinism*, *reductionism* and *functionalism* have been red rags to the theological bull! For the genetic constraints upon our nature and action are, from a theistic viewpoint, what God has determined shall provide the matrix within which freedom can operate. But is not this nothing other, in a new form, than the old theological chestnut of pre-destination and free will?

Where the Christian theist differs from the sociobiologist, as such, is in his affirmation of God as 'primary cause' or ground of being of the whole evolutionary process and, indeed, of God as the agent in, with, and under this process of creation through time. What constitutes the challenge to theology is a new apprehension and explication of God's presence and agency in the processes that biology, in general, and sociobiology, in particular, have unveiled. Of course, many sociobiologists will be opposed to setting their science in such a wider, theistic framework; for Wilson, for example, 'no species, our own included, possesses a purpose beyond the imperatives created by its genetic history. . . . If the brain evolved by natural selection, even the capacities to select particular esthetic judgments and religious beliefs must have arisen by the same mechanistic processes', and 'scientists cannot in all honesty serve as priests'.[6]

Here conflict between religion and a particular philosophical interpretation of biology is inevitable, but the theologian should not enter the lists with destructive ambitions. Indeed some theologians have even argued that theology must come to terms with the domination of the biological process by the prime requirement for *survival*, whether it be of genes, individuals, groups or species. Philip Hefner, for example, argues[7] that, in the light of biological evolution in general and the sociobiological critique in particular, the whole discussion of the is/ought dichotomy – which for too long (he thinks), as the naturalistic fallacy, has prevented us from seeing how the biological process generates human values – has moved into the arena of survival and nonsurvival. He uses the categories of A. J. Dyck[8] to elaborate the 'ought' as 'moral requiredness' which is described as a 'gap-induced requiredness': moral requiredness is a gap we feel compels us (moral obligation) to act so as to fill it in order to improve some situation. So Hefner then argues that: 'The most urgent gap experienced by humans [in relation to its value-requirements] – and therefore the most pressing gap-induced requiredness – is the gap created by the possibility of not surviving. Theology, therefore, has no alternative but to speak its truth about what is and ought to be in terms relevant to survival – the survival of the species, of the world, *of values, of human worth, of all the conditions upon which the human spirit is dependent*' (italics added).[9] But the question is: Can the values, and so on, whose survival is spoken of in the italicized end of this quotation, be regarded as derivable simply from contemplation of the sociobiological facts (if they are facts)? Mary Hesse comments on this prescription of theology's task by Hefner as follows: 'But whatever facts may be discovered about the conditions of survival by sociobiology, the conclusion that the survival of the human species is the most urgent *value* may itself be regarded as *morally* repugnant. This is surely a sufficient rebuttal of the claim that the facts alone permit the "ought" to be derived from the "is" . . . God in his wisdom may have ordained values which are consistent with earthly extinction; to suppose otherwise is to embrace some form of materialism.'[10] Whether or not this is a 'sufficient rebuttal' will certainly be argued, but I quote this interchange as an example of a new kind of question regarding *survival* and what it means that is raised for theology by sociobiology.[11]

There is an application of sociobiology which is relevant to theology and which has been taken up by a number of evolutionary naturalists sympathetic to religion in general, if not especially to Christian theology as such. This is the view that the religions have had a function in enabling human societies (and genes?) to survive and, to that extent, can be justified as useful, functional mythologies – even if they are now ripe, according to Wilson, for replacement by 'the evolutionary epic' as 'probably the best myth we will ever have'.[12] Donald T. Campbell[13] and Ralph Burhoe[14] both argue for a positively selective role for religion in the survival of cultures (which is their unit of survival, and so of selection); and Burhoe especially, unlike Wilson, argues for its continuing role in the development and survival of human culture, providing it can incorporate the scientific world view. No doubt Christian theologians will be grateful for this attribution of a survival function to religion in human culture, but the attribution again raises the questions of 'Survival for what?' Is survival a value? What kind of survival? However, theologians will (or should, in my view) first want to ask questions about the *truth* of religious notions, regardless of the contribution of religion to the survival of human culture(s). And one could argue that it is the ultimate commitment to the truth which is in God and Jesus the Christ that characterises the Christian faith without regard to survival calculations – think too of Job's 'Though he slay me, yet will I wait for him'.[15] Is not that the core of a religion which has a cross as its central symbol and historical focus?[16]

A new nuance has recently[17] been given by Michael Ruse and Edward Wilson to these somewhat more sympathetic sociobiological interpretations of morality and its conventionally presumed religious basis. They urge[18] that the possession of a moral code, of moral beliefs, in short of ethics, is 'an illusion fobbed off on us by our genes to get us to cooperate . . . ethics is a *shared* illusion of the human race' – albeit a useful illusion enforced by biology. For 'by making us think that there is an objective higher code, to which we are all subject', biology inculcates the motivations that encourage altruism and reciprocity, and hence furthers our reproductive ends. 'We function better [presumably biologically] because we believe [in an objective ethical code].'[19]

But, I wonder, does this really provide a new basis for understanding ethics as such, that is, the *content* of ethical codes, our actual ethical beliefs? For these latter can, in developed societies, be given, on reflection, some rational justification on bases other than that of reproductive efficiency in a purely biologically competitive milieu. And this is not surprising for evolution has now become 'psychosocial', as Julian Huxley used to put it,[20] that is, the factors affecting the development of human culture now depend not only on the interaction of *homo sapiens* with the physical and biological environment, but also on the knowledge and customs transmitted by culture. Human beings radically alter their environment at their own will and so alter their own development in a way that transcends that of all other living organisms. Evolution has become history.

It may well be true that long ago in human history, natural selection operated to favour genes which gave us brains that disposed us to act in those ways the sociobiologists denote as 'altruistic' and 'reciprocal'. However, it seems to be the case that this early stage of our biological history also, no doubt by the processes of natural selection, endowed us with brains that had the capacity to think rationally and to evolve belief systems of our own devising. The biologically selective process cannot of itself prescribe the *content* of these ratiocinations and reflections on our own behaviour, in the light of various belief systems that now constitute the ethical codes of humanity. For these develop by the procedures and constraints upon coherent, rational *thinking*.

The ethical codes so developed are, in any case, not uniform, and are often counter-biological, as in the Christian ethic which, while urging one to 'love one's neighbour as oneself', explicates this in the classic parable of the Good Samaritan from which it becomes clear that our 'neighbour' is anyone in need – and not at all our genetic kin. Indeed the story was told precisely to deny this latter. We may well have a capacity for acknowledging constraints on our behaviour 'wired-in', as it were, by our early biological origins, but the justification of the content of beliefs about such constraints in developed cultures goes far beyond, and often does not at all correspond with, the prescriptions for survival of the individual, of the community and, least of all, of the genes as such, that biology alone would predict.[21] It seems that this new twist to 'evolutionary ethics' is still guilty of the well-known, and in the circumstances ironically and ambiguously designated, 'genetic fallacy', whereby the ultimate form of a human cultural development is thought to be reductively entirely explained in terms of its biological or cultural origins. Just as science is not magic, so ethics, on the same grounds, is not genetics.

A more fruitful way of relating our biological origins and constraints to our developed rationally informed perceptions of ourselves may well be found in the publications of those who wish to emphasise, in a positively holistic fashion, the physical and biological rooting of the mental and spiritual lives of human beings (in addition to those of Burhoe, Campbell, Crook, Midgley and even Wilson, one could also cite Altner,[22] Jaynes,[23] Pugh[24] and Sagan[25]). To varying degrees these works see human mental and spiritual life as continuous with, and a development and elaboration of, the physical and biological (especially genetic) substratum through which evolution has operated. We have also witnessed the recognition by at least one eminent biologist, Sir Alister Hardy, of the religious experience of human beings as one of their natural characteristics and amenable to scientific investigation, at least in the style of natural history.[26] Our mental and spiritual life, it seems, must fulfil at least basic, evolutionary requirements long established, but we then go on to interpret ourselves to ourselves at our own culturally developed level. The pressure from the ideas of sociobiology in particular, and of biology and cosmic evolution in general, is towards a franker recognition of our natural relatedness to the physical and biological worlds and an acknowledgment that our mental and spiritual aspirations are so grounded. But what we should aspire to is not thereby prescribed and so it is that theology has, in my view, a new and exciting role to play if it will only recognise its new brief.

9 *Matter in religion and science*

There was a tendency amongst some Christian thinkers, but not those highlighted in Chapter 5, to find their way out of the impasse created by the Darwinian controversies by reverting to a naive dualism in which the physical and biological world was assigned to science and that of 'mind' and 'spirit' to religion in general and Christianity in particular. This saved Christians from thinking too hard about the developing sciences and salved the consciences of the scientists who were thereby freed to get on with their work. This they did and the scientific and Christian communities continued, and still continue, to go their separate ways. Yet Christians should not have delegated to science all the responsibility for formulating ideas concerning the stuff, the matter, of the cosmos. For Christian teaching about the 'two natures' in the one 'person' of Jesus has profound implications about what was possible in the material universe which includes human bodies and personalities. Moreover, by their character some of the central practices of the Christian faith predispose and point to, even if they do not logically compel, a certain way of regarding the material aspects of the cosmos. This applies particularly to its sacramental use of bread, wine and water.[1]

In these sacramental communal acts of worship a particular significance is being attributed to these very material objects in a Christian context. Coherent with and, to some extent, implicit in this usage there is a teaching concerning the meaning to be attached to matter, the stuff of the cosmos – answers to the questions 'What is matter doing?', 'What is matter for?' For it is a generally recognized feature of a sacrament that it is something singled out and set apart, yet of a universal character. Hence we might reasonably hope that from an understanding of the significance of the Christian use of the matter of bread and wine in the eucharist, in particular, further insight into the meaning of the material cosmos might be derived. *Mutatis mutandis*, we might hope that light will be thrown on the meaning of the sacraments by our scientific understanding of the behaviour and potentialities of matter. It must be stressed that these hopes are not certain of fulfilment, but nevertheless it seems worth exploring, in the following two sections, possible answers to the two questions that have been implicitly posed: 'What is the role of the matter in a sacrament, in general, and in the eucharist in particular?' and 'How does the scientific perspective affect our understanding of matter?'

Matter in the eucharist and other Christian sacraments

We are accustomed in our mutual interactions to use material things in ways which both express our mind, or intentions, and which simultaneously effect what is in our mind, or fulfil our intentions. Thus a signed order form both expresses the desire of the one who signs it to purchase, say, a book and sets the sequence of events in motion which leads to his possessing it; a deed of covenant both expresses the mind and attitudes of benevolence of an individual to some project and itself contributes to the realization of that project. Analogously, in the Christian understanding of God's relation to physical reality, the world of matter is seen as both expressing and revealing the mind of God, its Creator, and as effecting his purposes. For the physical, material world which he has brought into existence is the matrix within which and the means whereby autonomous, personal agents can be brought into existence and into harmony and union with himself. Thus, in the Christian understanding, the world of matter, in its relation to God, has both the *symbolic* function of expressing his mind and the *instrumental* function of being the means whereby he effects his purpose.

We could perhaps put it thus: the created world is seen by Christians as a symbol because it is a mode of God's revelation, an expression of his truth and beauty which are the 'spiritual' aspects of its reality;[2] it is also valued by them for what God is effecting instrumentally through it, what he does for men in and through it. But these two functions of matter, the symbolical and instrumental, also constitute the special character of the use of matter in the particular Christian sacraments.[3] Hence there is, in each particular sacrament, a universal reference to this double character of created physical reality and, correspondingly, meaning can be attached to speaking of the created world as a sacrament or, at least, as sacramental. However, it must be recognized that this sacramental character is only implicit, and that it is obscure and partial both because of man's limited perception and sensitivity and because of evil. The significance of the incarnation of God in a man within the created world is that in the incarnate Christ the sacramental character of that world was made explicit and perfected. In this sense, it seems legitimate to regard the incarnate life of Christ as the supreme sacrament. For in this outward historical life, there is both uniquely expressed and uniquely operative that purpose of goodness which is the purpose of God himself that all life and all nature should fulfil.

In the sacraments of the Church, these two ultimate sacraments, the created order and Christ as God incarnate, regularly come together and are brought into one focus in time and place. At the Last Supper, which developed into the Church's eucharist, Jesus identified the mode of his incarnation and reconciliation of God and man (his 'body and blood') with the very stuff of the universe when he took the bread, blessed, broke and gave it to his disciples saying,[4] 'This: my flesh for you', and similarly the wine, saying, 'This: my blood of the (new) covenant', or, in parallel to the other saying, and more simply, 'This: my blood for you (and for many)'. It seems to me that it is a legitimate extension and development of the ideas and symbolic references which are implicit in these features of this original historical act to affirm that, in this act, a new value was explicitly set upon the bread and wine, obstinately molecular as they are, an intimate part of the natural world (corn and grapes) and a product of men's cooperation with nature (bread and wine). His words and these acts seem to me to have involved a revaluation of the things themselves, a new value assigned by God himself in Christ. A further development seems natural in the light of what has been said above about the universal reference of sacramental acts: that to which a new value was imputed was not only these particular elements of bread and wine used in *this* way, but the whole created material world. For a sacrament has significance only as a part of a whole, of which the true relation to God is being represented and effectively realized.[5]

This value was implicit, though not available to man's observation, in the act of creation. It remained a potentiality of matter, only partially realized by man. It was the ground of the incarnation, the root of its possibility, for it was in his own world that God was incarnate in a man, that world of which he was already the formative principle. Even at the historic Last Supper, he was still largely incognito to his disciples, but to Christians he is now no longer unknown. So in Christian thinking the sacraments as a whole, especially the eucharist, manifest continually the ultimate meaning of matter as a symbol of God's being and as an instrument of his purpose.

The participants in the eucharist consciously and humbly offer their own lives in service to God and man in unity with the self-offered life of Christ which is believed to be present in and with the elements of bread and wine in the context of the total communal act. Thus, in this act, Christians believe they are participating in that re-formation and new creation of humanity which the coming of Jesus initiated through his incarnation and self-offering, cogently represented by the bread and wine offered with sacrificial reference both at the original Last Supper and at every eucharist of the Church since then. This union with the offering of Christ is not self-directed, but 'for others', and it is worth noticing that what Christ took and what is used in the eucharist is the product of man's action on nature, bread not corn, wine not grapes. So the whole life and work of man may be regarded as offered in this act which is so closely associated with the historic initiation of the new humanity 'in Christ'.

Many themes interlock and interweave in this central act of Christian worship, and all of these themes have immense significance for our attitude to the stuff of the cosmos of which we ourselves are part. It is interesting to note that the eucharist of the Christian Church which, like a parabolic mirror, focuses so many parallel rays into one point of time and space, from the earliest times contained overt references to God's creative activity, although this insight has been somewhat obscured since then. For the 'words of institution' of Jesus, already referred to, took place within the context of the Jewish mealtime blessing over bread and wine (the 'cup of blessing'). These blessings took the form of a thanksgiving to God for creation.[6] Similarly directed thanksgivings appear in the earliest liturgies of the church's eucharist[7] and are referred to by Irenaeus (c. AD 130 – c. 200), whose words are worth quoting more fully.[8] He speaks of Jesus as:

> Instructing his disciples to offer to God the first-fruits of his own creation, not as though he had need of them, but, that they themselves might be neither unfruitful nor ungrateful. He took that bread which comes of the [material] creation and gave thanks saying, This is my body. And the cup likewise, which is [taken] from created things, like ourselves, he acknowledged for his own blood, and taught the new oblation of the New Covenant . . . we ought to make oblation to God . . . offering first fruits of those things which are his creatures.

These prayers of thanksgiving in the eucharist developed naturally into an offertory of other foods, in addition to bread and wine. In the course of a complex history this basic feature has been fragmented and overlaid, but still survives in the ' . . . these thy *creatures* of bread and wine . . .' in Holy Communion in the Book of Common Prayer of the Church of England and in the ' . . . *haec dona, haec munera, haec sancta sacrificia illibata* . . .' of the traditional Latin Mass – and has been restored to some extent in most modern rites, though not enough in my view.

Matter in the scientific perspective – from the inorganic to the personal

The ability of human beings to survey their surroundings as subjects, to regard everything other than themselves as objects of their own consciousness, and so, as it were, to transcend the world, has long dominated their view of themselves. They have tended, and still do so, to regard their surroundings as a kind of stage on which their own personal drama is enacted, themselves in the foreground. This natural, everyday approach to the external features of man's life has played, in a variety of sophisticated forms, a dominant role in his reflections on his own nature and destiny. But in the last hundred years the perspective of the sciences concerned with the origin and development of the physical and biological worlds has, as we have seen, altered this outlook in a way which is, or should be, changing profoundly the way humans are coming to regard themselves. Our familiar environments of stone, water, air, earth, grass, birds, animals and so on are seen both to share with us common molecular structures and to be stages in a common development in time. The very stuff of which we are made and the way it has become organized as ourselves is an inherent part of the ongoing development of the physical cosmos which we survey. We, and all other living creatures, have emerged in time out of the non-living world of water, air and rocks which seem so distinct and different from us.

Although this continuity of man with the organic world had sometimes been accepted in principle (e.g. Gen. 2:7: 'And the Lord God formed man out of the dust of the ground and breathed into his nostrils the breath of life; and man became a living soul'), it was not until the Darwinian revolution and the work it stimulated that the scientific evidence of man's relation to other species began to appear, and it is only in the last few decades that the emergence of primitive living organisms from inorganic matter could be delineated in any fashion which has a scientific basis. The broad sweep of the cosmic development from the 'hot big bang' onwards is now generally known and part of twentieth-century conceptions (some would say mythology) and the fact and distinctive features of the evolutionary process have been outlined in earlier chapters.[9] If we are to interpret the whole cosmic development honestly, then we are bound to look at all the facts. The presence of persons in the universe is just such a fact – the fact of the emergence in the cosmos of the new features and properties of matter which appear when it is organised in the form we call a person. Briefly, with man evolution has become 'history', for man shapes his own physical environment and intellectual and cultural inheritance by his own choices based on his own inner drives and values which determine how he applies his unique awareness of that environment. Sir Julian Huxley calls this form of evolution 'psycho-social' although, as hinted above, the term 'history' is available for use in this sense.

It is because the biological evolution of man has now been superseded by this psycho-social development, which involves an interplay of the Darwinian combination of heredity, environment and mutation with man's conscious choice of what he makes of his environment, and what he makes of himself, that one can only see the next stage of development as some kind of inner transformation of man himself – of his values and his ability to attain their true expression. But this is precisely what the Christian gospel is, namely, that in and through Christ men have the opportunity of attaining their true ends, those for which God made them, and of experiencing that inner transformation which constitutes the essence of 'eternal life' in the Holy Spirit of God. In Christ, God the Word was made *our* flesh (John 1:14), the Word to us as men, whatever form his Word may be to other intelligent beings who may exist now or in the future in the universe.

To revert to the general development: the new features and behaviour which have emerged in man within the cosmic development can only be described by their own appropriate language and concepts, and necessitate modes of enquiry peculiar to themselves in accordance with the anti-reductionist epistemology developed in Chapter 1. There are no grounds for rejecting, on a supposedly scientific basis, those words and modes of speaking which men have developed to describe the uniquely human experience of the world and of their understanding of themselves and their mutual relationships. The language of personal relationships, of the terms used to denote intellectual and aesthetic activities, the nature of the consciousness viewed from within, and all these and many more are, as we saw, as legitimately applied to describe and understand human beings as the language of chemistry for molecules, of physiology for the inter-relation between organs in living creatures, of ethology for animal behaviour and so on. This is not to say such language will not need to be refined and clarified, but the fact of its existence and the existence of the human experience which has evoked its formation are part of the givenness of the cosmic development and cannot be ignored in any account of the cosmos which claims scientific objectivity. For the stuff of the world, the primeval concourse of hydrogen atoms or sub-nuclear particles, has as a matter of fact, and not conjecture, become persons who possess not only a social life and biological organization but also an inner and an inter-personal life that constitutes personhood. How are we properly to speak of the cosmic development if after aeons of time the atoms have become human beings, persons? Paradoxically, knowledge of the process by which they have arrived in the world seems to be confined to human beings. We alone reflect on our atomic and simpler forebears and we alone adjust our behaviour in the light of this perspective.

To ignore the glory, the predicament and the possibilities of man in assessing the trend and meaning of the cosmic development would be as unscientific as to endorse the former pre-Copernican account of the universe which was based on the contrary prejudice. Apparently, developing under the control of the regular processes of natural laws, new forms of matter have creatively emerged out of the nuclear particles and atoms of several thousand million years ago and have now in man become conscious both of the processes by which they have been brought into existence and of themselves. From man's consciousness new creativities of a specifically human kind have erupted, notably in men of genius but, equally significantly, in the very real individual creativity of each human being within his own social environment which, however humble, far transcends that of the highest animal. The presence of man and the fact of human personalness is therefore part of the givenness of the developing cosmos which science has unfolded.

A sacramental view of the cosmos

In discussing the continuity of the cosmic development, it was suggested (Chapter 6) that we need to revise what we mean by 'matter' and its associated adjective 'materialistic'. For just as the wetness of water, or the viscosity of a nucleic acid solution, are not properties of their constituent atoms but features of their higher molecular and macro-molecular levels of organization, so the properties and behaviour of living organisms can be regarded as manifestations of the potentialities of matter if incorporated into certain organized structures. How such incorporation can come about and how the 'boundary conditions' of the structures are established are problems to which we have adverted already. However, once they are established, each level of organization displays its character-istic features. To be consistent, one would say that matter organized in the way we call man, notably, of course, in the labyrinth which consti-tutes his brain, is capable of activities which we describe as those of conscious thought, of self-reflection (self-consciousness), of communi-cation with other human beings, and all the inter-relations of personal life and ethical behaviour, of creativity in art and science and, indeed, of all the activities individual and social which characterize and differen-tiate man from the rest of the biological world.

At each emergent level in evolution, matter in its newly evolved mode of organization manifests properties which could not, in principle, be discerned in the earlier levels from which the new emerges. In a sense, therefore, one could say that the potentialities of matter have been, and still are being, realized in the cosmic development. However, matter has evolved into persons and it seems we cannot avoid concluding, even from the most materialistic viewpoint, that the culmination of evolution in *homo sapiens* demonstrates the ability of matter (a long-hidden poten-tiality now realized) to display functions and properties for which we have to use special terms such as 'mental', 'personal', 'spiritual'. We have to employ these special terms (which cannot, without gross qualific-ation, be transferred even to the higher mammals) because these emergent properties are uniquely and characteristically human. Such an affirmation of, for example, the reality of human conscious and self-conscious activities, is not dependent, as we saw (Chapter 6), on any particular philosophy of the relation of an entity called 'mind' to one called 'body'. This problem remains open, on this view, to philosophical analysis: it is the fact that the problem arises and can be posed on which attention is here being focused. For it seems that by taking seriously the scientific perspective, we cannot avoid arriving at a view of matter which sees it as manifesting mental, personal and spiritual activities.

If we were unashamedly metaphysical and were to regard these quali-ties as pertaining to a different mode of existence, we might reasonably describe matter as the vehicle or means of expression of this mental, personal and spiritual mode. However, whether or not we adopt this more ontological view of mind, persons and spirit, there is a real convergence between the implication of the scientific perspective on the capabilities of matter and the sacramental view of matter which Christians have adopted as the natural consequence of the meaning they attach to Jesus's life and the continued existence of the Church. For, as explained above, Christians have had to understand matter both in the light of their conviction that matter was able in the man Jesus to express the being of God, who is nevertheless regarded as supra-mental, supra-personal and supra-spiritual, so that his mode of being lies beyond any sequence of 'mental', etc., superlatives we can delineate; and in the light of their understanding of the sacramental acts of Jesus, made in the context of his death and resurrection, and in which the continuing life of Christian humanity originates. Briefly, it looks as if Christians, starting, as it were, from one end with their experience of God in Christ through the Holy Spirit acting in the stuff of the world, have developed an insight into matter which is consonant with that which is now evoked by the scientific perspective working from matter towards persons, and beyond.

This congruence, for which I argue, between the perspective of the cosmos which science has developed and the Christian understanding of God's cosmic purposes as expressed ('symbolically') and effected ('instrumentally') through nature, the incarnation and the eucharist, is not meant to imply any identity in the way they impress themselves on us – even within the terms of Christian discourse. For science is *par excellence* a human activity of ratiocination based on experimental, empirical observations; while, for the Christian, there is a certain givenness about our encounter with God in Christ in the eucharist which cannot finally be subsumed under purely human, psychological terms. This givenness of the eucharist is quite distinctive but, it is urged, it is also intelligible and congruent with the scientific perspective.

The nature of this givenness of God in Christ in the eucharist can tentatively be elaborated, in terms akin to those used earlier in discussing the cosmic development, as follows. In the eucharist, a conjunction occurs of a group of baptized Christians, who are committed to fulfilling God's purposes in the world and who are consciously acting corporately in communion with each other, with the elements of bread and wine which are present because of their historical continuity with the Last Supper of Jesus. We thus have in such events unique, though temporary, configurations of Christian persons, corporately relating to each other, and of bread and wine taken, blessed, broken and given in accord with the intention of the historical Jesus. The assertion that God gives himself uniquely to human beings in this situation can be expressed as the assertion that in this unique configuration there emerges, in accordance with the divine purpose, a new potentiality of the stuff of the universe – just as it has in all the previous stages of the cosmic development, except that here it is mediated to men through the living Christ – and that this new potentiality is characterised by God being able to act in and through this corporate event in ways denoted by such terms, *inter alia*, as 'real presence' and 'sacrifice'.

This way of looking at and speaking of the eucharist can, of its very nature, be only tentative, but what is clear is that there can be a mutual enrichment of Christian incarnational and sacramental insights by the scientific perspective and vice versa. Each approach remains distinctive and autonomous, but the relationship developed above indicates at least the possibility of convergence into a new unified vision, even if the parallel lines converge only at the infinity of the divine. This approach gives a new relevance to Christian sacramental worship which is now seen not to be representing some magical, cabbalistic and esoteric doctrine, but expressing, in a communal context, the basic nature of the cosmic process which has brought man to this point and in which he is now invited by his Creator to participate consciously and willingly.

A summary of this sacramental view,[10] which incorporates the Christian understanding of God's trinity of being and which takes seriously the scientific perspective, might be expressed thus. The world is created and sustained in being by the will of God, the will of perfect Love. The Son, or Word of God (the Logos), is the all-sufficient principle and form of this created order. At every level, this order reflects in its own measure something of the quality of deity. 'From atom and molecule to mammal and man each by its appropriate order and function expresses the design inherent in it, and contributes, so far as it can by failure or success, to the fulfilment of the common purpose.'[11] The continuing creative power which is manifest as a *nisus* at all levels of existence to attain its intended form is, in the Christian tradition, God as 'Holy Spirit'.

The process of creation has been unfolded by the natural sciences as one in which new qualities and modes of existence continuously emerge out of simpler forms of matter by the operation of natural laws (Chapters 3, 4). The newer forms depend for their existence on the regularity of behaviour of the simpler entities out of which they are constructed but manifest properties and activities which are specific to that level of organisation of matter (Chapter 1). The level of organisation which is reached in man represents not only a new summit in this evolutionary process but a new departure in the way in which change is initiated. For the mode of organisation which constitutes man is characterized by activities and purposes which are only describable in terms of mind and self-consciousness. What appear to be freely-willed decisions determine how the individual and society develop and how they alter their environment, which then interacts on each succeeding generation. By his intelligent apprehension of his environment, man has become the controller and arbiter of the future of other forms of matter (Chapter 7). He is nevertheless incomplete and unfulfilled and is tragically aware of the lack of fulfilment of his own potentialities. Thus it can be said that in man matter has become aware of itself, of its past, and of its unfulfilled potentialities.

The Christian claim (Chapter 5, 6), and here it differentiates itself from secular 'humanism', then amounts to the affirmation that this whole process is the outworking of the creative being of God in the world and goes on to assert further that this process has culminated in the manifestation of God as a man within the created world. Only in a human being totally open to God could God express explicitly his character as creative Love: all other levels of created being up to this point were inadequate for this purpose and but implicit manifestations of a God still *incognito*. Thus, on the one hand that which God has brought into existence, the stuff of the cosmos, is seen through the sciences to be the matrix and necessary condition for the appearance of purpose, mind, self-consciousness and values – all that characterises the human person; and, on the other hand, the Christian revelation affirms that this character of the stuff of the cosmos is so fundamental that God expressed his being in, and acted through, the perfect culmination of this process in the person of Jesus of Nazareth.[12]

Indeed, in Jesus we really see what personalness amounts to. The two enterprises converge in a view of the cosmos which can therefore properly be called 'sacramental'. This technical theological term may be uncongenial to some (and not only to agnostics), but none other seems to be available which expresses so succinctly the simultaneous recognition of both the duality in our experiences represented by our familiar body-mind, subjective-objective, etc., dichotomies and the observed fact, in our own experience and in the evolutionary development revealed by the sciences, that all the 'higher' qualities of existence which characterise personal and mental life are qualities of matter in particular forms and *only* appear when matter is so organised. The term recognises bluntly the duality necessary in our talk about ourselves and about the character of the evolutionary process, but also recognises that the mental and spiritual features of existence are always features of, and only of, the organised matter which constitutes the observable cosmos.

It is not pretended that description of the cosmos as 'sacramental' represents any real solution of the body-mind and related problems. Nevertheless, the use of this term not only avoids both idealism and the grosser forms of materialism (in the old sense) but also serves to stress the consonance between the scientific understanding of the nature of human being and what Christians think is revealed of nature, man and God through the life and actions of Jesus, himself the culmination of that historical process which was at work in the Hebraic culture and which has been attested in its literature.

At the historical crisis of the human life of the Jesus who was God incarnate, at the moment before 'the love which moves the sun and all stars' culminated in the self-offering of the cross, Jesus himself gave a new significance to that characteristic act of man's creaturehood, his need to imbibe the world of matter in order to live. Eventually, that common meal became the symbolic meal of a potentially new humanity stemming from and one with Christ ('in Christ', as the New Testament puts it) – one might almost say of a new level of 'evolution' of human potentialities. For the Church believes that in the eucharist God acts to re-create both the individual person and society, to bring to fruition the purpose of his creation, manifest in the incarnation. In the eucharist, God expresses the significance of the created material order, and through that sacramental act of the restored humanity 'in Christ' he is achieving his purpose for protons, atoms, molecules, proteins, amoeba, mammals and humanity.

10 *Retrospect*

The prophets of Israel often interpreted the history of their people in such a way that apparent scourges, such as Cyrus,[1] were seen as blessings in disguise from the good Lord leading his people through experiences that alone would enable them to apprehend new truths. Thus it might come about that the new biology – and indeed the larger perspective of all the sciences – could, in fact, enlarge our comprehension and apprehension of the God who is always greater than that which we can at any time conceive. I have already in this volume expressed how I think the new biology, in the evolutionary setting which is afforded it by cosmology and the earth sciences, has large implications for our theology of nature, man and God. The new biology raises questions for us in a new way, in a new form and in a new context. If theological affirmations are not to be meaningless – not to be the mere inner musings of a religious ghetto – they simply have to articulate responses to the questions so raised. They must respond in the terms relevant to the context of the new knowledge, and not in the language of the intellectual framework that originally provided the setting for classical Christian dogmatic formulations, whether that of the late Roman Empire, or sixteenth-century Germany or nineteenth-century England.

To have the questions raised in this way is a new stimulus, in my view, for theology. For when the biological, and other, sciences prompt these questions they do so in a way that reveals they cannot answer them with the resources of the scientific method and the intellectual procedures of the sciences. So that, at last, theology has a chance to respond to questions that are actually being asked within the context of our present scientific culture. In responding, I think theology will find there is scarcely any one of the main 'heads' of Christian doctrine, as they used to be called, that is not affected by the new perspective. Perhaps one day a new coherent theology might emerge prompted by this stimulus and so continue in our own day what, for example, the Cappadocian Fathers and St Thomas Aquinas did in their times in relation to contemporary philosophy and science.

Nature

We now see nature as multi-levelled and hierarchical with new emergents developing in time among which, significantly, are consciousness and self-reflective self-consciousness. The natural physical, biological, human and social worlds are the realm of God's immanent activity, indeed the manifestation of his creative presence – and sacraments are particular focused instances of what is happening all the time. For one should speak of the world, of nature, of all-that-is, as being 'in God', rather than of God as 'in the world'. Nothing happens apart from God, but God is more and other than what happens. Awareness of the continuity of the physical, non-biological, and biological with the distinctive life of man and realisation that our mental and spiritual life is an emergent from this natural matrix provide a vision in which the whole world takes on a new value and significance – not simply because it resulted in us, but because it is an expression of God in action in the way appropriate to the levels in question, and we are that part of the cosmos consciously capable of being aware of and of responding to that immanent Presence. Man's most intellectual and spiritual activities are part of the created order and an aspect of them. 'That there should "emerge" in the cosmic process a capacity to apprehend, even in a measure to comprehend, that process is the most remarkable characteristic of the process itself . . . . That the world should give rise to minds that know the world involves a good deal concerning the nature of the world.'[2] This assessment and way of raising the question of God finds, in my view, increasing and ample justification in today's biological perspective.

Humanity

The scientific fact that matter, after a succession of levels of self-transcendence, can in man become self-conscious and personal, self-transcendent, and corporately self-reflective is a fundamental feature of the cosmos and must be regarded as a clue to its meaning and intelligibility. So the capacity for consciousness and then self-transcendence gradually increasingly manifests itself immanently within the natural order and reveals itself for what it is; and thereby what it also becomes capable of revealing is the immanence of the transcendent Creator – 'In the beginning was the Word . . . and the Word was God . . . all things were made by him . . . in him was life and the life was the light of men'.[3] But that light shone in darkness and was not comprehended. Human potentialities – qualitatively so far removed from even those of the highest mammal in respect of the possible creation of value, of beauty, truth and goodness – are not fulfilled and man is conscious of, indeed self-reflective on, his need to come to terms with death, finitude and suffering. In man, it almost appears as if the evolutionary process has faltered, for man's tragedy is both to be aware of his potentialities and to be unable to attain them.

Humanity needs redemption, not in the sense of any time-reversal to restore a pristine state of original innocence, but so that human beings can – with their peculiar combination of self-transcendence, self-consciousness, freedom to choose the good and their biological limitations – yet fulfil their potentialities and attain harmony with their Creator and so *pari passu* with the created natural world. In this view of the implication of the evolutionary perspective, it is with reference to such a placing of humanity that the 'redemption' made possible in Christ will henceforth have to be proclaimed. The role in human redemption of explicit sacraments in a sacramental universe in which the spiritual is known *only* 'in, with and under' the physical stuff of existence will clearly need further exploration – as will the implications of this perspective on humanity for our approach to the ethical problems raised by modern science, technology and medicine in which the interlocking of the material, personal and spiritual constitutes the very crux of the issues.

God

What about God and his action in the world in the light of the knowledge of it provided by the sciences? From the continuity and creativity of the processes of the natural world we inferred that God's creative relation to the world must be conceived of as a continuous, sustaining creative action within these natural processes. This is what we meant by saying that the Creator is *immanent* in his creation, and that is why we look for his 'meanings' *within* the world of which we are part.

But the natural processes of the world have led to the emergence within it of human beings who possess a sense of transcendence over their environment which serves to sharpen the quest for One who makes intelligible the fact that there is anything at all – the One who is ultimate Being and who gives being to all else. So we continue to postulate God the Creator as *transcendent* over all matter-energy-space-time, over all-that-is.

However, the concept of God the Creator as both immanent and transcendent was not entirely satisfactory when applied to One who is the Creator of that in which he is immanent. Traditional 'models' (*Logos*, spirit) need supplementing today in the light of the perspective of our present scientific knowledge of the world by models whereby the world is regarded as being, as it were, 'within' God, but the being of God is regarded as not exhausted by, or subsumed within, the world. (In this connection, a feminine image of God as Creator proves to be a useful corrective to purely masculine images by its ability to model God as creating a self-creative world *within* God's own Being.[4]

We would also have to say, as a consequence of the created order being continuously God in action, that although God is not more present at one time or place than at others (he is not a substance), all is of God at all times, nevertheless man finds that in some sequences of events in created nature and history God unveils his meaning more than in others. There are *meanings* of God to be unveiled but not all are read: some events will be more revealing than others. Moreover, any 'meanings' unveiled in the *various and distinctive levels* of the world must be complementary.

We have found that the processes of the world are *open-ended* and that there are *emergent* in space-time new organisations of matter-energy which often require epistemologically *non-reducible* language to expound their distinctiveness. Thus it was that I ventured the idea of God as 'exploring' in creation, of actualising all the potentialities of his creation, of unfolding fugally all the derivations and combinations inherently possible. The meanings of God unveiled to and for *man* will be the more partial, broken and incomplete the more the level of creation being examined departs from the human and personal, in which the transcendence of the 'I' is experienced as immanent in our bodies. The more personal and *self*-conscious is the entity in which God is immanent, the more capable it is of expressing God's *supra*-personal characteristics.

This stress on emergence would be one-sided without a balancing emphasis on the *continuity* that is perceived in the scientific observation of natural processes. Any new meaning which God is able to express in a new emergent should thus not be discontinuous with the meanings expressed in that out of which it has emerged. So it is that the transcendence-in-immanence of man's experience raises the hope and conjecture that in man, in *a* human person adequate for the purpose, immanence might be able to display in a uniquely emergent mode a transcendent dimension to a degree which could *unveil*, without distortion, the transcendent *Creator* (which is what the Christian tradition has meant by 'incarnation', is it not?).

So God, who is the Transcendent One immanent in the creative process, can no longer be regarded as the sublimely indifferent Absolute remote from all the pangs of the creative process. For in that process new life, new forms, only emerge through death of the old, and suffering and death are frequently the only gateway to new life and new creation. From a consideration of the character of the natural processes of suffering and death and from a recognition that God has put his own purposes at risk in creating free self-conscious persons, we have to recognise tentatively that *God suffers with creation and in the creative process* – that is, to say 'God is Love'[5] is as close as we are likely to be able to get in expressing the mystery of the divine life in itself, the ultimate nature of God's being-in-itself. We have then to conceive of God suffering in and with and indeed, through creation. When ultimately the transcendence-in-immanence and immanence-in-transcendence are fused in a manifestation that is both human and personal, that manifestation in the Word-made-flesh himself goes through the door of suffering and death to fullness of life and the consummation of humanity within the presence of God – so the final agony and apogee of the evolutionary process is the paradox of a man on a cross exalted by God into the divine life.

Appendix
Thermodynamics and life

'All kinds of private metaphysics and theology have grown like weeds in the garden of thermodynamics'[1]

This pungent judgement of a distinguished historian of science serves to remind us that, although thermodynamics has an austere and lofty intellectual and architectonic framework, it has nevertheless frequently generated a plethora of often gloomy emotions in those who have attempted to apply it on a cosmic scale. The much-quoted noble peroration of Bertrand Russell in his 1903 essay on a 'Free Man's Worship', where he urges 'unyielding despair' upon mankind as he contemplates the demise of all its achievements 'beneath the debris of a universe in ruins', as the Second Law of Thermodynamics pronounces the inevitable heat-death of the cosmos, is matched even by the cooler statement of the founder of cybernetics, the mathematician Norbert Wiener:

> We are swimming upstream against a great torrent of disorganisation, which tends to reduce everything to the heat-death of equilibrium and sameness described in the second law of thermodynamics. What Maxwell, Botzmann and Gibbs meant by this heat-death in physics has a counterpart in the ethics of Kierkegaard, who pointed out that we live in a chaotic moral universe. In this, our main obligation is to establish arbitrary enclaves of order and system. These enclaves will not remain there indefinitely by any momentum of their own after we have established them. . . . We are not fighting for a definitive victory in the indefinite future. It is the greater possible victory to be, to continue to be, and to have been. No defeat can deprive us of the success of having existed for some moment of time in a universe that seems indifferent to us.[2]

Here we have echoes, too, of Jacques Monod's 'The ancient covenant is in pieces; man at last knows that he is alone in the unfeeling immensity of the universe out of which he emerged only by chance'.[3]

What, in fact, is this aspect of modern physics and physical chemistry to which are attributed such dire consequences? Harold Macmillan, the former Prime Minister of Great Britain, wrote a book about politics a few years ago which he called *The Art of the Possible*; thermodynamics is the *science* of the possible – it stands in relation to science as a whole very much like logic does to philosophy. It doesn't invent; it proscribes. Paradoxically, classical thermodynamics has been most successful in deriving the relationships that characterise physical systems at equilibrium, that is, just those systems in which all processes are reversible, unlike most actual systems which always involve natural irreversible processes. The state of equilibrium is that to which all processes tend to lead any actual system. So classical thermodynamics deals accurately and powerfully with a kind of limiting world – that to which the actual tends. It is not, on that account, to be underestimated. It was, for example, by purely thermodynamic arguments that Max Planck, thinking about the observed features of the equilibrium between matter and radiation, in the famous 'black body' problem, came to the heretical and impossible conclusion that energy was exchanged in discrete units ('quanta') and not continuously; more recently it has been by the application of thermodynamics to 'black holes' that Stephen Hawking at Cambridge has been able to make a start on that ultimate goal of physics, a 'unified field theory'; and, more modestly and pedagogically, I myself recall the astonishment with which I, as a chemistry student, realised that classical thermodynamics allows, from purely thermal measurement (heat capacities, heats of transitions and reaction), the calculation of the equilibrium composition of a chemical reaction mixture at *all* temperatures, given measurement of the equilibrium constant at *one* temperature (and this latter can itself be calculated by statistical thermodynamics from spectroscopic data in certain cases). So the thermodynamic account of equilibrium and its interpretation of natural processes (which we shall come to later) may be regarded as one of the best-established pillars of modern science.

The edifice of classical equilibrium thermodynamics has rightly been likened by G. N. Lewis and M. Randall to that of a medieval cathedral, through which, in their own classic and pellucid exposition, they conceived of themselves as conducting their readers:

> There are ancient cathedrals which, apart from their consecrated purpose, inspire solemnity and awe. Even the curious visitor speaks of serious things, with hushed voice, and as each whisper reverberates through the vaulted nave, the returning echo seems to bear a message of mystery. The labor of gener-

ations of architects and artisans has been forgotten, the scaffolding erected for their toil has long since been removed, their mistakes have been erased, or have become hidden by the dust of centuries. Seeing only the perfection of the completed whole, we are impressed as by some superhuman agency. But sometimes we enter such an edifice that is still partly under construction; then the sound of hammers, the reek of tobacco, the trivial jests bandied from workman to workman, enable us to realize that these great structures are but the result of giving to ordinary human effort a direction and a purpose.

Science has its cathedrals, built by the efforts of a few architects and of many workers. In these loftier monuments of scientific thought a tradition has arisen whereby the friendly usages of colloquial speech give way to a certain severity and formality. While this may sometimes promote precise thinking, it more often results in the intimidation of the neophyte. Therefore we have attempted, while conducting the reader through the classic edifice of thermodynamics, into the workshops where construction is now in progress, to temper the customary severity of the science in so far as is compatible with clarity of thought.[4]

But, since that was written, the workmen have been brought in again, this time to work on irreversible processes and dissipative systems, indeed those very aspects which are pertinent to living systems. Thus thermodynamics continues to develop and the reek of tobacco is still to be discerned – not to mention the jests of the workmen!

The basic features of thermodynamics

In its classical form, as developed in the nineteenth century culminating in J. Willard Gibbs' great monograph on 'The Equilibrium of Heterogenous Substances'[5, 6] thermodynamics operated with a 'black box' and phenomenological approach in which exchanges of matter, heat, and other forms of energy were related to macroscopic properties (pressure, temperature, volume, etc.) of the system in question. It referred to matter in bulk (note that pressure and temperature have no meaning for only one or a few molecules). The *state* of a system (macroscopic state) is determined by its *properties* just in so far as these properties can be investigated directly or indirectly by experiment. As Gibbs put it:

> So when gases of different kinds are mixed, if we ask what changes in external bodies are necessary to bring the system to its original state, we do not mean a state in which each particle shall occupy more or less exactly the same position as at some previous epoch, but only a state which shall be undistinguishable from the previous one in its sensible properties. It is to states of systems thus incompletely defined that the problems of thermodynamics relate.[6]

The *properties* of a substance describe its present state and do not give a record of its previous history. So when a system is considered in two different states, the difference in volume or in any other property between the two states depends solely upon those states themselves, and not upon the manner in which the system may pass from one state to the other. Furthermore, classical thermodynamics distinguished between 'extensive properties', dependent on the amount of matter in the system (e.g., volume), and 'intensive properties', not so dependent (e.g., temperature, pressure, density, composition). The values of the parameters that denote these properties are characteristic of the system in a given state – that is, they are 'properties of the state of a system' – and if the system changes from, say, state A to state B, each of these properties changes by a definite amount (e.g., volume $V_A \rightarrow V_B$, i.e., by $(V_B - V_A) = \triangle V$, where $\triangle$ represents a positive increase in the value of that parameter), regardless of what the intervening states may be *en route*. Because of this, properties of the state of a system can be related mathematically, at least in principle, and their concomitant variation handled by the differential and integral calculus. A *Zeroth Law* underlies the whole edifice, to the effect that if two systems are in thermal equilibrium with a third system, then they are in equilibrium with each other. All systems in such mutual thermal equilibrium are said to have the same 'temperature', an absolute scale of which it is one of the purposes of the exercise to devise. Systems not in thermal equilibrium are said to have different temperatures.

The *First Law* of thermodynamics is simply the formalisation of what is more familiar as the law of conservation of energy which simply affirms that an entity 'energy' has many forms (thermal, electrical, mechanical ('work'), etc.) which are interchangeable with conservation of its total amount. More formally, this issues in the assertion that there exists a property of the state of the system, called the 'internal energy' (U, or E), such that changes in this property are the sum of the heat absorbed by the system and the mechanical work done on it during any change of state (when only these two forms of energy are involved.) Subsequently, to involve the quantity U(E) in equations characteristic of the state of the system and to apply the calculus to it with respect to any changes it may undergo is then equivalent to assuming the First Law without any further ado.

The *Second Law* is more elusive and multiple in its expression and formulations. It is concerned with the uni-directional nature of our experience – dropped eggs do not re-assemble and fly back into our hands and we cannot re-fill the petrol tanks of our cars by pushing them backwards! There is a universal tendency for work, and all forms of energy convertible to work, to degenerate into uniform thermal energy (e.g., in any mechanical device, some of the original energy *always* goes to thermal energy, heat, from friction). All real processes are uni-directional, and although local changes can be reversed at the expense of irreversible processes elsewhere, no real process is ever reversible in its entirety.

Notice immediately the special role of heat ('thermal energy') as that form of energy least available for conversion into directed mechanical work. The earlier developments in the nineteenth century involved the formulation of how much of the heat contained in a body could be converted into work and how the efficiency of this conversion was related to a temperature scale. Another concern arose from the recognition that degrees of irreversibility in natural processes needed to be quantitatively compared. The ideal, or fully reversible, process was taken as the base-line, and so to represent a process manifesting minimum irreversibility. Hence the change in the quantity, S, the 'entropy', that was postulated to measure degrees of irreversibility, was assigned a zero value for such ideal processes (dS, or $\Delta S = O$).

Careful analysis of the relationships between heat, work and temperature both in natural, irreversibly-operating and in ideal, maximally efficient, reversibly-operating heat engines showed that the property, S, could be a 'property of the state of the system' if it was equated, for reversible processes, to the ratio of heat absorbed reversibly divided by the temperature. By definition it remained unchanged in reversible, adiabatic processes and increases in natural, irreversible processes in an isolated system (no heat or matter exchange across its boundaries). Since natural processes always tend to a state of equilibrium, it follows that the entropy of an isolated system reaches its maximum when that system reaches internal equilibrium.

Because this analysis, one of the great achievements of nineteenth-century science, led to the formulation of a property, the entropy (S), that not only measured the extent of irreversibility in a natural process in a particular system but was also a property of the state of that same system, the quantity S could be related to other properties of the state of the system (internal energy (U), pressure (P), volume (V), temperature (T), composition, etc.) and changes in it could be handled by the calculus, as for those other properties.[7] The Second Law could then be stated in the form 'In any real process, there is always an increase in entropy'. The greater the value of the increase in entropy (Δ S) in a natural process occurring in a particular system, the greater the extent of its irreversibility – that is, the more 'degraded' and less available for performing mechanical work had the energy become in the process, and the more it had become chaotic, *thermal* energy. Thus changes in entropy measured something to do with the 'character', not simply the quantity of energy, in a system.

What this 'character' was, that was related to availability to perform directed mechanical work, only became clear with the later development of *statistical* thermodynamics, particularly at the hands of L. Boltzmann. This development is most easily understood in the context of the realisation that the energy states of any system are all discrete and not continuous (even for translational energy). The 'character' of the energy that is related to the entropy was proposed by Boltzmann to be the 'spread' or distribution of matter over the possible available energy states – the degree of randomness or 'disorderliness', as it were, of the matter-energy distribution. To be more precise, the entropy (S) is related to a quantity, denoted as W, which is the 'number of complexions' of the system, i.e. the number of possible dispositions of matter over the (equi-probable) available energy states (or, more precisely, the number of *micro*-states corresponding to a given *macro*-state identified through its macroscopic properties). The Boltzmann relation was simply

$$S = k_B \ln W$$

where k_B = the Boltzmann constant and is the gas constant (R)/Avogadro's number (N_o); and the logarithm is a natural one, to exponential base e. Note that $W = 1$ represents a maximum state of 'order' in this respect, with minimum entropy, namely zero, since $\ln 1 = 0$.

'Disorderliness' is, in this context, the zero value of a variable, 'orderliness', which is the extent to which 'any actual specimen of an entity approximates to the "ideal" or pattern against which it is compared'.[8] Such 'orderliness' reaches its maximum extent in the 'state of order' which is 'an ideal reference state, laid down and specified, according to certain rules or conventions, which is taken as having 100% orderliness'.[8] This 'state of order' might well be that of the geometrical order of a crystal lattice at absolute zero and orderliness would decrease (i.e., disorderliness would increase) according to the extent to which the atoms or molecules of the crystal were displaced from the lattice points and/or the greater were the spread of its quantised energy states relative to the ground state. For populations rather than single entities, 100% order with respect to any parameter or property would be characterised by all the members of the population exhibiting the same value of that parameter, or the same property. So when, loosely, entropy is said to be a measure of 'disorder' or 'randomness' it is this kind of orderliness that is being referred to. It is, to use an example of Denbigh,[8] the kind of order exemplified by a perfect wall-paper pattern rather than that of an original painting. Such 'order' is therefore scarcely adequate as a measure of the complexity and *organization* of biological systems. Nevertheless it could be affirmed that the kind of *dis*order measured by entropy is incompatible with biological complexity and organisation and, indeed, the state of maximum entropy, of maximum disorder in the sense defined, is equivalent to biological death. Thus we may say that a state of low entropy is a necessary but not sufficient condition for biological complexity and organization to occur.

Note that the above equation could have been written as

$$- S = k_B \ln (1/W),$$

in which case increase in the 'negentropy' $(-S)$ could be regarded as parallel to an increase in 'order' measured by $(1/W)$, a way of speaking popularised by E. Schrödinger[9] but in my view needlessly obfuscating, especially if an increase in order does not necessarily entail an increase in biological complexity and organisation.

Evolution and Thermodynamics – the Problem?

One of the implications of the classical thermodynamic account of natural processes, just outlined, is that time has, in relation to natural events, a uni-directional character so that entropy has often been called 'time's arrow', for the increase in entropy displayed by natural processes apparently specifies (or, better, is closely linked conceptually with) the direction of the flow of time. All of this has a curious and apparently problematic relation with that other great scientific development of the nineteenth century – namely the 'discovery of time' in biology, more precisely, the idea of biological evolution.

Time had already been 'discovered' in the eighteenth century in the sense that the development of geology as a science had vastly extended the time-scale of the history of the Earth as a planet and of the living organisms, including man, upon it. Then, with Darwin and Wallace and the activity their proposal engendered, an understanding of both the interconnectedness of all living forms and of their progressive development from single cells (themselves not *so* simple) to more and more complex forms was surprisingly rapidly established, in spite of the opposition we all know about. Yet, according to one version of the laws of thermodynamics (Clausius), 'The energy of the universe is constant; the entropy of the universe is increasing to a maximum'.

As we saw, entropy, and so 'disorder', in the sense we have defined, increases in all natural processes. So how is it that living organisms can come into existence and survive, swimming, as it were, against the entropic stream carrying all to thermal equilibrium and 'heat-death'? In living organisms, we see natural objects in which, while they are alive, complex organisation is being maintained, and even enhanced, against the universal tendency of all processes to occur with an overall increase in 'disorder'. Are living organisms actually, in some way, breaking the second law of thermodynamics by maintaining systems in a high state of organisation and so a low state of disorder, of low entropy? The brief answer to this question is 'No', when one recalls that, for a natural process or change, one must take into account everything that changes. Now living organisms are *open* systems exchanging energy and matter with their surroundings, and the changes in entropy in both the organism and the surroundings have to be assessed: So it is perfectly possible for there to be a *decrease* in entropy associated with the processes of metabolism, etc., occurring in a living organism while at the same time this decrease is more than offset by an *increase* in the entropy of the surround-

ings of the organism on account of the heat that passes to these surroundings from the organism (recall the basic classical definition of entropy
increase as heat absorbed divided by temperature, for a reversible
process).

So living organisms, once in existence, do not in any sense 'break' the
second law of thermodynamics – any more than these laws are broken
in certain purely physical processes when a more ordered form of a
system is generated with the evolution of heat, e.g., the freezing of super-
cooled water to form ice, or the generation of a density gradient in the
molecular concentration along a tube of gas which is in contact with a
source of heat at one end of the tube and a sink for heat at the other
end. In these latter systems, a steady state is eventually reached with
respect to the throughput of heat and the distribution of the molecules
and in this state there is both energy flow and a steady rate of production
of entropy in the flow processes. In these physical samples it is, of course,
an 'ordering' that is occurring, at the expense of a 'disordering' (=
increase in entropy) of the surroundings – and not strictly an increase in
organisation of the kind required to maintain living systems. But at least,
an increase in order, thus physically defined à la Boltzmann is a necessary
prerequisite, if not a sufficient one, for the maintenance of biological
organization.

But it also has to be recognized[10] that there are some natural processes,
in which there is an overall increase in entropy, which nevertheless
manifest an increase in molecular 'complexity' of a kind not simply
captured by the simple concept of 'order' already defined, though related
to it. Molecular complexity *can* increase in chemical reactions that involve
association to more complex molecular forms, in full accordance with
the Second Law. This is because any decrease in entropy that results
from the decrease in the number of complexions (W, above) when atoms
or molecules combine, that is consequent upon the loss of translational
modes of molecular motion, with their closely packed energy levels, to
(by and large) vibrational modes, with their more widely spaced levels,
is offset: (i) by an increase in the entropy of the surroundings resulting
upon the heat generated by a decrease during the chemical combination
in the potential (electronic) energy of chemical bonds; and (ii) by an
increase in entropy due to the increase in configurational possibilities
that occur, in spite of reduction in the number of molecules, when there
is an increase in molecular heterogeneity with the formation of new
chemical species (and this contribution is greater the greater the number
of possible new chemical structures).

Wicken [10-12] denotes (i) and (ii), respectively, as 'energy-randomisation' and 'matter-randomisation' to emphasise that it is the randomising tendencies which the Second Law of thermodynamics formalises that drive forward the formation of more complex structures. The Earth's biosphere is in a steady-state of free energy flux, from the Sun to the Earth (with its biosphere) to outer space, with the rhythm of the Earth's diurnal rotation. Within the biosphere itself there is a continuous steady flow of energy through the various trophic levels of the ecologist, with concomitant transfer of heat to the non-living environment and so to outer space. [13, 14]

The formation of chemical bonds by process (i) then, entirely in accord with the Second Law and in conjunction with (ii), provides the opportunity for the increase in molecular, and so organisational, complexity upon which natural selection then operates. Wicken [12] has further argued that, for these reasons, the biosphere must evolve toward a stationary state of maximal structuring and minimal dissipation with respect to the (solar) applied free energy gradient. Wicken's general argument I have expressed here in terms of entropy rather than in his terms which are those of 'information', by which he means simply the negative of entropy as thermodynamically and statistically defined (see below), and so related to 'order' in the strict sense (and not to 'organisation'). So the Second Law of thermodynamics, far from prohibiting any increase in complexity, necessitates its increase at the molecular level. But does the recognition of this provide any thermodynamic basis for the actual coming into existence, in the first place, of living, organised systems of matter, as distinct from providing an interpretation of their continued existence, growth and death?

In the first half of the twentieth century, classical thermodynamics had been extended to natural irreversible processes at the hands of Onsager, Meixner, A. Katchalsky, de Groot, de Donder and Prigogine and his colleagues of the Brussels school. Although this extension reaped many rewards in other fields, it did not assist much in the interpretation of biological processes. For the thermodynamics of irreversible processes was developed for the situations in which the flows and rates of the processes were linear functions of the 'forces' (temperature, concentration, chemical potential gradients) that impelled them. Such linear, non-equilibrium, processes can, as we just saw, lead to the formation of configurations of lower entropy and higher order – so that non-equilibrium can be a source of order. But the 'order' so created is not really structural and far from the organised intricacies of biology. Moreover, and more pertinently, biological processes depend ultimately on biochemical ones and these, like all chemical reactions not at equilibrium, are intrinsically non-linear (in the relation between reaction rates and driving forces, the 'affinity', or free-energy difference) and fell outside the scope of irreversible thermodynamics at this stage of its development.

To show the Boltzmann equilibrium ordering principle (coupled with $\exp(-E/k_B T)$ being proportional to the probability of occupation of a state of energy E at temperature T) is inadequate to explain the origin of biological structures, it suffices to take an example of Eigen.[15] Consider a protein chain of 100 amino acids, of which there are 20 kinds – and biological systems are orders of magnitude more complex than this. The number of permutations of the possible order of amino acids in such a protein, and on which its biological activity and function depend, is $20^{100} \simeq 10^{130}$, assuming all sequences are equally probable. This is the number of permutations necessary to obtain a given arrangement starting from an arbitrary initial distribution. If a change of structure occurred at the (impossibly) high rate of one every 10^{-8} seconds, then 100^{122} seconds would be needed altogether to produce a given sequence – yet the age of the earth is 10^{17} seconds. So the chance of 'spontaneous' formation of the protein, à la Boltzmann, through processes at equilibrium, is indeed negligible. Equilibrium cannot give rise to biological order. There is no chance of an increase in 'order' of the Boltzmann kind by equilibrium considerations.

However, account now has to be taken of the Earth not being a system in equilibrium but being, and always having been, an *open* system through which there is a major flux of energy inwards from the Sun and outwards into space (and perhaps some minor flux of matter, too, though this seems in practice to be negligible). Thus, at present, the Earth receives energy from the Sun during the day and absorbs this heat both physically and chemically through the green chlorophyll of plants: at night-time much of this energy is radiated out again but some is stored in the carbohydrates of plants and so finds its way into other living organisms (including ourselves) as the intermediate source of their energy – before again being given up as heat to the atmosphere, and so to space again. Hence biological evolution has to be considered thermodynamically in relation to the openness of this whole system, and, in particular, of the biosphere located near to and on the Earth's surface. So it will be a thermodynamics of natural, irreversible processes in open systems that will be relevant to biological evolution and the coming into existence of living systems. There have been a number of other approaches for quantifying the evolutionary process and these have often been intricately interwoven in discussion of the relation of thermodynamics to the evolutionary process. They are described more fully in the original article[16] from which this Appendix is derived. But it is, in the end, in my view, the concepts of complexity and organisation that are the most pertinent and their relation to the thermodynamic interpretations of evolution are considered in the following section.

Thermodynamics and the evolution of biological complexity and organization

Increase in complexity and organisation. The biological complexity we actually observe now in the natural world is the product of a long evolutionary history and different levels in the hierarchy of biological complexity have appeared at successive stages in the history of the Earth, as illustrated by Table 1 devised by G. I. Stebbins.[17]

TABLE 1

The major levels of organisation in organic evolution

Level	Examples	Years ago when first appeared
8. Dominance of tool-using and conscious planning	Man	50,000
7. Homoiothermic metabolism (warm blood)	Mammals, Birds	150,000,000
6. Organised central nervous system, well-developed sense organs, limbs	Arthropods, Vertebrates	600,000,000 450,000,000
5. Differentiated systems of organs and tissues	Coelenterates, Flatworms, Higher Plants	1,000,000,000 400,000,000
4. Multicellular organisms with some cellular differentiation	Sponges, Algae, Fungi	2,000,000,000

TABLE 1 (continued)

Level	Examples	Years ago when first appeared
3. Division of labour between nucleus	Flagellates, Other Protozoa (Eukaryotes)	??????
2. Surrounding cell membrane with selective permeability and active transport of metabolites	Bacteria, Blue-Green Algae (Prokaryotes)	3,000,000,000?
1. Earliest self reproducing organic systems	Free living viroids (none still living)	??????

(From: Stebbins [17])

Table 1 emphasises the truism that today's biological structures are the result of a long process of development from earlier forms, a fact which is disregarded in the kind of calculations that try to estimate, say, the chance of a molecule of a typical protein being formed *de novo* from its constituent atoms, or even amino acids. Such calculations (*a fortiori* if complete organisms are considered) usually result, as we saw, in the conclusion that this probability is so low that the planet Earth has not existed long enough for such a complex assembly to appear by the random motion of atoms and molecules – whether this period be that of the total 4–5 thousand million years of the Earth's life, or the 1.1 thousand million years between the formation of the Earth (4.6 thousand million years ago) and the oldest known rocks (3.5 thousand million years ago) containing the remains of living cells (blue-green algae) found in rocks at Warrawoona, Australia.

The fallacy of such calculations lies in their ignoring the actual processes whereby complex self-reproducing (initially molecular and macromolecular) systems might self-organise themselves entirely consistently with currently known thermodynamics and chemical kinetics;[18] in ignoring the role of selection of organizations of macromolecules that have favoured reproduction rates and, once established, irreversibly channel the evolutionary process in one particular direction;[13, 19] and in ignoring the fundamental analyses of the architecture and evolution of complexity made by many authors, and in particular, H. A. Simon.[20] His story of the two watchmakers, Hora and Tempus, illustrates the evolutionary advantages of the modularisation that can occur in the assembly of a hierarchy and is worth quoting in full.

> There once were two watchmakers, named Hora and Tempus, who manufactured very fine watches. Both of them were highly regarded, and the phones in their shops rang frequently – new customers were constantly calling them. However, Hora prospered while Tempus became poorer and poorer and finally lost his shop. What was the reason? The watches the men made consisted of about one thousand parts each. Tempus had so constructed his that if he had one partly assembled and had to put it down – to answer the phone say – it immediately fell to pieces and had to be reassembled from the elements. The better the customers liked his watches, the more they phoned him the more difficult it became for him to find enough uninterrupted time to finish a watch. The watches that Hora made were no less complex than those of Tempus. But he had designed them so that he could put together sub-assemblies of about ten elements each. Ten of these sub-assemblies, again, could be put together into a larger sub-assembly; and a system of ten of the latter sub-assemblies constituted the whole watch. Hence, when Hora had to put down a partly assembled watch in order to answer the phone, he lost only a small part of his work, and he assembled his watches in only a fractioon of the man-hours it took Tempus. (Simon[20])

Simon went on to take a more quantitative analysis of the relative difficulty of the tasks of Hora and Tempus. If there is one chance in a hundred that either watchmaker would be interrupted while adding one part to an assembly, then a straightforward calculation showed that it would take Tempus, on the average, about four thousand times as long to assemble a watch as Hora! Although, Simon points out, the numerical estimate cannot be taken too seriously (and indeed it can be shown to be too low) the lesson for biological evolution is quite clear. The time required for the evolution of a complex form from simple elements depends critically on the number and distribution of potential, inter-mediate, stable forms: in particular if there exists a hierarchy of poten-tially stable 'sub-assemblies'.

A more detailed argument shows that in a hierarchy of potential stable sub-assemblies, the time required for a system containing 10^{25} atoms to evolve from one containing 10^{23} atoms is the same as that for a 1000-atom system to evolve from a 10-atom one. Or to put it (with Simon[20]) more broadly and only illustratively, it might well be that the time of evolution of multicellular organisms from single cells is of the same order of magnitude as the time required for the evolution of single-celled organisms from macromolecules. Indeed, some such principle must lie behind the strong impression that evolution develops exponentially and that only a logarithmic time-scale can spread out its many stages in any evenly-spaced manner.

Simon showed that complex systems will evolve from simple systems much more rapidly if there are stable intermediate forms than if there are not, and that the resulting complex forms will then be hierarchic in organization. The requirement for stability of an atomic or molecular structure reduces to the requirement that the free energy of the structure be less by virtue of its structure than that of its component atoms or molecules. The complex structures that emerge in the evolution of the first living forms, and of subsequent forms, may be presumed to have a stability of this kind, although, since living systems are open, the stability attributed to them must not be identified directly with the net free energy of formation of their structures. The point that is essential to make here, in relation to the possibility of formation of complex forms, is that natural selection speeds up the establishment of each new stratum of stability in the succession of forms of life. Each stratification of stability is only a temporary resting place before random mutation and natural selection open up further new possibilities and so new levels of (temporary) stability – rather as if the free energy profile were a switchback with any given form stable only to the immediate environment of the controlling parameters and always with a finite chance of mounting the next barrier to settle (again temporarily) into a new minimum.

Bronowski[21] has also pointed out that this 'stratified stability', which is so fundamental in living systems, gives evolution a consistent direction in time towards increased complexity. He used the metaphor of evolutionary time as a 'barbed arrow', because random change will tend in the direction of increasing complexity, this being the only degree of freedom for change – and Saunders and Ho[22] have also produced a neo-Darwinian argument along similar lines for the inevitability of increases in complexity in evolution.

Thermodynamic interpretations of evolution   Living systems are *open* in the thermodynamic sense, that is, they exchange matter and energy with their environment. It is possible for such open systems to evolve towards a *steady state* in which the total entropy (and indeed all other macroscopic parameters) of the system remains unchanged since it is then constituted by two balancing and exactly cancelling components: an increase in entropy in any time interval resulting from the irreversible processes occurring in the system; and a decrease in entropy due to loss of heat to the surroundings (which thereby undergo an increase in entropy). 'Internal' entropy production ($d_i S/dt$) due to the natural processes occurring in the steady state of an open system is a characteristic feature of such a system. It was an early discovery of irreversible thermodynamics (Prigogine[23]) that, when driving forces have a linear relation to resulting fluxes (and when certain other, not unduly restrictive conditions apply), the entropy production can be shown to be constant and at a minimum with respect to its values as it approaches the steady state (e.g., see ref. 18, p. 35–40).

This requirement for linearity restricts the applicability of the above principle to real systems not far removed from equilibrium, for only then can forces and fluxes be related linearly in all instances. H. J. Hamilton[24] assumes that open[25] systems that involve non-linear irreversible processes (which means in practice most real systems, including living ones) also obey this principle of the entropy production being minimal in the steady state. He then goes on to show that, on this basis, the probability that a particular kind of complex will be formed by the addition of one or another kind of element to an existing large complex (or the frequency of occurrence of such a complex in a large population of systems) is greater the lower the value of specific entropy production of the new complex.[26] He calls this thermodynamic criterion for the coming into existence of a new complex 'the principle of thermodynamic selection' and then applies it to the spontaneous creation and hierarchical evolution of all ordered structures – and in particular to the successively and increasingly complex living system of biological evolution, so that 'the principle of natural selection thus may be formulated in terms of fundamental thermodynamic laws and will be seen to be a special application of the principle of thermodynamic selection' (ref. 24, p. 316). He goes even further, affirming that

> The principle of natural selection, thus formulated, has the character of a fundamental physical law. Self-reproducing systems with suitably open hereditary programs may combine to form stable social systems, which may grow and reproduce

as a unit. In this way self-reproducing systems of increasing
hierarchical order, size, and organizational complexity may
evolve through processes of thermodynamic (natural) selection.

(ref. 24, p. 289)

These ideas of Hamilton constitute a thoroughgoing attempt to interpret the form (and even the behaviour) of living systems and the processes
by which they have evolved in terms of thermodynamics – and so in
terms of fundamental physical laws. Its principal weakness is that it rests
on an unproven and, so far, not adequately empirically substantiated
premise, namely, that the steady state(s) of *nonlinear* open (and 'closed')
systems are characterised by having a minimum entropy production.
Indeed, the time variation of the entropy production has no special
properties for such non-linear systems and only part of the entropy
production (that due to changes in the forces operative) may be used as
a criterion of evolution according to the Brussels school.[27, 28] So the status
of Hamilton's 'principle of thermodynamic selection' remains problematic and, for the moment, does not provide a secure enough basis for a
uniquely thermodynamic interpretation of biological evolution. Broadly,
it seems thermodynamically feasible to associate a reduction in entropy
production with a decrease in the dissipation of energy and so with
maximising the utilisation of energy, which must help survival of a living
system. However, the argument is not yet really rigorous enough, in my
opinion, to affirm confidently that there is such a 'principle of thermodynamic selection' with respect to minimal entropy production that is operative in biological evolution and uniquely determinative of its course.

That the biosphere is one of the temporary 'residences' of (free) energy
in its flux from the Sun via the Earth's surface on its way again to outer
space has already been stressed. Over the time-scale of existence of most
biological organisms (even that of the species rather than of the individual
organism), this flux corresponds to a steady state, with overall inward
flow balanced by flow outward. However, just as in a stream passing
down a rocky gorge, flows can vary within the overall movement, yet
nevertheless the general movement be in one direction, so too it is
pertinent to relate these energy fluxes to the general direction of biological
evolution. Thus, in his now classic work, *Elements of Physical Biology*,
A. J. Lotka wrote as follows in 1924:

Collective Effect of Individual Struggle for Energy Capture. Our
reflections so far have been directed to the selfish efforts of each

organism and species to divert to itself as much as possible of the stream of available energy. But . . . we shall be led to enquire: What must be the effect, upon the world-as-a-whole, of the general scrimmage for available energy? . . . . If we had only the animal kingdom to consider we should in the first instance be disposed to conclude that the cosmic effect of the scrimmage for available energy would be to increase the total energy flux, the rate of degradation of the energy received from the sun. But plants work in the opposite direction . . . . There are thus two opposing tendencies in operation, and it is difficult to see how any general principle can be applied to determine just where the balance will be struck.

The Law of Evolution Adumbrated as a Law of Maximum Energy Flux. This at least seems probable, that so long as there is an abundant surplus of available energy running 'to waste' over the sides of the mill wheel, so to speak, so long will a marked advantage be gained by any species that may develop talents to utilize this 'lost portion of the stream'. Such a species will therefore, other things equal, tend to grow in extent (numbers) and this growth will further increase the flux of energy through the system. . . . Every indication is that man will learn to utilize some of the sunlight that now goes to waste. The general effect will be to increase the rate of energy flux through the system of organic nature, with a parallel increase in the total mass of the great world transformer, of its rate of circulation or both.

One is tempted to see in this one of those maximum laws which are so commonly found to be apt expressions of the course of nature. But historical recollections here bid us to exercise caution; a prematurely enunciated maximum principle is liable to share the fate of Thomsen and Berthelot's chemical 'principle of maximum work'.[29]

The note of caution at the end is certainly worth taking to heart, for it is not at all clear how this flux and its associated entropy increase, i.e., 'randomisation' of energy with time, is to be related to biological development or evolution. We saw above that 'order', in the strictly thermodynamic sense, as related to W, *can* be generated in purely physical systems while operating strictly under the mandate of the Second Law, that is, with entropy increasing in a natural, irreversible process.

Moreover, we saw too that such order can arise spontaneously in a system (technically a closed one), such as a tube containing a gas in contact with a source of heat at one end but not at the other, through which thermal energy is flowing. The 'structure' so formed – in this instance, merely a gradient of increasing molecular concentration in the same direction as the energy flow – serves to reduce the *rate* at which the energy flows, and so decreases the rate of energy dissipation and the rate of production of entropy, to levels which both Morowitz[13] and Hamilton[24], in describing this system, affirm must be minimal. Certainly there is a reduction and therefore an increase in the 'residence time' of the energy in the system itself. Morowitz[13, 14] argued that in biological evolution, these thermodynamic effects will favour the emergence of new species that have an increased residence time before it is passed out as heat to the surroundings.

Of course, the total overall flow of energy from the Sun via the Earth to outer space is not, in the long run, affected by living organisms on the Earth's surface, but (as in Lotka's mill wheel analogy, or as for eddies in a stream) this does not prevent particular living organisms from existing in their own adaptive niches by having an increased efficiency of energy utilisation, a decreased dissipation of energy and entropy production, and so a longer 'residence time' for the energy in the organism. Here a difficulty arises. Is one referring in this to the individual organism or to a population of organisms? For there are grounds for thinking (see, e.g., Wicken[12]) that as evolutionary expansion into new adaptive zones (or individual biological development) proceeds, the total dissipation of the evolving ecosystem or developing organism often increases rather than decreases. It becomes crucial to decide to which unit one is referring: individual organisms or populations, in the context of evolution; or the individual embryo or the whole organism, in the context of development? Wicken affirms that 'If the principle of decreasing dissipation applies in biological evolution, it can only be with respect to the whole, quasi-closed ecosystems, to interacting webs of populations, rather than to individual species' (Wicken, ref. 12, pp. 14–15).

Many other factors are involved in success in competition, as the sociobiologists would be quick to point out, but Wicken nevertheless regards it as safe to affirm that, considered as wholes, the evolution of ecosystems is bound by the general thermodynamic principle of decreasing energy dissipation. More particularly, when there is a constant overall energy flux in a particular ecosystem, he affirms that this principle predicts that further increases in the total mass of organisms can occur only through reductions in the mean specific (i.e., per unit) dissipation of its energy-transforming components (presumably the individual organisms).

As with Hamilton's extension of the principle of minimum entropy production from linear to non-linear open and closed systems, this is all plausible and, indeed, probable. The bother is that it lacks a coerciveness that can come only from experimental studies on the energy fluxes and rates of entropy production in actual biological systems, whether a developing embryo or organ in relation to an organism, or an organism in relation to a population of organisms, or the latter in relation to its whole ecosystem. Until these are forthcoming we are perforce in the realm of reasonable conjecture and not of proven and tested application of thermodynamic principles. However, what does emerge from these and other proposals is the broad consistency and coherence with thermodynamics of the possibility and direction of biological evolution. In particular, in the light of the way in which the energy-randomising character of irreversible processes – the basis of the Second Law – drives transformations in the actual existing world of atoms and molecules to structures of greater complexity, a thermodynamic interpretation renders more intelligible the tendency for there to be an increase during evolution both in complexity and in any functional organisation that enhances efficiency of energy utilisation in individual organisms and minimises energy dissipation (entropy production) in whole ecosystems.

The origin of living systems from the non-living and from dissipative structures One of the particular achievements of thermodynamic theory in the last few decades has been its provision of a basis for understanding the spontaneous *coming into existence*, as distinct from the maintenance, of organized structures (which may be as much kinetically as topologically organised) in open (and closed) systems far from equilibrium when flux-force relationships are non-linear. This analysis by the Brussels school, under the leadership of Ilya Prigogine, has significance especially for understanding the emergence of functionally and structurally organised living matter from non-living, i.e. non-self-copying, matter (for references see ref. 18, chap. 2). They have been able to show how, on a strictly thermodynamic basis, new organised forms of systems can (but not necessarily will) come into existence and be stable, if matter and energy are flowing through to maintain them.

These new ordered forms are called *dissipative structures* and are radically different from the 'equilibrium structures' studied in classical thermodynamics, the 'order' of which is attained only at low enough temperatures in accordance with Boltzmann's ordering principle (as described above, and coupled with exp $(-E/k_B T)$ being proportional to the probability of occupation of a state of energy E at temperature T). In this non-linear range, non-equilibrium can indeed be the source of an order that would not be predictable by the application of Boltzmann's principle. In such states there can occur, under the right conditions, fluctuations that are no longer damped and that are amplified so that the system changes its whole structure to a *new* ordered state in which it can again become steady and imbibe energy and matter from the outside and maintain its new structured form. This instability of dissipative structures has been studied by these workers who have set out more precisely the thermodynamic conditions for a dissipative structure to move from one state to a new state which is more ordered than previously, i.e., for 'order through fluctuations' to occur.

It turns out that these conditions are not so restrictive that no system can ever possibly obey them. Indeed, a very large number of systems, such as those of the first living forms of matter which must have involved complex networks of chemical reactions, are very likely to do so, since they are non-linear in the relationship between the forces and fluxes involved. The ordered configurations that emerge beyond such an instability of the thermodynamic branch of non-linear systems were called dissipative structures, because they are created and maintained by the entropy-producing 'dissipative' processes occurring inside the system through which, being open, there is a continuous flux of matter and energy.

Model physical systems undergoing such transitions are now well-known, e.g., the famous Bénard phenomenon wherein a hexagonal organisation at right angles to the vertical heat flow is observed, at a certain critical point, in a column of liquid heated from below – and others cited by H. Haken[30] who, because the awareness of them has now become so widespread, and because they share common features in the 'bifurcation' of the solutions of the differential equations controlling these phenomena, has invented a new name for the study of such systems, namely 'Synergetics'.

Even more pertinent to biological systems is the observation of order-through-fluctuations in chemical systems. Chemical networks can be of a very high degree of complexity through incorporating one or more autocatalytic steps and they are often non-linear (in the sense above) when not close to equilibrium. Then various kinds of oscillating reactions and other features can occur. One of the most striking of these is the so-called Belousov-Zhabotinsky reaction, the oxidation of malonic acid by bromate in the presence of cerium ions in solution (Tyson[31]). With the right combination of solution conditions, and at constant temperature, the original homogeneous reaction mixture changes into a series of pulsing waves of concentration of cerium ions, moving up and down the tube, until eventually a steady state is reached in which there are static, banded layers of alternating high and low concentrations of ceric ions. From an originally homogeneous system, a highly ordered structure has appeared through the fluctuations that are possible in a non-linear system far removed from equilibrium.

What has happened is that fluctuations in such a system have been amplified and, consistently with the laws of chemical kinetics, a new structure has appeared that is ordered, at first in time and then finally in space – representative of an alliance of chance and law. Under the conditions of this reaction the structural formation has a probability of unity, provided that the initial fluctuation arises from within the system. The causal chain leading to this fluctuation, although it cannot be discerned by ourselves, must itself be the result of law-like processes occurring at the micro-level. Because of the discovery of these dissipative systems, and of the possibility of 'order-through-fluctuations', it is now possible, on the basis of these physicochemical considerations, to regard as highly probable the emergence from non-living matter of those ordered and articulated molecular structures that are living. Instead of them having only an inconceivably small chance of emerging in the 'primeval soup' on the surface of the earth before life appeared, we now see that ordered dissipative structures of some kind will appear in due course.

One has to presume that before life had evolved there existed in this prebiotic stage a system containing replicating macromolecules that could both maintain itself by means of some simple copying mechanism and have a potentiality of change incorporated into its very structure and function so as to facilitate its multistage evolution to more complex forms more efficient in survival and reproduction. Some of the kinetic and stochastic problems associated with such prebiotic systems have been very fully investigated by M. Eigen and his colleagues at Göttingen.[15, 19, 32] In the present context, we raise the question asked by Prigogine and his colleagues from a more thermodynamic perspective which may be put thus: 'How can each step in an evolutionary process in which each stage leads to more orderly, or at least more complex, configurations contain within itself the potentiality to change by other, later transitions to yet more ordered, complex configurations?'

Each transition, to be part of a *continuous*, multistage evolution, cannot become a 'dead-end', that is, it must contain within itself the possibility of yet further changes – otherwise the system is simply eliminated in the competition for limited 'food' reserves (of simpler monomers, in this case). What is needed is for change to occur in such a non-linear open system in a way that increases its non-linearity and distance from equilibrium and thereby both ensures and enhances the possibility of further change. This could come about by the change, however brought about, being of such a kind that it increased the interactions between the system and its external environment, such interactions being one of the causes of non-linearity. If this were to happen, this increase of interaction would be reflected in an increase in the entropy production per unit mass, i.e., there would be an increase in the 'dissipation' in the system as an immediate consequence of the transition. This increased dissipation would then, temporarily at least, characterise a system which had the potentialities of undergoing further instabilities when appropriate thresholds were passed, and so of forming new structures, with again increased dissipation, and so on. A kind of 'feedback' in evolution of such non-linear systems has therefore been postulated by the Brussels group[27] that may be depicted as:

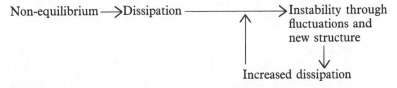

Once this instability has been initiated, it is proposed, the system can increase its specific entropy production[26] which they take as a suitable index of the level of dissipation in a system. Each instability would be followed by a higher level of energy dissipation which would mean some of the irreversible processes in the system would be working more intensely, would therefore depart further from equilibrium, and so would enhance the probability that there should occur those kinds of fluctuations that would again render the processes unstable. They have been able to show that quite large classes of systems in which biological macromolecules are being synthesised can display this 'evolutionary feedback', principally because the transitions that increase the relative numbers of copies of such macromolecules must have certain autocatalytic properties.

Further calculations suggested to them that those systems that display an *increase* in dissipation, as manifest in the specific entropy production, do so only transiently, after the initial threshold fluctuation. For once it is in the new regime that can display this initial enhancement of dissipation, it seems, from the available thermal data, that the system adjusts itself to the constraints and the dissipation then tends to decrease to a new level characteristic of the new non-linear steady state (now further than before from equilibrium). As Prigogine *et al.* say: 'one is tempted to argue that only after synthesis of the key substances necessary for its survival (which implies an increase in dissipation) does an organism tend to adjust its entropy production to a low value compatible with the external constraints' (ref. 27, box inset).

As already mentioned, for a non-linear system to evolve it must undergo changes which are of such a kind that they still, after the change, possess the potentiality of further change. However, this state of affairs could not continue indefinitely, and indeed there was evidence that eventually the entropy production could decrease to a new value characteristic of the new (dissipative) structure. The creating of structure leads to an increase in entropy production whereas maintenance of the structure once formed, it is suggested, could obey the theorem of minimum entropy production. On this interpretation, entropy production would pass through a series of decreasing minima, transitions between which occur via a temporarily enhanced increase before falling to the next lower minimum.[27]

The idea of a succession of temporarily stabilised states as being a useful perspective on evolution was also proposed by J. Bronowski[21] when he pointed out that 'stratified stability' was the principal feature of the evolutionary sequence, both inorganic and organic. Each more complex form represents a new stratum of stability which has a finite chance of forming under the conditions appropriate to it. His picture of evolution is: once formed, each stratum of complexity has a stability which allows the possibility of the next stratum appearing by providing the structures (atomic, molecular, organic, or whatever) which form the constituent building blocks of the next level.

> Because stability is stratified, evolution is open and necessarily creates more and more complex forms. . . . So long as there

remains a potential of stability which has not become actual, there is no other way for chance to go. It is as if nature were shuffling a sticky pack of cards, and it is not surprising they hold together in longer and longer runs (ref. 21, p. 32).

Bronowski speaks here of chance (which is related to entropy) but the strata to which he refers are levels of *energy* minima, successive ones higher in energy than the preceding, and each reached over an energy barrier – rather like ascending and descending a succession of cols into a series of valleys in a mountain range, the level of each valley bottom being higher than its predecessors.

This interpretation is given a more sophisticated thermodynamic content in the treatment of the Brussels school. In their exposition, too, it is not instability but a succession of instabilities of dissipative systems, now appearing under the aegis of thermodynamic laws, that bridges the gap between the non-living and the living. This succession of instabilities can be a process of self-organisation, and so of evolution, provided there are fulfilled certain conditions that emerge clearly from the foregoing thermodynamic considerations. They are that a process of self-organis- ation can occur in a system if: (i) the system is *open* to the flux of matter and energy; (ii) the system is not at equilibrium and preferably *far from equilibrium* and (iii) the system must be *non-linear* in its flux-force relationships, i.e., there must be strong coupling between its processes. These simple requirements underlie the ideas developed above, notably by the Brussels school, and are certainly satisfied by all biological systems and organisms and so the following 'theorem', formulated by G. Nicolis, is applicable to them and serves to summarise the whole analysis:

> Consider a single phase system satisfying the above three prerequisites [(i)–(iii)], whose entropy can be defined in terms of macroscopic quantities. Under these conditions, steady states belonging to a finite neighbourhood of the state of thermo- dynamic equilibrium are *asymptotically stable*. Beyond a *critical distance* from equilibrium they *may* become unstable.[33]

The evolution to order through an instability induced by fluctuations, referred to in this last sentence, is only a possible, not a certain, develop- ment and in fact requires, along with the subsequent stabilisation to a dissipative structure, that some other very stringent conditions be fulfilled.

Thermodynamics and kinetic mechanisms The existence of these other conditions reminds us that, like patriotism, thermodynamics 'is not enough'. For thermodynamics is always the science of the possible: it can allow, it can forbid, but it cannot prescribe. What actually occurs in any system obeying the conditions described above for it to become (more) self-organising depends on the ability of the actual molecules and higher structures present, on their spatial and temporal arrangement and on the numerical parameters specific to these features. In a molecular system, this means the patterns generated will depend principally on chemical reaction rate constants and on diffusion constants, controlling movement across space.

Similar parameters characteristic of higher order structures will also operate at other levels – e.g., in the patterning in predator-prey, herbivore-plant and host-parasite systems (Lotka[29]). Ever since the seminal paper of A. M. Turing (1952), *The Chemical Basis of Morphogenesis*,[34] it has become increasingly clear that suitable combinations of rates of chemical reactions and diffusion processes can spontaneously generate patterns in space and time, both permanent and oscillating according to conditions. This separate development of dynamical theory, of kinetics and of fluctuation theory opens up new vistas of interpretation of pattern formation at many levels of biology (and even in social structures, according to the Brussels group (Lepkowski[35])). These interpretations cannot be described here (see ref. 18, chap. 4) but, the point is, it is now possible to understand the detailed mechanisms in actual dissipative systems that lead to new ordered ('self-organized') forms appearing.

Particularly striking biological examples of such forms are provided by the oscillations in time and the patterning in space of the concentrations of intermediates in glycolysis that have been observed by Benno Hess and his colleagues, and the quite extraordinary ability of individual unicellular slime mould organisms (in particular *Dictyostelium discoideum*) to come together, under conditions of starvation, in organised spiral and annular patterns in a colony that then behaves, temporarily, as an organised whole until new food sources are found (references in ref. 18, chap. 4).

So, one may well ask, what *is* to be gained from the application of irreversible thermodynamic concepts and criteria to biological systems? The primary and overriding gain is undoubtedly in the ability of thermodynamics to provide, as it were, an architectonic framework which limits but does not in detail prescribe. One can then build on this framework by using other resources of dynamical theory, of kinetics, of fluctuation theory – and of precise experimental information and new knowledge of modes of control and regulation at all levels in biology. Structural order comes from the existence of constraints and the macroscopic and phenomenological approach of thermodynamics is uniquely fitted to handle such factors. Thus it is that the thermodynamic analyses we have been describing can serve to eliminate some putative models of biological situations as being incompatible with macroscopic physical laws, while permitting others, if not actually determining the choice between them. This can be a useful role, since so much of theoretical biology is concerned with formulating and testing mathematical models of the phenomena in question and thermodynamics can be a help, for example, in restricting the rate laws that might be relevant. Indeed, for some areas of theoretical inquiry, the thermodynamic constraints on the building of models are often the most reliable knowledge of the situation available – for example, in any modelling of prebiotic evolution.

So thermodynamics can never work in isolation from other approaches based on the theory of fluctuations, of stability, of stochastic processes and of non-linear differential equations. However, it has its own unique insights which serve to link reflection on biological systems with the whole corpus of physicochemical theory. For the new concepts in irreversible thermodynamics of non-equilibrium as the source of order, of 'order through fluctuations', of the decisive role of non-equilibrium constraints and of dissipative structures (spatial, temporal and both) in open systems, broaden and deepen immeasurably our perspective on biological systems and whole organisms and, indeed, have already proved to be a stimulus for the kind of detailed work that is required to give them a 'local habitation and a name'.

Conclusion

At the beginning of this Appendix I quoted a paragraph of Norbert Wiener in which he seemed to be suggesting that a thermodynamic perspective provoked the feeling that the universe was somehow against the experiment of life and that in nurturing our little enclave of organised existence, as biological and as social systems, we were swimming against the entropic stream that was in fact sweeping all to randomness and 'dark night'. But the picture that is emerging in more recent thermodynamic analyses of dissipative systems and of living organisms has a different tenor. Certainly the stream as a whole moves in a certain general, overall direction which is that of increasing entropy and increasing disorder, in the specific sense I have defined. However, the movement of the stream *itself* inevitably generates, as it were, very large eddies *within* itself in which, far from there being a decrease in order, there is an increase first in complexity and then in something more subtle – functional organisation. Now there could be no eddies without the stream in which they are located and so may it not be legitimate to regard this inbuilt potentiality for living organisation that the entropic stream manifests as being its actual point – namely, why it *is* at all? There could be no self-consciousness and human creativity without living organisation, and there could be no such living dissipative systems unless the entropic stream followed its general, irreversible course in time. Thus does the apparently decaying, randomising tendency of the universe provide the necessary and essential matrix (*mot juste!*) for the birth of new forms – new life through death and decay of the old.

Notes

Chapter 1: The sciences and reductionism

1. By Herbert Dingle, I believe, though I have not been able to trace this remark.
2. Francis H. C. Crick *Of Molecules and Man* (Univ. of Washington Press, Seattle, 1966), p. 10.
3. E. O. Wilson, *Sociobiology* (Belknap Press, Harvard Univ., Cambridge, Mass., 1975), p. 4.
4. Sir William Paton, in discussions in Oxford, 1971–2.
5. R. S. Cohen, 'Causation in History' in *Physics, Logic and History*, ed. W. Yourgrau and A. D. Breck (Plenum Press, New York, 1970), pp. 231–45.
6. J. D. Lambert, Oxford discussions, 1971–2.
7. J. A. Russell, Oxford discussions, 1971–2.
8. D. W. Millard, Oxford discussions, 1971–2.
9. F. J. Ayala, in the Introduction to *Studies in the Philosophy of Biology: Reduction and Related Probles*, ed. F. J. Ayala and T. Dozhansky (Macmillan, London, 1974), p. ix.
10. Even in 1979, W. C. Wimsatt (in an article entitled 'Reduction and Reductionism' in *Current Research in Philosophy of Science*, ed. P. D. Asquith and K. E. K. Kyburg, Jr, (PSA, East Lancing, Michigan, 1979), pp. 352–80) could instance 132 papers that had appeared concerning these themes in the previous two or three years.
11. Crick, *op. cit.*, pp. 13, 14.
12. K. F. Schaffner, *Science* 157 (1967), 646.
13. K. R. Popper, 'Scientific reduction and the essential incompleteness of all science' in *Studies in the Philosophy of Biology: Reduction and Related Problems*, ed. A. J. Ayala & T. Dobzhansky (Macmillan, London, 1969), pp. 259–84.
14. Theodosius Dobzhansky, 'On Cartesian and Darwinian Aspects of Biology' in *Philosophy, Science and Method*, ed. S. Morgenbesser, P. Suppes and M. White (Macmillan, New York, 1969), pp. 165–78.
15. Ayala (n. 9 above), p. viii.
16. C. N. Hinshelwood, *The Structure of Physical Chemistry* (Clarendon Press, Oxford, 1951), p. 449.
17. Note that the ambiguity of 'nothing' has to be guarded against at this point. Sometimes 'thing' is used generally (as in 'something', 'anything',

'everything', 'nothing') of any possible entity that could be referred to by a referring expression within some context of discourse. But sometimes 'thing' means a visible and tangible object.

18. D. M. MacKay, *The Clockwork Image* (Inter-Varsity Press, London, 1974), pp. 42–4.

19. Theodosius Dobzhansky, *The Biology of Ultimate Concern* (New American Library, New York, 1967); Ian Barbour, *Issues in Science and Religion* (SCM Press, London, 1966), esp. pp. 324–37; J. C. Eccles, *Facing Reality* (Longman, London, 1970); Arthur Koestler and J. R. Smythies, eds, *Beyond Reductionism* (Hutchinson, London, 1969); A. R. Peacocke, *Science and the Christian Experiment* (Oxford Univ. Press, London, 1971); Marjorie Grene, ed., *Interpretations of Life and Mind* (Routledge & Kegan Paul, London, 1971); William H. Thorpe, *Animal Nature and Human Nature* (Methuen, London, 1974).

20. Ernest Nagel, 'Wholes, Sums and Organic Unities', *Philosophical Studies* 3 (1952): 17–32. His treatment may be summarized as follows: The word 'whole' is used to refer to something with a spatial extension, to some temporal period, to any class of elements, to a property of an object or process, to a pattern of relations, to a process, to any concrete object, or to any system whose spatial parts stand to one another in various relations of dynamical dependence. Corresponding to each of these meanings, the reference of the word 'parts' can be explicated, and this suffices to indicate at once not only the ambiguity of these words themselves but also of the word 'sum', which is being attributed, or not attributed, to the relation of the 'wholes' to the 'parts', and so also the ambiguity of the word 'addition', which is the process whereby wholes are putatively derived from parts. 'Organic wholes' or 'organic unities' are those systems which exhibit a mode of organization that is often claimed to be incapable of analysis in terms of an 'additive point of view' (p. 26). Two kinds of this supposed 'addition' have furthermore to be distinguished: 'The question whether a given system can be *overtly constructed* in a piecemeal fashion by a seriatim juxtaposition of parts, and the question whether the system can be *analyzed in terms of a theory* concerning its assumed constituents and their interrelations. . . . However, this difference between systems does not correspond to the intended distinction between functional and summative wholes; and our inability to construct effectively a system out of its parts, which in some cases may only be a consequence of temporary technological limitations, cannot be taken as evidence for deciding the second of the above two questions' (p. 28).

21. *Ibid.*, p. 29.

22. *Ibid.*, p. 30.

23. Nagel (n. 20 above), pp. 24–25.

24. *Ibid.*, pp. 29–30.

25. Peacocke (n. 19 above), chaps. 1–3; W. H. Thorpe in 'Reductionism in Biology' in Ayala & Dobzhansky (n. 9), pp. 111ff.; H. H. Pattee, 'The

Problem of Biological Hierarchy' in *Towards a Theoretical Biology*, ed. C. H. Waddington (Edinburgh Univ. Press, Edinburgh), 3:117–36.

26. M. Beckner, 'Reduction, Hierarchies and Organicism' in ref. 9, above, pp. 163–76.

27. *Ibid.*, pp. 164–5.

28. *Ibid.*, p. 166.

29. Ernest Nagel, *The Structure of Science* (Harcourt Brace & Co., New York, 1961), chap. 11.

30. These conditions are (1) the condition of connectability – that all the concepts or terms of T_h can be systematically connected with some of the terms of T_l (by synthetic-identity statements, explicit definitions, or some other semantic relation) – and (2) the condition of derivability – that each law L_h is deducible from T_l, together with statements which connect the respective concepts or terms of the two levels L_h and L_l and a description of relevant boundary conditions in the vocabulary of T_l. It should be noted that, according to this definition, reduction is distinctively linguistic, for it is the deduction of one set of empirically confirmable statements from another such set – and not the derivation of the properties of one subject matter from the properties of another – because the 'nature' of things (especially the elementary constituents of things) is not accessible to direct inspection (Nagel, *op. cit.*, p. 364). Nagel regards it as 'hopelessly and irresolvably speculative' to try to make reduction the deduction of properties or 'natures' from other properties or 'natures'. For notation here and in notes 31 and 33, see Fig. 1.

31. The 'oversimplification' to which Hempel objects arises, in the case of the mechanistic programme for the reduction of biology (as T_h) to physicochemistry (as T_l), in the claim that, in applying the condition of connectability, all biological concepts and terms can be extensionally characterised in physicochemical concepts and terms. This has to be insisted upon, in this programme, for otherwise the 'connecting principles' (cf. Nagel[30]) would merely constitute additional biological laws if they expressed only the necessary or sufficient physicochemical conditions for biological concepts, so that the reduction would then be incomplete at the first stage of connectability. However, since the connecting principles which are presently available do not begin to suffice to characterize all concepts and terms of biology (T_h) in physicochemistry (T_l), the programme of mechanistic reduction appears untenably oversimplistic in Hempel's view.

32. Conveniently grouped and summarised into four paradigms by K. F. Schaffner in 'Approaches to Reduction', *Philosophy of Science* 34 (1967), 137–47, where he elaborates a general reduction paradigm yielding the earlier ones as special cases.

33. If, like one group of authors (Karl R. Popper, Paul K. Feyerabend and Thomas R. Kuhn), one considers that a complete reduction of a T_h to a T_l is not likely, then in the development of sciences new theories will tend to be seen as making cataclysmic breaks with the old; whereas, if

one thinks reduction is possible, then old theories may be regarded as reduced by the new ones which replace them. (E.g., Schaffner [*ibid*]; cf. also the stretching of reduction to deal with cases where there is abrupt contradiction [and not a deductive relation] between the old and the superseding new theory by relating them both to the observations they both explain [J. G. Kemeny and P. Oppenheim, 'On Reduction', *Philosophical Studies* 8 (1956), 6–19].) The latter position represents some widening of the scope of what is meant by reduction, although the central idea is always that of explaining a theory T_h in terms of a theory T_l from a different branch of science, corresponding (usually) to a different level in the hierarchy of systems which the sciences study. E.g., from this more historical perspective, Popper ('Scientific Reduction and the Essential Incompleteness of All Science' in Ayala and Dobzhansky [n. 9 above], pp. 259–84) asserts that, while in all the sciences the attempt to make reductions is justified on methodological grounds and must continue because we learn so much that is fruitful even from unsuccessful attempts and while nothing is as great as successful reduction, yet hardly any major reduction in science has ever been completely successful, for there is, he argues, almost always an unresolved residue left by even the most successful attempts at reduction. There is an unresolved residue even in the reduction of chemistry to physics since the heavier elements have an evolutionary history and their coming into existence is rare in the cosmos, so that cosmological considerations enter in addition to those of quantum physics – and a theory of evolution is even more indispensable in biology. The 'deductions' involved in reducing one branch of science to another are not, in practice, strict, for they involve all sorts of approximation, simplications and idealisations.

34. C. F. A. Pantin, *The Relations between the Sciences* (Cambridge Univ. Press, Cambridge, 1968); P. W. Anderson, 'More Is Different: Broken Symmetry and the Nature of the Hierarchical Structure of Science', *Science* 77 (1972), 393–6; A. R. Peacocke (n. 19 above), chap. 2, and *The Physical Chemistry of Biological Organization* (Clarendon Press, Oxford, 1983), chap. 1; Peter Medawar, 'A Geometric Model of Reduction and Emergence' in Ayala and Dobzhansky (n. 9 above), pp. 57–63; and L. L. Whyte, A. G. Wilson and D. Wilson, eds, *Hierarchical Structures* (Elsevier Publishing Co., New York, 1969).

35. Medawar, *op. cit.* (n. 34), p. 61.

36. Beckner, *op. cit.* (n. 26), p. 170 and Nagel, *op. cit.* (n. 29).

37. Beckner, *op. cit.* (n. 26), p. 170.

38. *Idem, ibid.*

39. *Idem, op. cit.*, p. 174.

Chapter 2: Is biology nothing but physics and chemistry?

1. P. Medawar ('A geometric model of reduction and emergence' in F. J. Ayala and T. Dobzhansky (eds), *Studies in the Philosophy of Biology: Reduction and Related Problems* (Macmillan, London, 1974), pp. 57–63) cites 'heredity', 'infection', 'immunity', 'sexuality' and 'fear' (p. 57), but many others were also pointed out in the same volume by other authors who develop this emphasis in their own particular ways. Ernest Boesiger ('Evolutionary Theories after Lamarck and Darwin') stresses that the patterns of explanation of the adaptive or 'purposeful' character of organisms which invoke use and disuse or natural selection are distinctive of biology and are 'organismic' (p. 42). Gerald M. Edelman ('The Problem of Molecular Recognition by a Selective System', *ibid.*, pp. 45–8) has described how, methodologically, the current selective theory of antibody formation emerged only when attention was focused on two levels in the system, that of the cell and that of antibodies at the molecular level; the latter alone failed as an explanation. G. Ledyard Stebbins ('Adaptive Shifts and Evolutionary Novelty: A Compositionalist Approach', *ibid.*, pp. 285–306) sees the study of organic evolution as polarised around two widely distinct forms: evolution in the broad sense ('a succession of events that took place over billions of years of time, and gave rise successively to living matter . . . and finally to man . . .' [p. 285]), which can be studied only by a compositionistic activity drawing on information from a wide variety of sources (systematics, paleontology, population genetics); and evolution at the level of populations, which looks for changes that can be observed by a scientist in a much shorter time through quantitative, experimental methods. Theodosius Dobzhansky ('Chance and Creativity in Evolution', *ibid.*, pp. 307–38) shows that evolutionary theory requires concepts that play no part outside biology ('Mutation, sexual recombination and natural selection are linked together in a system which makes biological evolution a creative process' [p. 336]). Henryk Skolimowski ('Problems of Rationality in Biology', *ibid.*, pp. 221–2) emphasises that evolved man is cognitive, comprehending evolution; and this itself is life enhancing and involved in evolution, so that ideas such as 'feedback', 'information', 'environment', and 'past experience' become normative, to be made sense of only in a system that admits values and norms. This necessitates an 'evolutionary rationality' introducing 'open-ended concepts', 'growth concepts', and 'normative concepts'.

2. F. Jacob, *The Logic of Living Systems* (Allen Lane, London, 1974), pp. 406–7 (emphasis added). An 'integron', in Jacob's terminology, is each of the units in a hierarchy of discontinuities formed by the integration of sub-units of the level below. An integron is formed by assembling integrons of the level below it; it takes part in the construction of the integron of the level above (*op. cit.*, p. 302).

3. J. J. C. Smart, *Philosophy and Scientific Realism* (Routledge & Kegan Paul, London, 1963), chap. 3.
4. Michael Polanyi, *Personal Knowledge* (Routledge & Kegan Paul, London, 1958); *The Study of Man* (Routledge & Kegan Paul, London, 1959); *The Tacit* Dimension (Routledge & Kegan Paul, London, 1967); 'Life Transcending Physics and Chemistry', *Chemical and Engineering News* (August 21, 1967), pp. 54–66; 'Life's Irreducible Structure', *Science* 160 (1968), 1308–12.
5. Much is sometimes made of the distinction that machines are artefacts and biological organisms are not. Clearly, machines are designed by man to have certain relationships and interactions among their components, so that we can predict how they will behave, within limits determined partly by our lack of knowledge of what we need to know about the components and their properties over a period of time and under stress. The labyrinthine organisation of biological organisms is only gradually becoming apparent to us, and we are profoundly ignorant of it at most levels – only a small, though central, part has been unveiled by the molecular biology of the last few decades. We are largely ignorant of the organisation of biological systems; we are unable to predict any but the smallest fraction of their behaviour; and we have to admit that we are ignorant even of how we ought to think about them, what conceptual tools are needed, at different levels. But this relative difference in our knowledge of mechanics and organisms need not of itself invalidate Polanyi's arguments, even if they are vulnerable on other counts, as discussed in this Chapter. It is interesting to note that even systems composed of molecules, etc., obeying the essentially deterministic laws of classical physics can be shown to have behaviour which is predictable only within limits: e.g., in meteorology, it is becoming clear that 'no conceivable improvement of the observing network can increase this period [of weather prediction] to longer than a value lying somewhere between ten days and three weeks. . . . The atmosphere is a physical system which is demonstrably unpredictable in practice beyond a certain time, even though it is composed of a finite collection of objects whose interactions are governed by the laws of physics' (R. S. Harwood, Oxford discussions, 1971–2).
6. K. P. Schaffner, 'Anti-Reductionism and Molecular Biology', *Science* 157 (1967), 644–7, and 'The Watson-Crick Model and Reductionism', *British Journal for the Philosophy of Science* 20 (1969), 325–48.
7. Schaffner, 'Watson-Crick Model', pp. 345–6 (my italics).
8. Polanyi, 'Life Transcending Physics and Chemistry' and 'Life'-s Irreducible Structure) (n. 43 above).
9. A. R. Peacocke, *The Physical Chemistry of Biological Organization* (Clarendon Press, Oxford, 1983).
10. *Idem, op cit.*, chap. 2; see also ch. 4, n. 13, below.
11. *Idem, op. cit.*, chap. 5.
12. Q.v., *idem, op. cit.*, chap. 3; see also ch. 4, n. 13, below.

13. *Idem, ibid.*, see especially chap. 6 on 'The interpretation of biological complexity'.
14. B. Hess, 'Oscillators: a property of organized systems' in *Frontiers in physico-chemical biology*' (Academic Press, New York, 1978), p. 418.
15. W. C. Wimsatt, 'Robustness, reliability and multiple-determination in science' in *Knowing and validating in the social sciences: a tribute to Donald T. Campbell*, ed. M. Brewer & B. Collins (Jossey-Bass, San Francisco, 1981); see also pp. 61–2 and ch. 4, n. 13.
16. 'Multiple determination' Wimsatt calls it.
17. See above, p. 6.
18. Q.v. *Reductionism in Academic Disciplines*, ed. A. R. Peacocke (NFER – Nelson, London, 1985).
19. H. H. Penner & E. A. Yonan, *J. Religion* 52 (1972), 128.

Chapter 3: The new biology – holistic

1. This *methodological* distinction – a useful one – was made, inter alia, by T. Dobzhansky in relation to biology in S. Morgenbesser, P. Suppes and M. White eds, *Philosophy, Science and Method* (Macmillan, New York, 1969), 165–78.
2. F. Jacob, *The Logic of Living Systems* (Allen Lane, London, 1974), p. 13. *Nature, Lond.* 290 (1981), 82.
3. H. W. Bell *et al.* (members of the British Museum (Natural History)), *Nature, Lond.*, 290 (1981), 82.
4. F. Jacob, *op. cit.*, ref. 2, p. 13.
5. This universality can still be confidently maintained in spite of slightly deviant codes operating in the small genomes of mitochondria and those more recently discovered in ciliated protozoons and mycoplasms (as reported by T. D. Fox, *Lond.* 314 (1985), 132). These minor variations throw light on some early divergencies from the common stock but do not affect the general argument in the text.
6. See M. O. Dayhoff, *Atlas of Protein Sequence and Structure* (National Bio-medical Research Foundation, Washington, DC, 1972), vol. 5, 8 and D55.
7. A. C. Wilson, S. S. Carlson and T. J. White, *Ann. Rev. Biochem.* 46 (1977), 573–639.
8. V. M. Sarich and A. C. Wilson, *Science* 158 (1967), 1200–3; M.–C. King and A. C. Wilson, *Science* 188 (1975), 107–16.
9. C. R. Woese, 'The primary lines of descent and the universal ancestor' in *Evolution from molecules to men*, (ed) D. S. Bendall (Cambridge University Press, Cambridge, 1983), p. 209–33.
10. A. Efstratiadis, J. W. Posakong, T. Maniatis, R. M. Lawn, C. O'Connell, R. A. Spritz, J. K. DeRiel, B. G. Forget, S. M. Weissman, J. L. Slighton,

A. E. Blechl, O. Smithies, F. E. Baralle, C. C. Shoulders and N. J. Proudfoot, 'The structure and evolution of the human beta-globin gene family', *Cell* 21 (1980), 653–68.

11. A. C. Jeffreys, S. Harris, P. A. Barrie, D. Wood, W. Blanchetor and S. M. Adams, 'Evolution of gene families: the globin genes' in D. S. Bendall (ed.), *op. cit.*, ref. 9, p. 175–95.

12. F. Perler, A. Efstratiadis, P. Lomedico, W. Gilbert, R. Kolodner and J. Dodgson, *Cell* 20 (1980), 555–566.

13. H. B. D. Kettlewell, 'Selection experiments in industrial melanism in the lepidoptera', *Heredity* 9 (1955), 323.

14. Hugh Montefiore, *The Probability of God* (SCM Press, London, 1985), chap. 6.

15. See Peter J. Bowler, *Evolution: the history of an idea* (University of California Press, Berkeley, 1984), p. 317.

16. Bowler, *op. cit.*, ref. 15, p. 318.

17. For one of the most vivid and informed accounts of these legal battles, see the narrative of the theologian-witness Langdon Gilkey, *Creationism on Trial* (Winston Press, Minneapolis, 1985).

18. *Nature, Lond.* 289 (1981), 735; 290 (1981), 75–6, 82.

19. I am thinking of such works as: *Darwinism Defended: a guide to the evolution controversies* by Michael Ruse (Addison-Wesley, Reading, Mass., 1982); and *Abusing Science: the case against creationism* by Philip Kitcher (MIT Press, Cambridge, Mass., 1982). A useful perspicacious recent account, with a full bibliography, is to be found in the book by P. J. Bowler (ref. 15 above), chap. 12, pp. 338–48. The theological case against 'creation-science' is well presented by Protestant, Catholic and Jewish authors in *Is God a Creationist?*, R. M. Frye (ed.) (Charles Scribner's Sons, New York, 1983) and the intellectual roots of creationism have been examined sociologically by M. A. Cavanaugh in 'Scientific creationism and rationality', *Nature* 315 (1985), 185–9.

20. A. J. Cain, in an address critical of cladism to the 1981 British Association meeting at York, reported in *Nature, Lond.* 293 (1981) 15–16. Cladism has been expounded by M. Eldredge and J. Craecraft in their *Phylogenetic Patterns and the Evolutionary Process* (Columbia University Press, New York, 1980).

21. C. Patterson, letter to *Nature* 288 (1980), 430 – replying to a letter of L. B. Halstead, *ibid.*, 208.

22. C. Patterson, *Biologist* 27 (1980), 234–40.

23. ' . . . the most important outcome of cladistics is that a simple, even naive method of discovering the groups of systematics – what used to be called the natural system – has led some of us to realize that much of today's explanation of nature, in terms of neo-Darwinism, or the synthetic theory, may be empty rhetoric', C. Patterson, *op. cit.*, ref. 22, p. 240.

24. J. Maynard Smith, *Evolution Now* (Macmillan, London, 1982), p. 109.

25. See the full report by R. Lewin in *Science* 210 (1980), 883–7.

26. N. Eldredge and S. J. Gould in T. J. M. Schopf (ed.), *Models in Palaeobiology* (Freeman, San Francisco, 1972), 82–115; *idem.*, *Palaeobiology* 3 (1977), 115–51; N. Eldredge, *Time Frames: The rethinking of Darwinism evolution and the theory of punctuated equilibrium* (Simon & Schuster, New York, 1985; Heinemann, London, 1986).

27. *The Living Stream* (Collins, London, 1965), 161ff., 189ff.

28. J. Maynard Smith, *op. cit.*, ref. 24, p. 126.

29. S. J. Gould, *Palaeobiology* 6(1) (1980), 119–30.

30. P. J. Bowler, *op. cit.*, ref. 15, p. 323.

31. J. S. Jones, *Nature, Lond.* 293 (1981), 427–8. However, it *is* puzzling that so little evolution actually occurred over hundreds of thousands to millions of generations in a diverse range of species and this demands an explanation, so G. A. Dover argues (*Nature, Lond.* 318 (1985), 19). Reasonable proposals have been made and the debate continues.

32. P. G. Williamson, *Nature, Lond.* 293 (1981), 437–43.

33. L. R. Halstead, *Nature, Lond.* 288 (1980), 208.

34. See J. Maynard-Smith, *The Theory of Evolution*, 2nd ed. (Pelican Books, London, 1966) for one of the best accounts of these subtleties. An excellent assessment of the question is to be found in 'Is a new evolutionary synthesis necessary?' by G. L. Stebbins and F. J. Ayala, *Science* 213 (1981), 967–71. They conclude that the 'modern synthesis' does not preclude the kind of emphasis made by the 'punctualists', and their article is notable for a particularly lucid perception of the relation of different levels of theory (from the *micro-* to the *macro-*evolutionary) which are assessed in relation to the issues concerning reduction, along lines very similar to those outlined in Chapter 1.

35. R. M. Gorczynski and E. J. Steele, *Nature* 289 (1981), 678. See also R. B. Taylor, *Nature* 286 (1980), 837; an article entitled 'Too soon for the Rehabilitation of Lamarck', in *Nature* 289 (1981), 631–2; and an account (R. Lewin, *Science* 213 (1981), 316–21) of the subsequent controversy about the interpretation of these and other experimental observations, and of the personal conflicts involved.

36. P. J. Bowler, *op. cit.*, ref. 15, p. 321.

37. H. Montefiore, *op. cit.*, ref. 14, pp. 79–80.

38. A. Koestler, *The Ghost in the Machine* (Hutchinson, London, 1967).

39. R. C. Lewontin, 'Gene, organism and environment' in B. S. Bendall (ed.), *op. cit.*, ref. 9, 273–85.

40. Sir Alister Hardy, *The Living Stream* (Collins, London, 1985), 161ff., 189ff.

41. M. Kimura, *Nature, Lond.* 217 (1968), 624–6; M. Kimura, *Proc. Nat. Acad. Sci., USA* 76 (1979), 3440–4.

42. R. C. Lewontin, *The Genetic Basis of Evolutionary Changes* (Columbia Univ. Press, New York, 1974).

43. E. Nevo, 'Population genetics and ecology' in D. Bendall (ed.), *op. cit.*, ref. 9, pp. 287–321.

44. *The Encyclopaedia of Ignorance*, R. Duncan and M. Weston-Smith (eds)

(Pergamon Press, Oxford, 1977) gives frank and revealing accounts of many such areas.

45. F. H. C. Crick, *Of Molecules and Man* (Univ. of Washington Press, Seattle, 1966), p. 10.

46. R. Sheldrake, *A New Science of Life* (Bland & Briggs, London, 1981).

47. Because he claims it could, in principle, be falsified by experiments. However, this criterion of Popper is now widely recognised as insufficient as a criterion of what constitutes a scientific proposition – and frequently inapplicable to undoubtedly scientific statements (e.g., most of the affirmations of geology referring to long past changes in the Earth's crust).

48. Indeed, the chief merit of Sheldrake's book is, in my view, its cogent and accurate descriptions of many of the unsolved mysteries of biology.

49. A. M. Turing, 'The chemical basis of morphogenesis', *Phil. Trans. R. Soc., Lond.* B237 (1952), 37.

50. For a fuller account of these phenomena, with references, see A. R. Peacocke, *The Physical Chemistry of Biological Organization* (Oxford Univ. Press Oxford, 1983), chap. 4, and the Royal Society Discussion, London (1981) on 'Theories of Biological Pattern Formation', *Phil. Trans. Roy. Soc., Lond.* B. 295 (1981), 425–617.

51. J. D. Cowan, 'Symmetry breaking in embryology and in neurobiology' in *Symmetry in Sciences*, B. Gruber and B. R. Millman (eds) (Plenum Press, New York, 1980).

52. L. Wolpert, 'Pattern formation in biological development', *Scient. Am.* 239 (Oct. 1978), 124.

53. A. Gierer, *Progr. Biophys. Molec. Biol.*, 37 (1981), 1.

54. S. Wolfram, *Nature, Lond.* 311 (1984), 419–424.

55. See B. Hogan, *Nature, Lond.* 314 (1985), 670–1; G. Vines, *New Scientist* Jan. 10, 1985, 30–4; for an earlier survey and references, see J. Maddox, *Nature, Lond.* 310 (1984), 9, and G. Struhl, *Nature, Lond.* 310 (1984), 10–11; and for reports on 1985 developments see J. Maddox, *Nature, Lond.* 317 (1985), 571 and M. Robertson, *ibid.*, 318 (1985) 12–13.

56. G. G. Simpson, *The Meaning of Evolution* (Bantam Books, Yale Univ. Press, New Haven, 1971), 236.

57. See A. R. Peacocke, *Science and the Christian Experiment* (OUP, London, 1971), 91–102 for a fuller account of these features of evolution.

58. Simpson, *op. cit.*, ref. 56, pp. 258–9.

59. K. Denbigh, *An Inventive Universe* (Methuen, London, 1975), p. 98ff.

60. A fuller account of this and other attempts to quantify complexity is to be found in A. R. Peacocke, *op. cit.*, ref. 50, pp. 255–68.

61. Teilhard de Chardin, *The Phenomenon of Man* (Collins, London, 1959), 300–2.

62. J. Wicken, *J. Theor. Biol.* 72 (1978), 191–204.

63. See A. R. Peacocke, *op. cit.*, ref. 50, chap. 5.

64. *Idem, ibid.*, ref. 50, chap. 2 and the Appendix to this book.

65. T. Dobzhansky, *The Biology of Ultimate Concern* (New American Library, New York, 1967), 129.
66. G. G. Simpson, *op. cit.*, ref. 56, p. 201.
67. Etymologically, ecology is the science of our planetary home (Greek *oikos*), more specifically, the relations of living organisms to each other and to their environment.

Chapter 4: The new biology – 'reductionistic'

1. The whole area of brain research and the neuro-sciences, which could well be considered as reductionistic, is developing so rapidly and involves such a vast new philosophical literature on the body-mind problem that it has been impossible to include any assessment of it in this section, though it is considered more broadly, in its consequences for theology, in Chapter 9.
2. G. S. Stent, *Science* 160 (1968), 390–5.
3. *Ibid.*, 391.
4. N. Bohr, address on 'Light and Life' to the International Congress of Light Therapy in 1932 – *Nature, Lond.* 131 (1933), 421.
5. W. T. Astbury, *Harvey Lectures*, 1950–51 (Thomas, Springfield, Ill., 1952).
6. Stent, *op. cit.*, ref. 2, 391.
7. J. D. Watson, *The Double Helix* (Weidenfeld and Nicolson, London, 1968); R. Olby, *The Path to the Double Helix* (Macmillan, London, 1974); H. F. Judson, *The Eighth Day of Creation* (Jonathan Cape, London, 1979).
8. Stent concludes: 'I think it fair to say, by way of appreciation of the dogmatic phase, that there have been two great theories in the history of biology that went more than a single step beyond the immediate interpretation of experimental results; these were organic evolution and the central dogma' (*op. cit.*, ref. 2, p. 394).
9. S. Brenner, *Nature, Lond.* 248 (1974), 787.
10. G. S. Stent, *Nature, Lond.* 248 (1974), 779–81.
11. K. F. Schaffner, *Science* 157 (1967), 644–7; see the discussion of his and Polanyi's position in Chapter 2.
12. M. Beckner, 'Reduction, Hierarchies and Organism' in A. J. Ayala and T. Dobzhansky (eds), *Studies in the Philosophy of Biology* (Macmillan, London, 1974), pp. 63–76.
13. I. Prigogine in *From Being to Becoming* (W, H. Freeman and Co., San Francisco, 1980): 'There is a microscopic formulation that extends beyond the conventional formulations of classical and quantum mechanics and *explicitly* displays the role of irreversible processes. This formulation leads to a unified picture that enables us to relate many aspects of our observations of physical systems to biological ones. The intention is not to 'reduce' physics and biology to a single scheme, but to clearly define the

various levels of description and to present conditions that permit us to pass from one level to another' (pp. xiii, xiv). 'We start with the observer, a living organism who makes the distinction between the future and the past, and we end with dissipative structures, which contain, as we have seen, a "historical dimension". Therefore, we can now recognize ourselves as a kind of evolved form of dissipative structure and justify in an "objective" way the distinction between the future and the past that was introduced at the start. Again *there is in this view no level of description that we can consider to be the fundamental one. The description of coherent structures is not less "fundamental" than is the behaviour of the simple dynamical system'* (p. 213, my italics). And D. C. Mikluckecky, W. A. Wiegand and J. S. Shiner, 'A Simple Network Thermodynamic Method for Modeling Series-Parallel Coupled Flows. I. The Linear Case', *J. Theor. Biol.* 69 (1977), 471–510: 'The main question of interest . . . is whether the network [thermodynamic] approach will be of any help in resolving this philosophical dilemma [of reductionism versus 'wholism', namely that biology deals with a level of organization not found among the objects of study in physics and chemistry]. To the extent that it provides a method for dealing with more complicated organizational patterns, it must. On the other hand, reducing a living system to a network is not far from reducing it to a collection of molecules. *The networks, as models, are more models of our theories and hypotheses about how the living system works than of the living system itself.* By creating the appropriate network, various notions we have about the workings of an organism can be quantitatively tested' (p. 510, italics mine).

14. See Chapter 2 and Wimsatt, *op. cit.* (ref. 15 to Chap 1.).
15. J. Monod, *Chance and Necessity* (Collins, London, 1972).
16. *Ibid.*, p. 110.
17. For a fuller exposition see the Appendix (section on 'The origin of living systems from the non-living and from dissipative structures', pp. 152ff. and for a developed account, with the mathematical and thermodynamic arguments, see the account in A. R. Peacocke, *The Physical Chemistry of Biological Organization* (Oxford University Press, Oxford, 1983), chap. 2.
18. I. Prigogine and G. Nicollis, *Quart. Rev. Biophysics* 4 (1971), 132.
19. See A. R. Peacocke, *op. cit.* (1983), ref. 17, chap. 5.
20. M. Eigen and R. Winkler, *Laws of the Game* (Knopf, New York, 1981 and Allen Lane, London 1982).
21. M. Eigen, *Naturwissenschaften* 58 (1971), 519.
22. See May B. William, 'The Logical Status of Natural Selection and Other Evolutionary Controversies: Resolution by an Axiomatization' in *The Methodological Unity of Science* (Reidel Publ. Co., Dordrech, 1973).
23. E. O. Wilson, *Sociobiology – The New Synthesis* (Belknap Press, Harvard University Press, Cambridge, Mass., 1975), p. 4.
24. V. C. Wynne-Edwards, *Animal Dispersion in Relation to Social Behaviour* (Oliver and Boyd, Edinburgh, 1962).

25. The seminal work was that of W. D. Hamilton, 'The genetic evolution of social behaviour', *J. Theor. Biol.* 7 (1964), 1–16; 17–32.

26. J. B. S. Haldane, 'Population genetics', *New Biology* 18 (1955), 34–51.

27. R. Dawkins, *The Selfish Gene* (Oxford University Press, Oxford, 1976). Dawkins graphically summarises his way of looking at biological evolution and the behaviour of living organisms thus: 'Replicators began not merely to exist, but to construct for themselves containers, vehicles for continued existence. The replicators which survived were the ones which built *survival machines* for themselves to live in. The first survival machines probably consisted of nothing more than a protective coat. But making a living got steadily harder as new arrivals arose with better and more effective survival machines. Survival machines got bigger and more elaborate, and the process was cumulative and progressive. Was there to be any end to the gradual improvement in the techniques and artifices used by the replicators to ensure their own continuance in the world? There would be plenty of time for improvement. What weird engines of self-preservation would the millennia bring forth? Four thousand million years on, what was to be the fate of the ancient replicators? They did not die out, for they are past masters of the survival arts. But do not look for them floating loose in the sea; they gave up that cavalier freedom long ago. Now they swarm in huge colonies, safe inside gigantic lumbering robots, sealed off from the outside world, communicating with it by tortuous indirect routes, manipulating it by remote control. They are in you and in me; they created us, body and mind, and their preservation is the ultimate rationale for our existence. They have come a long way, those replicators. Now they go by the name of genes, and we are their survival machines. . . . We are survival machines, but "we" does not mean just people, it embraces all animals, plants, bacteria, and viruses' (Dawkins, pp. 21–2).

28. On any reckoning, it would have to be a *system* of concomitantly acting, linked genes, for inheritance of behavioural characteristics is likely to be polygenic. So in the text, as in the Dawkins quotation (ref. 29), take the singular 'gene' to refer to such a system.

29. 'For purposes of argument it will be necessary to speculate about genes "for" doing all sorts of improbable things. . . . We are saying nothing about the question of whether learning, experience, or environmental influences enter into the development of the behaviour. All you have to concede is that it is possible for a single gene, other things being equal and lots of other essential genes and environmental factors being present, to make a body more likely to save somebody from drowning than its allele would' (Dawkins, ref. 27, *The Selfish Gene*, p. 66).

30. J. Krebs, 'Sociobiology, ten years on', *New Sci.* Oct. 3 (1985), pp. 40–3.

31. J. Maynard Smith, 'The birth of sociobiology', *New Sci.* Sept. 28 (1985), pp. 48–50.

32. J. Maynard Smith, 'Evolution and the theory of games', *Amer. Sci.* 64

(1976), 41–5; *Evolution and the theory of games* (Cambridge University Press, Cambridge, 1982).

33. E. O. Wilson, 'Biology and the Social Sciences', *Daedalus* 106, no. 6 (Autumn 1977), 127–40.

34. Wilson, *Sociobiology*, ref. 23, p. 7.

35. 'Sociobiology is defined as the systematic study of the biological basis of all social behaviour. For the present it focuses on animal societies, their population structure, castes, and communication, together with all the physiology underlying the social adaptations. But the discipline is also concerned with the social behavior of early man and the adaptive features of organization in the more primitive contemporary human societies. . . . It may not be too much to say that sociology and the other social sciences, as well as the humanities, are the last branches of biology waiting to be included in the Modern Synthesis. One of the functions of sociobiology, then, is to reformulate the foundations of the social sciences in a way that draws these subjects into the Modern Synthesis. Whether the social sciences can be truly biologicized in this fashion remains to be seen' (Wilson, ref. 23, p. 4).

36. M. Sahlins, *The Use and Abuse of Biology* (University of Michigan Press, Ann Arbor, Mich., 1976), xi.

37. M. Sahlins, *ibid.*, x.

38. *Idem, ibid.*, 4–5.

39. *Idem, ibid.*, 7.

40. *Idem, ibid.*, 9

41. *Idem, ibid.*, 11.

42. *Idem, ibid.*, 61, 65.

43. V. Reynolds, *Times Lit. Suppl.* 13 Jan, 1978, p. 23.

44. Mildred Dickemann (*New Sci.* 10 Oct. 1985, pp. 38–41) cites *inter alia*: the role of genetic relatedness as one of the factors in the fissioning of villages and in fights between village hosts and guests, and in competition among men for women among the Yanomamo Indians (work of H. Chagnon of the University of California at Santa Cruz); and also that adoption in Pacific societies from outside the genetic kin group, which Sahlins had used as evidence against the theory of kin selection, has been shown by J. Silk (Emory University, Atlanta, Georgia) in fact to exhibit a tendency both to favour close relatives in adoption and genetic kin in bequeathals.

45. M. Dickemann (ref. 44) reports such studies on the patterns of assistance in middle-class Los Angeles women, on polygyny in US Mormons, in the propensity to rape among different groups of males and of child abuse in the US.

46. E. O. Wilson and C. J. Lumsden, *Genes, Mind and Culture* (Harvard University Press, Cambridge, Mass., 1981). Another important work in this regard is that of L. L. Cavalli-Sforza and M. W. Feldman, *Cultural Transmission and Evolution* (Princetown University Press, Princeton, NJ, 1981) and their earlier 'Towards a theory of cultural evolution', *Interdisci-*

plinary Science Review 3 (1979), 99–107. These latter, unlike Wilson and Lumsden, present a mainly logical structure and regard the empirical data as still lacking, whereas Wilson and Lumsden make significant assertions about human society.

47. Surveyed by R. Lewin, 'Cultural diversity tied to genetic differences', *Science* 212 (1981), 908–9.
48. E.g., P. B. Medawar, 'Stretch Genes', *The New York Review of Books*, July 16, 1981; C. R. Cloninger and S. Yokoyama, *Science* 213 (1981), 749, critical of the genetics; and E. Leach, 'Biology and Social Science: Wedding or Rape?', *Nature, Lond.* 291 (1981) 267–8 – a particularly polemical attack from a leading anthropologist.
49. J. Maynard Smith and N. Warren, 'Models of Cultural and Genetic Change', *Evolution* 36 (1982), 620–7.
50. J. H. Crook, *The Evolution of Human Consciousness* (Clarendon Press, Oxford, 1980), 162ff. In Crook's view: 'Sociobiology explains why human behavior is not arbitrary, why it is structured in a broadly characteristic way wherever people are, but it does not proceed to reduce all descriptions of individual human action to biological causation. . . . Cultural evolution thus comprises a historical process that provides human beings with the sociological environment within which the basic biological strategies of the species are worked out' (pp. 186–7).

A similar view is expressed also by Pierre L. van den Berghe in *Human Family Systems. An Evolutionary View* (Elsevier, New York, 1979) but in terms more critical of the purely cultural interpretations he attributes to Sahlins. 'The question is thus not who [the social and cultural anthropologists or the sociobiologists] is right and who is wrong, but the level of explanation sought. Sociobiology does very poorly in explaining conscious motivations of individuals, and the detailed culture idiom through which a behavior is expressed, such as the ceremonies of a wedding ritual. On the other hand . . . sociobiology goes a long way in accounting for basic, structural features of human societies. . . . Human systems of kinship and marriage conform to only a few basic types. Underlying a great deal of variety in detail, human societies share much of their basic structure of kinship and marriage. The variations, while they attest to our versatility in adapting to a wide range of environmental conditions, are themselves not random but adaptive' (p. 87). 'The modalities of our behavior are indeed importantly shaped by the cultural rules we invent for ourselves; but the rules themselves reflect an underlying biological reality. Human behavior in general, and mating and reproductive behavior in particular, are thus *both* cultural and biological, *both* genetically and environmentally determined, and it makes no sense to dissociate one aspect from the other. What we call kinship and marriage in humans is the cultural expression of our biologically predisposed system of mating and reproduction. We set up societies around mating and reproduction and we cook up rules of conduct about them because it was adaptive for us to do so. The few groups foolish enough to do otherwise failed to survive in competition with those that did. This may not remain true for all time, but it has been true everywhere so far; and "everywhere so far" is all the data we have with which to construct an explanatory social science' (pp. 88–9).

51. See, for instance, Mary Midgley, *Beast and Man: the Roots of Human Nature* (Methuen, London, 1980), her swingeing attack on Dawkin's *The Selfish Gene* in 'Gene-juggling', *Philosophy* 54 (1979), 439–58; and S. Hampshire's review in *The New York Review of Books*, Oct 12, 1978, pp. 64–9, of E. O. Wilson's *On Human Nature* (Harvard University Press, Cambridge, Mass., 1978).

52. See the appropriate sections in A. L. Caplan (ed.), *The Sociobiology Debate* (Harper & Row, New York, 1978); M. Ruse, *Sociobiology: Sense or Nonsense?* (Reidel, Dordrecht, 1979).

53. See Caplan (ed.), op. cit. (ref. 52), pp. 280–90. See also Wilson's rejoinder in Caplan, ref. 52, 291–303.

54. Not always *that* tentative with some authors!

55. Crook, ref. 50, pp. 189–90.

Chapter 5: Man, God and evolution: yesterday

1. For a recent discussion see the volume to which this chapter originally contributed, namely, *Darwinism and Divinity*, (ed.) J. Durant (Blackwells, Oxford, 1985).

2. Gertrude Himmelfarb, *Darwin and the Darwinian Revolution* (Norton Library, New York, [1959] (1968)).

3. See S. Daecke, 'Entwicklung, in *Theologische Realenzyklopädie*, IX, 5 (Walter de Gruyter, Berlin & New York, 1982), pp. 705–16, for a fuller exposition and for detailed references to the authors quoted, e.g., Haeckel, Seeberg, Uexküll, Titius, *op. cit.*, p. 710.

4. Karl Heim, *Das Weltbild der Zukunft* (Berlin, 1904).

5. W. Pannenberg, (1975) *Wissenschafts theorie und Theologie* (Frankfurt am Main, Suhrkamp Verlag); Eng. trans. *Theology and the Philosophy of Science* (Darton, Longmann & Todd Ltd, London, 1976).

6. W. Pannenberg, 'Theological questions to scientists' in A. R. Peacocke (ed.), The Sciences and Theology in the Twentieth Century (Oriel Press, London & Stockfield; Univ. of Notre Dame Press, Notre Dame, 1981), p. 11.

7. J. Moltmann, *The Future of Creation* (SCM Press, London, 1979); only since this was written has Moltmann's *Gott in der Schöpfung* (Ch. Kaiser Verlag, München, 1985) come to hand, and, more recently still, its English translation, *God in Creation* (trans. M. Kohl, SCM Press, London, 1985).

8. Stephen Toulmin and June Goodfield, *The Discovery of Time* (Hutchinson, London, 1965), pp. 214, 215.

9. H. Bergson [L'Evolution Creatrice 1907], *Creative Evolution*, Engl. trans. A. Mitchell (Macmillan, London & New York, 1911).

10. P. Teilhard de Chardin (1959)., Engl. trans. B. Wall, *The Phenomenon of Man* (Collins, London).

11. Z. Alszeghi, 'Development in the Doctrinal Formulations of the church concerning the Theory of Evolution', *Concilium* 6, No. 3 (1967), pp. 14–17.

12. E. Nemesszeghy and J. Russell, *The Theology of Evolution* (Mercier Press, Cork, 1971), p. 48.

13. K. Rahner, 'Christology within an evolutionary view', *Theological Investigations* V(III), chap. 8, pp. 157–192. Trans. K.-H. Kruger (Darton, Longman & Todd, London, 1966).

14. Rahner, *op. cit.*, ref. 12, p. 184.

15. *Idem, ibid.*, pp. 184–5.

16. *Idem, ibid.*, p. 166.

17. *Idem, ibid.*, pp. 162, 163.

18. *Idem, ibid.*, pp. 164–5.

19. *Idem, ibid.*, p. 168.

20. *Idem, ibid.*, pp. 160–1.

21. J. R. Moore, *The Post-Darwinian Controversies* (Cambridge University Press, Cambridge, 1979).

22. A. L. Moore (1889), *Science and Faith* (Kegan Paul, Trench & Co., London), p. 184.

23. A. L. Moore (1889), 'The Christian Doctrine of God' in *Lux Mundi*, C. Gore (ed.) (Murray, London, 12th edit., 1891), p. 73.

24. J. R. Illingworth, 'The Incarnation in relation to Development' in *Lux Mundi*, C. Gore (ed.) (Murray, London, 12th edit., 1891), p. 132.

25. *Idem, ibid.*, ref. 24, pp. 151–2.

26. C. Gore, *The Incarnation of the Son of God*, Bampton Lectures, Oxford (Murray, London, 1891), pp. 32–3.

27. F. R. Tennant, *The Origin and Propagation of Sin*, Hulsean Lectures, Cambridge, 1901–2 (Cambridge University Press, Cambridge, 1902).

28. A. N. Whitehead, *Process and Reality* (Macmillan, New York; Cambridge University Press, Cambridge 1929).

29. W. Temple, *Nature, Man and God*, 1932–3 & 1933–4 Gifford Lectures (Macmillan, London, 1934); see also my account in *The Experiment of Life*, ed. F. Kenneth Hare (Univ. of Toronto Press, 1983), pp. 27ff.

30. L. S. Thornton, *The Incarnate Lord* (Longmans, Green & Co., London, New York, Toronto, 1928).

31. F. W. Dillistone, *Charles Raven: Naturalist, Historian and Theologian* (Hodder & Stoughton, London, 1975).

32. C. E. Raven, *Natural Religion and Christian Theology*, Gifford Lectures, Vol. I: Science and Religion; Vol. II: Experience and Interpretation (Cambridge University Press, Cambridge, 1953).

33. A. R. Peacocke, *Creation and the World of Science* (Clarendon Press, Oxford, 1979), pp. 125–7.
34. For expositions of process theology, see (inter alia): J. B. Cobb, *A Christian Natural Theology* (Lutterworth London, 1966); J. B. Cobb & D. R. Griffin, *Process Theology* (Christian Journals Ltd., Belfast, 1976); N. Pittenger, *Process Thought and Christian Faith* (Nisbet, London, 1968).
35. R. W. Burhoe, *Towards a Scientific Theology* (Christian Journals, Belfast, 1981), p. 15.

Chapter 6: Man, God and evolution – today

1. A. R. Peacocke, Introduction to *The Sciences and Theology in the Twentieth Century*, (ed.) A. R. Peacocke (Oriel Press, Stockton and London; University of Notre Dame Press, Notre Dame, 1981), pp. ix–xviii.
2. A. R. Peacocke, *Intimations of Reality: critical realism in science and religion*, The Meldenhall Lectures, 1983, at De Pauw University (University of Notre Dame Press, Notre Dame, 1984).
3. *Christian Believing*, Report of the Doctrine Commission of the Church of England (SPCK, London, 1976), p. 1.
4. A. R. Peacocke, *Creation and the World of Science* (Clarendon Press, Oxford, 1979).
5. H. Wheeler Robinson, 'Hebrew Psychology' in *The People and the Book*, A. S. Peake (ed.) (Clarendon Press, Oxford, 1925), p. 362.
6. W. Eichrodt, *Theology of the New Testament*, trans. J. A. Baker (SCM Press, London, 1967), Vol. 2, p. 124. He expounds this subsequently in the following terms: 'Of the greatest consequence, however, is the realism in biblical psychology, which brings the body into organic connection with the psychic life. . . . For the body is not an object which we possess, but which stands outside our real being; it is not simply the natural basis and instrument to which we are assigned, but which does not belong to our essential self. It is the living form of that self, the necessary expression of our individual existence, in which the meaning of our life must find its realization. . . it is understood as in all its parts the medium of a spiritual and personal life, which stands under divine vocation, and finds its nobility in being God's image' (p. 149).
7. J. A. Baker has stressed both the 'earthiness' and the personal aspects of the Hebrew view which he expounds as follows: 'Man is formed of matter. His every thought, feeling, action, his most transcendental conceptions, have their origin in, and are made possible by, the same basic particles as those from which the whole cosmos is built. It is through the body, therefore, that man has to live. . . . But the paradox of man's being is that, though he is thus physical through and through, He is also something much more – a non-physical reality, a person. This truth is bound up

with his self-awareness, which is of such a kind that he can address himself as 'thou', ... This personhood is a different kind of fact from the fact of his body; indeed, it is the determinative, classifying fact about him.' – 'Man: his nature, predicament and hope, (1) The Old Testament' in *Man: fallen and free*, E. W. Kemp (ed.) (Hodder & Stoughton, London, 1969), p. 94.

8. The contrast in some Pauline passages of *sarx* (flesh) and *pneuma* (spirit) is not, as is commonly believed, that of body, conceived as evil, as against disembodied and eternal soul, conceived as good. For *sarx* possesses physical attributes and refers rather to man's total created nature in its weakness, by contrast with and distant from God, and sometimes as it deliberately turns away from God; whereas *pneuma* is that by virtue of which man is open and sensitive to the life of God. Living *kata sarka* ('after, or according to, the flesh') denotes wrong living not because matter or the body is in any way evil, but because living in this manner is living for the world and not for God, and is thus a distortion of man's relationship with God.

Cf. also in this context I. T. Ramsey's account of Pauline anthropology together with an interpretation of the meaning of 'soul' that takes into consideration current scientific knowledge: ' . . . there is for St Paul, at least in theory, the natural man, the man who is nothing but a combined topic of the natural and behavioural sciences, who receiveth not the things of the Spirit of God (I *Corinthians* 2:14), whose life is restricted to the natural world; the man who in one sense does not live as distinct from existing. But there is by contrast the "spiritual man" who discerns the things of the Spirit of God, who (we may alternatively translate) is braced by the wind of God blowing in his face, who realizes himself as he responds to the activity of God disclosed in Christ, who "sees" the deep things of God, the activities of God known in a situation of depth. Here is the spiritual man, defined by a specific kind of activity – the basic personality matrix which he realizes as he responds to the gospel – who finds his life and freedom in responding to what he discerns in depth. Here is the man who in theological terms is saved and made whole and who, under the inspiration of the haunting vision of the gospel, can pioneer whatever changes come to man or society as scientific exploration takes us further into unknown and exciting terrain. He goes forward in faith, confident that under the inspiration of his vision there can be a creative outcome to the travail in which we endeavour to match medico-scientific developments with the needs and possibilities of human life and society.

'Here, then, in a personality which each of us discovers is an active self-response to a disclosure of God's activity in Christ, is for the Christian that which unifies, that which is distinctive of each of us. This is that to which the word "soul" was meant to point; that which can be expressed in directed thought or bodily activity. Here is no metaphysical substructure or pin-cushion, no static centre, but that which we know in being active, in realizing ourselves. Here is the permanent complement of all scientific discourse, something implicit in all the strands of knowledge with which the natural and behavioural sciences supply us' (I. T. Ramsey, 'Human Personality' in *Personality and Science: An interdisciplinary discussion*, I. T. Ramsey & R. Potter (eds) (Churchill Livingstone, Edinburgh & London, 1971), pp. 130–1).

9. Ref. 6, p. 126.

10. Cf. D. Wiggins, 'Identity-Statements' in *Analytical Philosophy*, Second Series, R. J. Butler (ed.) (Blackwell, Oxford, 1965), p. 41.

11. S. Kripke, 'Naming and Necessity' in *Semantics of Natural Language*, G. Harman & D. Davidson (eds) (Reidel, Dordrecht, 2nd edit., 1972), pp. 253–355.

12. D. Davidson, 'Mental events' in *Experience and Theory*, L. Foster & J. W. Swanson (eds) (University of Massachusetts Press, Amherst, 1970).

13. Cf. J. A. Fodor, in *Psychological Explanations* (Random House, New York, 1968), ch. 3; and D. Davidson, *loc. cit.*

14. I. T. Ramsey, *loc. cit.*, pp. 127–8.

15. It should hardly need stressing that such a reappraisal of what has traditionally been called 'the Fall' of man should have a profound effect on how Christians ought to conceive of the innovatory and compensating 'redemption' wrought by Christ – it *should* hardly need stressing but for the fact that most Christian soteriology seems to wend its blissful way, whether as evangelical preaching or as systematic theology, in a state of even greater innocence than Adam himself of knowledge of the present state of understanding of *both* the evolution of man *and* the interpretation of the Genesis myths.

For a fuller statement of this position see the author's earlier works (*Science and the Christian Experiment*, Oxford University Press, London, 1971, pp. 148ff; and ref. 4 above, pp. 190ff.). For an interesting argument that the Adam and Eve story is a myth of an 'awakening' to free choice and thereby alienation with the loss of a childlike harmony with God and the gain of a harmony that is self-conscious and chosen, see J. Baker, *Expository Times* 92 (1981), 235–7.

16. A view often denoted as 'pan-en-theism', a word coined apparently by K. C. F. Krause in the nineteenth century (according to the *Oxford Dictionary of the Christian Church* (ed. F. L. Cross) (Oxford University Press, Oxford, 1957, 1st edit., p. 1010) entry). It is there defined as 'the belief that the Being of God includes and penetrates the whole universe, so that every part of it exists in Him, but (as against Pantheism) that His Being is more than, and is not exhausted by the universe'. See the discussion in ref. 4 above and references therein to process theology's espousal of this concept.

17. To use the Lutheran phrase about the mode of Christ's presence in the bread and wine of the Christian eucharist.

18. A universe under the iron grip of a law-like determinism at both the micro-

and the macro- levels would simply repeat all its past patterns and not allow the formation of new ones; whereas a universe in which randomness alone reigned would not contain any recognisable, enduring forms at all and could scarcely be a 'cosmos'.

19. See Chap. 3, pp. 52–3, and the Appendix.
20. A musical term which has come to mean 'the whole scale, range or compass of a thing' (Oxford English Dictionary).
21. Ref. 4, pp. 105–6.
22. K. Popper, *The Unended Quest* (Collins, Fontana, London, 1976) who also quotes Kepler to this effect; M. Capek, *The Philosophical Impact of Contemporary Physics*, 1961; M. Eigen & R. Winkler, *Laws of the Game* (Knopf, New York, 1981, and Allen Lane, London, 1982).
23. Ref. 4, pp. 106–8.
24. Harvey Cox, *The Feast of Fools* (Harvard University Press, Cambridge, Mass., 1969), p. 151.
25. J. S. Habgood, *A Working Faith* (Darton, Longman & Todd, London, 1980), pp. 18ff.
26. H. Montefiore, *The Probability of God* (SCM Press, London, 1985), p. 98.
27. D. J. Bartholomew, *God of Chance* (SCM Press, London, 1984).
28. *Idem, ibid.*, p. 97.
29. *Idem, ibid.*, p. 138.
30. See my review of ref. 27 in *Modern Theology* 2 (Jan. 1986) 157–161.
31. Actually, Montefiore after quoting myself and Dr Habgood[26] and suggesting our views are deistic, goes on to say that 'God could have created matter in such a way that it tends to assemble itself in increasingly complex ways which make it possible to produce as its end the kind of moral and intellectual and spiritual beings which have in fact emerged' (ref. 26, p. 100) and comes dangerously near to an explicit deism himself in his affirmation that ' . . . there seems nothing arrogant to me in believing that the process of creation and evolution *has been set in hand* to produce such creatures, for they alone are capable of conscious, rational, moral, spiritual and personal activity' (italics added, ref. 26, pp. 100–1). Whereas, in my own exposition, this 'process of creation and evolution' is in itself continually, and all the time, the immanent God in the act of creating.
32. As reproduced partly (it seems) in Rustum Roy, *Experimenting with Truth* (Pergamon, Oxford, 1981), p. 188.
33. A similar view has been urged by Paul Burrough, an Anglican bishop, in his *God and Human Chance* (Book Guild, Lewes, 1985).
34. Cf. 'Two men will be in the field; one is taken and one is left' (Mt 24:40). 'Does not God send his rain on the just and the unjust?' (Mt 5:45). And do *you* think the 18 who were killed by the fall of the Tower of Siloam were 'offenders above the men that dwell in Jerusalem?' (Lk. 13:4)?
35. 1 Cor. 1:23.
36. For an exposition of the specifically *Christian* perspective on man and the

cosmos, see A. R. Peacocke, 'The Nature and Purpose of Man in Science and Christian Theology', *Zygon* 8 (1973), 383–90.

37. D. E. Jenkins, *The Glory of Man* (SCM Press, London, 1967), pp. 53ff. Jenkins continues: 'Jesus Christ, because he is a man, is, like every other man, continuous as a physical organism with the whole of the rest of the universe. There is no more of an evolutionary break between the cooling of a spiral nebula and the man Jesus than there is in the case of any one of us. Between the cosmic dust and us there is no discontinuity. So Jesus Christ is all that is involved in being man including the possibility of analytical reduction to whatever are the units of the stuff of the universe. . . . in the purposes of the transcendent and independent God, and by the power of this God, a union has been achieved between that evolutionary product of cosmic dust which is a human being and that transcendent and wholly other purposeful personalness who is God. Transcendent and independent personalness is at one with derived, dependent and evolved personality whose whole basis can be reduced to that impersonal materiality out of which it has developed and on which it depends.'

38. W. Temple, *Nature, Man and God* (Macmillan, London, 1964; 1st edit. 1934), p. 478.

Chapter 7: Nature as creation

1. F. Capra, *The Tao of Physics* (Collins, Fontana, London, 1976).
2. A. R. Peacocke, *Creation and the World of Science* (Clarendon Press, Oxford, 1979), Appendix A.
3. One could instance, inter alia, the 'pan-en-theistic' creation-centred spirituality of Meister Eckhardt (e.g., see *Breakthrough: Meister Eckhardt's creation spirituality in new translation*, M. Fox (Image Books, Doubleday, Garden City, NY, 1980) and the wider tradition covered by books such as *The Perennial Philosophy*, Aldous Huxley (Collins, Fontana, London, 1958) and *Mysticism*, F. C. Happold (Penguin Books, London, 1963).
4. For the evidence for this interpretation of the Genesis narration see *Creation* by C. Westerman (SPCK, London, 1974), pp. 52–3, and J. Barr, 'Man and Nature – the Ecological Controversy and the Old Testament', *Bull. J. Rylands Lib.* 55 (1972), pp. 21ff. and p. 72.
5. Q.v., A. R. Peacocke, 'A sacramental view of nature' in *Man and Nature*, ed. Hugh Montefiore (Collins, London, 1975), pp. 132–42, 202–3, largely reproduced in Chapter 9, below.
6. G. Herbert, *Providence*, 11.5–16 (Works of George Herbert, Clarendon Press, Oxford, 1941 edn.), pp. 161ff.
7. Eric Ashby, *Reconciling Man with the Environment* (Oxford University Press, London, 1978), p. 84.
8. *Idem, ibid.*, pp. 84–5.
9. Dr Norman Moore, in a lecture delivered at St George's, Windsor, in September 1973.

10. Barbara Ward & Rene Dubos, *Only One Earth* (Penguin Books, Harmondsworth, 1972), p. 298.

Chapter 8: God and the selfish genes

1. K. Peters, *Zygon* 15 (1980), 213.
2. See A. R. Peacocke, *Intimations of Reality: critical realism in science and religion* (University of Notre Dame Press, Notre Dame, 1983), chap. I.
3. E. O. Wilson, 'Biology and the Social Sciences', *Daedalus* 106, 6 (Autumn 1977), 127–40.
4. R. Dawkins, *The Selfish Gene* (Oxford University Press, Oxford, 1976).
5. It needs, of course, much amplification along the lines I have developed elsewhere in *Creation and the World of Science*, 1979 (chapter 4 and Appendix C which outline the arguments against reductionist interpretation of human behaviour and attempt to establish a placing for theological discourse (see also Chapter 1, above). See also *The Shaping of Man*, by R. Trigg (Blackwell, Oxford, 1982).
6. E. O. Wilson, *On Human Nature* (Harvard University Press, Cambridge, Mass., 1978), pp. 2, 193, respectively.
7. P. Hefner, 'Is/Ought: a risky relationship between theology and science' in *The Sciences and Theology in the Twentieth Century*, ed. A. R. Peacocke (Oriel Press, Routledge & Kegan Paul, London and Notre Dame Press, Notre Dame, Indiana, 1981), pp. 58–78. The impossibility of deducing ethical norms from the character of the evolutionary process, what *ought* to be from what *is* (or has been) the case – the 'naturalistic fallacy' of G. E. Moore (*Principia Ethica*, Cambridge University Press, Cambridge, 1903) – still continues to have the support of philosophers, e.g. A. M. Quinton, 'Ethics and the theory of evolution', in I. T. Ramsey (ed.), *Biology and Personality* (Blackwell, Oxford, 1966) and A. G. N. Flew, *Evolutionary Ethics* (Macmillan, London, 1967). However, it does not bar us from allowing evolutionary considerations to bear upon our ethical judgments.
8. A. J. Dyck, 'Moral Requiredness: Bridging the gap between 'Ought' and 'Is' – Part I', *J. Rel. Ethics* 6 (1978), 293–318; see also, Eileen Barker, 'Value systems generated by biologists', *Contact* 55 (1976), 2–13.
9. P. Hefner, *op. cit.*, ref. 7, p. 76.
10. M. Hesse, 'Retrospect' in *The Sciences and Theology in the Twentieth Century*, (ed.) A. R. Peacocke (Oriel Press, Routledge & Kegan Paul, London, and Notre Dame Press, Notre Dame 1981), pp. 283–4.
11. For further discussion of this issue see P. Hefner, 'Survival as a Human Value', *Zygon* 15 (1980), 203–12 and W. H. Austin, 'Are Religious Beliefs "Enabling Mechanisms for Survival"?', *ibid.*, pp. 193–201.
12. E. O. Wilson, ref. 40, p. 201.
13. D. T. Campbell, 'On the conflicts between biological and social evolution

and between psychology and moral tradition', *Amer. Psychologist* 30 (1975), 1103–26, reprinted in *Zygon* (Vol. 11, No. 3, 1976) is a discussion of Campbell's thesis.

14. R. W. Burhoe, 'The Human Prospect and The Lord of History', *Zygon* 10 (1973), 299–375.

15. Job 13:15.

16. Hefner's reply to this question would be that 'the most fundamental affirmation in the Judeo-Christian traditions concerning God is that of his faithfulness to and love for his creation. . . . The theologian has no alternative but to assume God's faithfulness will not allow creation, including the human portion of that creation, to go unconsummated . . . when the term 'survival' is incorporated within the theological perview, it takes on the meaning associated with consummation and destiny under God. . . . Christian faith gives the created order very significant status within the purposes of God: if therefore it is determined that the survival thrust is a major motif operative within that order, a motif that gives shape and dynamic to the created order, even where that order includes human beings, the theologian must make the effort to discern how that motif is related to God' (Hefner, ref. 35, pp. 209–10).

17. M. Ruse and E. O. Wilson, 'The evolution of ethics', *New Scientist*, Oct. 17, 1985, pp. 50–2. See also M. Ruse, 'The morality of the gene', *Monist* 67 (1984) 167–99; and Michael Ruse and Edward O. Wilson, 'Ethics as applied science', *Philosophy*, 1986, in press.

18. M. Ruse and E. O. Wilson, 'The evolution of ethics', *op. cit.*, p. 52.

19. *Ibid.*, p. 51.

20. J. Huxley, 'The evolutionary process' in *Evolution as a Process*, ed. J. Huxley, A. C. Hardy, E. B. Ford (Allen & Unwin, London, 1954).

21. The incest taboo seems to be a case where a combination of its contragenetic character and early conditioning render it a universal feature of all ethical codes.

22. G. Altner (ed.), *The Human Creature* (Anchor Books, Doubleday, Garden City, NY, 1974).

23. J. Jaynes, *The Origin of Consciousness and the Breakdown of the Bicameral Mind* (Houghton Mifflin, New York, 1976).

24. G. E. Pugh, *The Biological Origin of Human Values* (Basic Books, New York, 1977).

25. C. Sagan, *The Dragons of Eden: Speculations on the Evolution of Human Intelligence* (Hodder & Stoughton, London, 1977).

26. Sir Alister Hardy, *The Spiritual Nature of Man* (Clarendon Press, Oxford, 1979).

Chapter 9: Matter in religion and science

1. Technically, these have been denoted as the 'matter' which constitutes the

appropriate sacrament in contrast to its particular 'form' and intention –
but in the present discussion 'matter' refers to physical reality at various
levels of complexity. (The word is notoriously ambiguous, and it is always
important to be clear with what it is being contrasted.)

2. Cf. William Temple, *Nature, Man and God* (Macmillan, London, 1934),
ch. IV.

3. Cf. O. C. Quick, *The Christian Sacraments* (Nisbet, London, 1932).

4. There has been much search for the authentic account of what Jesus actually
said over the bread and the cup. What is quoted represents the conclusions
of J. Jeremias (in *The Eucharistic Words of Jesus*, SCM Press, London, 1966)
which have received wide support. For other discussions of this complex
issue see: J. A. Baker, 'The "Institution" Narratives and the Christian
Eucharist' in *Thinking about the Eucharist*, Church of England Doctrine
Commission, SCM Press, London, 1972; and the survey by C. P. M. Jones,
pp. 148–69, in *The Study of the Liturgy* (ed. C. Jones, G. Wainwright and
E. Yarnold, SPCK, London, 1978).

5. Following Quick, *op. cit.*, ref. 3, p. 105.

6. Probably the word over the bread was very close to the form of the present
Hebrew prayer book: 'Blessed art Thou, O Lord our God, King of the
Universe, who bringest forth bread from the earth.'

7. See G. Dix, *The Shape of the Liturgy* (Dacre Press, London, 1945).

8. From Dix, *op. cit.*, ref. 7, pp. 113ff. (Irenaeus, *Adv. Haer.* IV, 17–18, 6).
It is not suggested, of course, that Irenaeus, in using such 'first-fruits'
terminology, had adopted the view developed here. No doubt he was much
more concerned with parallels between certain biblical texts. However, it is
suggested that this feature of the eucharist of the early Church to which he
refers does in fact represent a genuine insight and point of growth for a
legitimate further development.

9. A fuller account of this 'broad sweep of cosmic development' for the general
reader is given in A. R. Peacocke, *Science and the Christian Experiment*
(Oxford University Press, London, 1971), chapters 2, 3.

10. The approach outlined in this chapter has been adumbrated long since in
William Temple's *Nature, Man and God* (Macmillan, London, 1934),
ch. XIX, as I have developed in more detail in my article 'The New Biology
and *Nature, Man and God*' in the William Temple centenary volume *The
Experiment of Life* (ed. F. Kenneth Hare, University of Toronto Press,
Toronto, 1983), pp. 27–88). But in *Nature, Man and God* Temple writes in
somewhat Hegelian terms, and it is hoped that the approach offered here
provides a contemporary elaboration of Temple's penetrating insight into
the relevance of the Christian sacraments for providing the basis of a unified
view of matter and of 'spirit'. The approach is also similar to that presented
in L. S. Thornton, *The Incarnate Lord* (Longmans, London, 1928).

11. C. E. Raven, *Natural Religion and Christian Theology*, Gifford Lectures
(Cambridge University Press, Cambridge, 1953), Vol. II, p. 157.

12. See A. R. Peacocke, *Creation and the World of Science* (Clarendon Press,

Oxford, 1979), chap. VI, 'Evolved Man and God Incarnate', for a fuller elaboration of this perspective.

Chapter 10: Retrospect

1. Cf. Isaiah 41:2–4.
2. W. Temple, *Nature, Man and God* (Macmillan, London, 1934), pp. 129, 131.
3. John 1:1–3.
4. See A. R. Peacocke, *Creation and the World of Science* (Clarendon Press, Oxford, 1979), pp. 141–4.
5. 1 John 4:16.

Appendix

1. E. H. Hiebert, *Daedalus*, Fall, 95 (1966), 1075.
2. N. Wiener, *I am a Mathematician* (MIT Press, Cambridge, Mass., 1956), p. 325.
3. J. Monod, Chance and Necessity (Collins, London, 1972), p. 167.
4. G. N. Lewis and M. Randall, *Thermodynamics* (McGraw Hill, New York, 1923), p. vii.
5. J. Willard Gibbs, *Transactions of the Connecticut Academy of Science* 3 (1876), 228.
6. J. Willard Gibbs, 'Thermodynamics', *Collected Works of J. Willard Gibbs*, Vol. 1 (Longmans, Green & Co., New York, 1928).
7. Furthermore, new composite properties, a combination of U and S with P, V and T could be devised, e.g., the 'Gibbs free energy' = $G = U + PV - TS$ and heat content, $H = U + PV$. So $G = H - TS$ and this is an important criterion of equilibrium at constant temperature and pressure, for then $dG = 0$.
8. K. Denbigh, 'A non-conserved function for organised systems' in *Entropy and information in science and philosophy*, ed. L. Kubát and J. Zeman (Elsevier, Oxford, 1975).
9. E. Schrödinger, *What is Life?* (Cambridge University Press, Cambridge, 1944).
10. J. Wicken, *Journal of Theoretical Biology* 72 (1978), 191–204.
11. J. Wicken, *Journal of Theoretical Biology* 77 (1979), 349–65.
12. J. Wicken, *Journal of Theoretical Biology* 87 (1980), 9–23.
13. H. J. Morowitz, *Energy flow in biology* (Academic Press, New York, 1968).
14. H. J. Morowitz, 'Energy flow and biological organization' in *Irreversible*

thermodynamics and the origin of life, ed. G. F. Oster, I. L. Silver and C. A. Tobias (Gordon & Breach, New York, 1974), 25–31.

15. M. Eigen, *Naturwissenschaften* 58 (1971), 465–523.
16. A. R. Peacocke, 'Thermodynamics and Life', *Zygon* 19 (1984), 405–16.
17. G. L. Stebbins, *The basis of progressive evolution* (University of North Carolina Press, Chapel Hill, N.C., 1969).
18. A. R. Peacocke, *An introduction to the Physical Chemistry of Biological Organization* (Clarendon Press, Oxford, 1983).
19. M. Eigen, *Quarterly Reviews of Biophysics* 4 (1971), 149–212.
20. H. A. Simon, 'The architecture of complexity' in *Proceedings of the American Philosophical Society* 106 (1962), 467–82. (On natural hierarchies, see also: *Hierarchical structures*, ed. L. L. Whyte, A. G. Wilson and D. Wilson (Elsevier, New York, 1969); *Hierarchically organized systems in theory and practice*, ed. P. A. Weiss (Hafner, New York, 1971); *Hierarchy theory, the challenge of complex systems*, ed. H. Pattee (George Braziller, New York, 1973); and A. R. Peacocke, 'The nature and evolution of biological hierarchies' in *New Approaches to Genetics*, ed. P. W. Kent (Oriel Press, London, 1978), 245–304.)
21. J. Bronowski, *Zygon: Journal of Religion and Science* 5 (1970), 18–35.
22. P. T. Saunders and M. W. Ho, *Journal of Theoretical Biology* 63 (1976), 375–84.
23. I. Prigogine, *Étude thermodynamique des phénomènes irreversibles* (Desoer, Liège, 1947).
24. H. J. Hamilton, *Zygon: Journal of Religion and Science* 12 (1977), 289–335.
25. Or 'closed' (= energy transference to and from surroundings, but not matter) – as distinct from 'isolated' systems (no energy or matter transference). Here, and in what follows, 'open' will usually be taken to include 'closed' in this technical sense.
26. *Specific* entropy production (s.e.p.) = entropy increase per unit time per unit mass.
27. I. Prigogine, G. Nicolis and A. Babloyantz, *Physics Today* 25 (1972), 23–8, 38–44.
28. See the account given in ref. 18, pp. 42ff.
29. A. J. Lotka, [1924 *Elements of Physical Biology*] *Elements of Mathematical Biology* (Dover Publications, New York, 1956), pp. 356–8.
30. H. Haken, *Synergetics: non-equilibrium phase transitions and self organization in physics, chemistry and biology* (Springer-Verlag, Berlin, 1978).
31. J. J. Tyson, 'The Belousov-Zhabotinsky reaction' in *Lecture notes in biomathematics*, ed. S. A. Levin (Springer-Verlag, New York, 1976).
32. M. Eigen and P. Schuster, *The hypercycle* (Springer-Verlag, Berlin, 1979).
33. G. Nicolis, 'Patterns of spatio-temporal organization in chemical and biochemical kinetics' in *Proceedings SIAM-AMS Symposium on Applied Mathematics, American Mathematics Society* 8 (1974), 33.
34. A. M. Turing, *Philosophical Transactions of the Royal Society, London* B237 (1952), 37–72.

35. W. Lepkowski, 'The social thermodynamics of Ilya Prigogine' in *Chemical and Engineering News*, April 16, 1979, 30–3. But the cautionary note sounded by Wicken with reference to the transferring of thermodynamic concepts to the social sciences is worth noting (in his 'Entropy and Evolution: A Philosophic Review' in *Perspectives in Biology and Medicine*, Winter, 1979, 285–300, especially 299–300). Such a transference certainly looks, in the first instance, like an illegitimate application of principles valid in one domain to another where their application is inappropriate. However, cross-fertilisation by analogy and metaphor can often prove to be a creative stimulus as long as it is recognised as such – and is not a concealed reductionist ploy.

Index

Index

Index

Index